How You Can Help Your Child Learn Best

You, as a parent, can raise your child's lifelong level of intelligence and increase his or her joy in learning by how you care for your child the first six years after birth. This up-to-date, easy-to-follow guide provides the understanding, information, and simple activities that will help you nourish your youngster's mind well so he or she will grow up brighter and happier.

How to Raise
a Brighter Child

HOW TO RAISE
A BRIGHTER
CHILD

The Case for Early Learning

JOAN BECK

POCKET BOOKS
New York   London   Toronto   Sydney   Singapore

POCKET BOOKS, a division of Simon & Schuster Inc.
1230 Avenue of the Americas, New York, NY 10020

Libary of Congress Cataloging-in-Publication Data

Beck, Joan Wagner, 1923-
    How to raise a brighter child : the case for early learning /   Joan Beck
        p.   cm.
    This version includes new material, including information on changing
family lifestyles and the internet.
    Includes bibliographical references (p. 305).
    ISBN 0-671-03575-4
    1. Child rearing.   2. Education.   3. Education, Preschool—Parent
participation.   I. Title.
HQ769.B346   1999   99-26646
649'. 1—dc21   CIP

Revised Pocket Books trade paperback printing September 1999

10   9   8   7   6   5   4   3   2

POCKET and colophon are registered trademarks of
Simon & Schuster Inc.

Cover design by Anna Dorfman

Cover photo credits (l-r): Elizabeth Opalenik, Jack Reznicki, Don Mason, Steve
Prezant

Printed in the U.S.A.

The poem "My Sister Is a Sissy" is reprinted from
A New Kid on the Block, by Jack Prelutsky. Text copyright © 1984
by Jack Prelutsky. By permission of Greenwillow Books,
a division of William Morrow & Company, Inc.

To Ernie,
who shares the adventure

Contents

CONTENTS

Preface

This is a child-care book about your youngster's mind, not his body. It will tell you not how to feed, burp, diaper, and put your baby back to sleep but what you can do to stimulate her mind to learn and grow. It concerns the nourishment you should be giving his brain, not his stomach. It is devoted to thinking, not thumb sucking. It holds that parents should spend more time—and can have far more fun—sharing a youngster's delight in learning than fretting about toilet training.

We now know that parents can raise a child's useful level of intelligence substantially by the ways in which they care for him during the first six years of his life, long before he begins his formal education. Even the most skilled and loving parents, in the best of homes, have probably been stunting their children's mental development to a degree because they have not known what fast-growing brains need so urgently.

The purpose of this book is to report to parents about new research on the growth of children's intelligence during the first six years of life and to translate this research from scientific journals, professionals' symposiums, and experimental laboratories into a form that will be useful to those who live and work with small children daily. It aims to do for your child's mind what other books do for her physical and emotional growth.

When this book was first published in the 1960s, scientists had just begun to unlock the secrets of the developing brain, and a few pioneering educators had designed early-learning programs to capitalize on those discoveries. This book was the first ever written to report to parents about that research and how they could use it to help their children's brains grow better, to their lasting joy and benefit. Since then, hundreds of thousands of parents have tried these ideas, and many have written to say how much their youngsters have profited from this new understanding about the enormous and innate need to learn and how it could best be filled. Many of the letters echoed the key finding in early-learning research: Satisfying a child's mental hunger not only results in her becoming brighter but makes her happier and helps family life go more smoothly.

Now, an explosion of new discoveries has confirmed those basic ideas and given them new urgency. Even neuroscientists have been astounded to learn how rapidly a baby's brain grows, how literally trillions of neural connections form in the first few months of life, and how those connections disappear forever by about age 10 if they are not used. The brain, in effect, becomes hard-wired at an early age, and the learning opportunities a child has during those first few years can make a permanent difference in her lifelong level of intelligence.

In the 1960s, the ideas presented here were somewhat controversial. Now, they have attracted the attention of organizations like the Carnegie Corporation; have been the subject of a White House conference; and have sparked a new industry in books, videotapes, and computer software designed to help babies learn. Educators have conducted hundreds of studies with children at all socioeconomic levels and consistently found that early learning opportunities can raise their IQs and give them a better chance to succeed in school.

The new research and the years of experience that go into this latest edition reconfirm the book's first premise: Parents—

instead of being too emotionally involved to teach their own offspring—are the first and most influential teachers a child ever has. The most obvious evidence is, of course, the way in which mothers and fathers help a youngster master the complexities of his native language long before the age of six.

You won't be able to follow all of the suggestions in this book with one individual boy or girl. Children differ too much, one from another. So do homes, parents, and circumstances. No child is ever developed, like a recipe, by adding precisely so much of each ingredient. Every youngster comes with different inborn characteristics and temperament and potentialities that a parent must take into consideration in rearing her. Parents also vary in how much time they can spend on child care and what responsibilities they must take on outside the home.

But this book will give you broad guidelines to follow. It will help you see your child in a new light, give you a fresh perspective on what her growing mind needs, and suggest hundreds of specific ways in which you can help to provide for these needs. Once you begin to think of her as an eager, growing, exploring, budding intelligence as well as a small human being with urgent physical and emotional needs, your whole relationship with her will be different—richer, happier, and more satisfying.

In writing this book, I am functioning in my primary role as a journalist—not as an educator or child-care professional. The new research about early learning and the promise it holds for so many young lives is one of the most exciting ideas of the last several decades and one about which I have been fortunate to do considerable reporting. I am deeply grateful to the physicians, educators, psychologists, and behavioral scientists who have shared their knowledge and explained their work to me so that I could report it to readers in a form most useful to them in their lives with small children. The names of parents and children and identifying details used in illustrative examples have been changed, although all of the incidents are factual.

I appreciate the encouragement I received from my editors at the *Chicago Tribune* and permission to include in this book some material from my articles and columns about children published by that newspaper and by the Chicago Tribune–New York News Syndicate, Inc. The information in this book comes from many sources, including research reports, professional journals, government studies, interviews, scientific meetings, physicians, child-care professionals, educators, psychologists, and parents; I am grateful to all of them for sharing their expertise and experience. Leon Shimkin, who was chairman of the board of Simon & Schuster when this book was first published, played a major role in making this book a best-selling success, and I will always be appreciative of his interest and enthusiasm. I also wish to thank James Ertel for his advice and help and Debra Bass for helping to assemble the latest research. Norma Howard, of the ERIC Clearinghouse on Early Childhood Education, contributed much by making computer searches for relevant research. The March of Dimes Birth Defects Foundation has provided information and help; I have learned much from their experts and, in particular, from Dr. Virginia Apgar when she was the foundation's medical director. Physicians and staff at the American Academy of Pediatrics have been helpful in providing research and insight, as always. Todd Hallenbeck deserves thanks for his generous and cheerful help in setting up my computer. And so does my father, Roscoe Wagner, for myriad reasons.

My two children, Christopher and Melinda, indelibly shaped my feelings about the satisfactions of being a mother and first taught me unmistakably about the eager insistence with which babies and young children seek to learn. I am grateful to them for what they taught me and for the joys they have given me all of their lives and to my husband, Ernest Beck, for taking such a loving and liberated share in parenting.

HOW TO RAISE
A BRIGHTER
CHILD

1

Your Child's First
and Best Teacher: You

How much is your child capable of learning before he's six years old and ready for first grade? What happens to his brain during these preschool years when his body is growing and changing so rapidly?

Is your youngster's intelligence level fixed for life by the genes she inherits? Or can it be raised by the way you care for her at home, long before she ever meets a teacher in a classroom?

As a parent, what can you do to give your child ample opportunity to grow in intelligence during these irreplaceable early years of life?

An explosion of new research into how the brain grows is yielding exciting answers to these questions. The discoveries add up to a larger, happier, and extremely important role for parents in fostering the mental development of their children before school age and to the promise of lifelong higher intelligence for these youngsters.

Most child-care books concentrate on helping parents learn

1

how to raise children who are physically healthy and emotionally well adjusted. They have detailed directions about how to become a competent diaper changer, tantrum stopper, rash identifier, bathroom attendant, and referee between rival siblings. But parents receive almost no help or information or credit for their role as teacher and nurturer of their offspring's developing intelligence. Much more has been written about what should go into a baby's stomach than what should go into her growing mind. More emphasis has been put on teaching a child to use the bathroom than to use her brain.

Today, the evidence is overwhelming that the quantity and quality of learning experiences your baby has—even before he is out of diapers—can greatly influence how well his brain works all the rest of his life. Scientists have made astounding discoveries about how rapidly a baby's brain grows in the first few years of life—forming trillions of connections every second that will later serve as the pathways of thought. Learning experiences and loving, one-on-one attention strengthen those connections, actually shaping the neurological structure of the brain. But scientists also know conclusively that without ample, appropriate stimulation, those neural connections will wither and die. In fact, the optimum time for many kinds of learning may already be past by the time a child reaches age six and enters first grade.

These findings provide important information for families trying to balance work and child care. More than half of mothers with young children now work outside the home and fear missing out on some of the best learning opportunities. Fathers increasingly want to play a bigger role in their children's development but face time pressures of their own. Yet helping enhance a child's mind often takes no more time than caring for her physical needs, as later chapters of this book show.

The new neurological discoveries have profound implications for national policy as well. Growing numbers of children are at serious risk of not getting proper stimulation that will

2

help their brains grow. Today, nearly 3 million infants and toddlers under age three live in poverty. More than 25 percent are born to unwed mothers, many of whom are still adolescents themselves. Yet study after study has shown that the benefits of early learning can go a long way toward making up for those early setbacks and help children of all socioeconomic levels grow up more intelligent and capable than they otherwise would have been.

Not surprisingly, these discoveries have infused new passion into the old political debates over day-care and family-leave policies. They have also attracted the attention of educators, philanthropists, and politicians who see a rare opportunity, and an urgent need, to help ensure that children grow to their full intellectual potential. Governors in several states have championed expanded preschool programs. First Lady Hillary Rodham Clinton sponsored a White House conference calling for greater investment in young children aged zero to three. Even the prestigious Carnegie Corporation of New York has focused its resources to call fresh attention to the critical years between birth and age three, calling for a "national investment" in the nation's youngest children to give all babies and toddlers the opportunity for optimal neurological development.

"The risks are clearer than ever before: an adverse environment can compromise a young child's brain function and overall development, placing him or her at greater risk of developing a variety of cognitive, behavioral, and physical difficulties," a Carnegie task force concluded. "In some cases these effects may be irreversible. But the opportunities are equally dramatic: a good start in life can do more to promote learning and prevent damage than we ever imagined."[1]

What is perhaps most exciting in these discoveries is the critical role that you, as a parent, can play as your child's first and most important teacher. You have the unique opportunity to boost your youngster's intelligence when it is most subject to change, to teach her individually, at her own pace and by what means she is most likely to learn, to shape your relationship with her in ways that can actually help her become brighter. It's time you got more help in this vital role. That is the purpose of this book.

Parents who have tried using early-learning techniques with preschool children often report delightedly about the results. Some cases in point:

• In a small town in Indiana, Jeanne Jenkins is giving a birthday party for her four-year-old daughter and six friends. Toward the end of the party, Ms. Jenkins leaves the young guests alone in the living room while she dips up the ice cream and lights the candles on the cake. From the kitchen, she hears nothing but a worrisome quiet. Anxiously, she peeks into the living room and sees that one of the guests has pulled a Smokey the Bear book from the shelf and is reading with great delight to the other children, who are fascinated by the story.

 After the party, Ms. Jenkins telephones the small guest's mother. "Oh yes, Meagan learned to read last summer," replies the four-year-old's parent. "No, she'd never read a Smokey the Bear book before. But she does read everything she can get her hands on."

• In a New York City park, 22-month-old Emily is exploring a large bronze statue of Alice in Wonderland. She announces to her baby-sitter a surprisingly complex thought for someone still in diapers: "I'm going to climb up on mushroom and say hello to mouse."

• In suburban Connecticut, Andrea, age five, scrambles into her father's desk chair, switches on the family computer, and uses her own password to sign onto the Internet. In the space for *key word*, she types in *dogs* and is soon clicking through Web page after Web page, printing out color pictures of the breeds that catch her eye. "This is the one I want!" she triumphantly tells her father.

- In Ann Arbor, Michigan, a third-generation Armenian couple—she a grade-school teacher on extended maternity leave and he a teaching assistant finishing work on his Ph.D.—want their son, Jack, to appreciate and profit from his Armenian heritage. So they have spoken only Armenian to him since his birth. Outside his home, Jack hears—and learns—English effortlessly. Now, at age four, he is happily fluent in both languages and switches from one to the other when it is appropriate.

- In a nursery school outside Los Angeles, Danny, four, walks purposefully over to a supply cupboard and pulls out a box of beads and numbered cards. Sprawling on a little rug on the floor, he arranges a set of the numbers in order from 0 to 9. Beside each he places a little glass dish and into each he drops a corresponding number of beads.

  Next, Danny puts another set of numbers in "tens place," making his figures read 11 to 99. With ready-made chains of 10 beads each, he lays out matching rows of 10 to 90 beads beside the tiny dishes. Then he adds a third set of numbers in "hundreds place" and the right number for 100-bead units. When he finishes, he has correctly created and labeled rows for 111, 222, 333, 444, 555, 666, 777, 888, and 999—and, with obvious satisfaction, taught himself a major lesson in number concepts.

None of these children was born a genius. But because someone who loved each youngster knew about the importance of early learning experiences, each had the opportunity to learn more than most children usually do at the age when their fast-growing minds could absorb knowledge readily. All of them appear to be developing above-average intelligence and a joyous love of learning as a result.

Meagan's mother taught her to read for fun, using a series of phonetic games and cartoons published by a Chicago newspaper. "We had no idea a four-year-old could learn so fast or enjoy reading so much," she wrote to the newspaper's editor.

Emily's attentive baby-sitter—and her busy parents, both professionals—made a point of conversing with her as much as possible and expressing their delight whenever she learned new words and put them to use in sentences.

Andrea has played games on the family computer since she was three and watched her older sister use the Internet for research. Her parents let her set up her own password and watched—at a safe distance—as she explored the Internet on her own.

Jack's parents are deliberately using early-learning principles to preserve an ethnic heritage that is important in their own lives and that they want to pass on, with all its cultural richness, to their children.

Danny attends a Montessori school, where he can choose freely from a wealth of early-learning materials.

Interest in early learning and research about it are coming from many different scientific fields and forging exciting new connections among them. Neuroscientists are using new imaging technology to actually watch the brain in action, and they are finding neurological explanations for what pioneering educators had long noticed about how eagerly young children learn. Biologists are conducting experiments probing the effects of early stimulation on young animals and demonstrating how experience shapes the brain. Psychologists are learning more about the biological basis of behavior and studying how a "bad upbringing" may actually change the chemistry of the brain.

Sociologists and teachers are urgently searching for ways to help disadvantaged children, many of whom reach first grade with learning abilities already stunted for lack of adequate stimulation during the first six years of life. Educators are reaching out to some of those children and contributing to the growing volume of evidence that preschool learning experiences can raise their intelligence levels. Many parents are discovering upon thoughtful observation that their own small children are ready and eager for learning previously assigned only to first grade level or beyond.

Computer experts are looking with fresh excitement at the potential that computers offer young children for unprecedented kinds of learning opportunities. "Children take to programming like ducks to water, especially if they are offered a gentle approach to it," wrote Seymour Papert, the Lego Professor of Learning Research at the Massachusetts Institute of Technology and developer of LOGO, a computer programming language.[2]

Research about early learning emerging from all of these sources, from the fields of neurology, physiology, psychology, biology, and education, and from specialists working from many divergent points of view, can be summed up like this:

- We have greatly underestimated what children under age six can and should be learning.

- It is possible, by changing our methods of child rearing, to raise the level of intelligence of all children and to have happier, more enthusiastic youngsters as a result.

- That chance does not last forever. Without ample, appropriate stimulation, unused neurons in a young child's brain atrophy and disappear. Vital connections between brain cells never develop. The brain loses much of its capacity and potential—permanently.

"To get to the heart of the matter, it appears that a first-rate educational experience during the first three years of life is required if a person is to develop to his or her full potential," said Dr. Burton White, who founded and directed the Harvard

Preschool Project, a research study focused on how children develop during the first six years.[3]

Early learning doesn't mean that you should try to teach your three-year-old to read to make him a status symbol, or because your neighbor's four-year-old can read or because you want to be sure he gets into Harvard 15 years from now. You aren't trying to make a six-year-old out of a four-year-old or turn a nursery school into a first grade or deprive your youngster of the chance to be a child.

Early learning does mean that you try to understand your youngster's innate drive to learn, to explore, to fill her developing brain's urgent needs for sensory stimuli and satisfying learning experiences, just as you try to understand and fill the needs of her body for nourishing foods. You aren't stuffing his brain with facts so he'll make Phi Beta Kappa at Yale any more than you give him vitamins to force his growth so he'll make the Chicago Bears' backfield.

Early learning simply means using new knowledge about what your youngster's brain needs during the crucial first years of life so that his mental development will come nearer to reaching its potential and your child will be brighter and happier for it.

Research is showing that traditionally accepted child-care practices may even be inadvertently curtailing children's mental development in some ways. Parents may leave an infant alone and crying with boredom in his crib or playpen, in an attempt to train him to be "good" and undemanding. Yet a baby's needs for sensory stimuli and motor activity—to look at a variety of things, to listen to myriad sounds and voices, to move and be moved about, to touch, to hold—are as great as her hunger for food and for love.

Parents may spank the hands of a toddler who is not trying to be destructive but merely trying to satisfy some of her insatiable desire to explore, to climb, to push, to pull, to take apart, to taste, to experiment.

"Curtailing the explorations of toddlers between nine and eighteen months may hamper the children's rate of development and even lower the final level of intelligence they can achieve," wrote Dr. Joseph McVicker Hunt, professor emeritus of psychology at the University of Illinois.[4]

Researchers have discovered that even well-read, educated, and intelligent parents have probably handicapped their children in the past because of child-rearing practices that ignored the needs of the developing brain. These are the parents who were most aware of prevailing child-care theories, who heeded the warnings about not "overstimulating" a child, and who read the books that said a youngster would develop "readiness" for learning on his own inner timetable regardless of the amount of stimuli in his environment. Many of these parents feared to stimulate their children intellectually for fear of "pushing" or "pressuring" them and because they had heard that fathers and mothers are "too emotionally involved" with their youngsters to do an adequate job of teaching.

Much new research now shows that the idea of "readiness" has been overrated and that a child's ability to acquire many skills depends on the stimulation and opportunity in his environment as well as his inner schedule of growth. In fact, some kinds of brain development may actually be dependent on a child's having certain kinds of environmental stimulation, some researchers now say. Most of the experimental programs concerned with early learning have been deliberately designed to remove any kinds of pressures—or even extrinsic rewards—from the learning activities and have been set up so that the young children participate only if they wish and stop whenever they choose and are never praised or criticized for what they do or do not do. Yet even under these circumstances, children of three and four eagerly teach themselves such intellectual activities as reading and writing.

Observers in almost all early-learning research projects comment on the joy and happiness and enthusiasm of the children involved. And the most careful follow-up studies do not detect any ill effects on these youngsters' personality, emotional well-being, behavior, eyesight, or general health.

When Dr. Dolores Durkin, professor of education at the University of Illinois, made studies of children who learned to read before they entered first grade, she was surprised to find that few of them came from professional or upper-middle-class families. In fact, more than half of the early readers in her California study had parents she classified as being lower socioeconomic class. One fourth more she identified as lower middle class.[5]

Studies of the home backgrounds of these early readers— and of a control group with similar IQs who could not read before first grade—pointed up an important difference. The better-educated parents in higher socioeconomic groups knew the theories that reading should be taught only by trained teachers and that parents should keep hands off the whole process.

Families less informed about these traditional concepts had happily and enthusiastically welcomed their children's questions about words, answered them, helped them, and accepted their preschoolers' ability to read. None of these parents felt guilty about their youngster's reading skill, as did two or three of the parents with professional backgrounds.

Dr. Durkin's research showed that the early readers consistently outscored the control group with equal IQ in the elementary grades. (But part of the careful scientific design of the research—which intended to keep each early reader matched with a nonreader of equal IQ as they advanced through several grades—was upset because many of the early readers were double-promoted.)

The widely accepted idea that a preschooler's only occupation should be "play" and the attitude that play is the direct opposite of learning have also tended to deprive youngsters of desirable mental stimulation. Small children love to learn.

They are born with an innate hunger for learning. And they keep on having an insatiable desire to learn—unless you bore, spank, train, or discourage it out of them.

If you think carefully about what most interests your baby or your toddler, you'll observe that it is seldom "play," as adults use the word. It's much more apt to be learning. In fact, sometimes you can't seem to stop your baby from working hard at learning in order to persuade her to play or eat or rest, no matter how hard you try.

A four-month-old baby, for example, who is just learning to roll from her stomach onto her back works harder at pushing herself up and over than does a runner trying to shave seconds off a marathon time. Once she manages to flop over, she usually screams until you put her back on her stomach so she can try again. If you offer her a rattle or a cuddly animal so she will quiet down and play and you can get back to your own work, she usually bats it away in her eagerness to resume her difficult learning activity. No one is forcing her or pressuring her or hurrying her or grading her or making her compete or threatening not to love her unless she learns to roll over. She wants to learn, urgently, on her own.

You can see this same phenomenon clearly when your baby is trying to pull himself up on his feet. He grunts and grimaces and struggles and works harder than a weight lifter. At first, when he finally does pull himself up on his feet, he doesn't know how to let go and sit down. So he screams. You lower him gently to the floor and give him a toy to play with. But he doesn't want to play. He wants to stand up. He wants to learn.

How long does a baby practice vowel and consonant sounds, stringing them together in delightful nonsense before he hits on a single word that brings recognition from his mother? No one pressures him into that concentrated practice, which typically goes unrewarded for months. Yet this is what babies and toddlers do endlessly, of their own free choice.

How many questions do two- and three-year-olds ask in a

single day? They're trying to find out all they can about the world around them, about cause and effect and all the fascinations of existence. This is not what an adult considers play. Yet a busy, impatient, tired mother can't turn off the torrent of why's even for an hour.

Three- and four-year-olds love what preschool educators call "imitative play"—pretending to be grown up. But they seldom copy grown-ups at play. They imitate adults at work: washing dishes, caring for babies, going off to work, driving a truck, as doctor, nurse, soldier, mother, father, grocer, firefighter, police officer, teacher.

You can think more objectively about this entire question of preschoolers' play if you keep track of your child's activities for just one day. What makes her happiest? What stimulates her to the greatest concentration? What holds her interest longest? Almost always, it's an activity in which she is learning something that increases her competency or satisfies her curiosity—especially if her mother or her father is right beside her sharing her excitement about learning.

Countless interactions like these lay the foundation for your child's intellectual development. Very early in a youngster's life, he begins to learn about the world via his five senses: vision, hearing, touch, taste, and smell. An environment rich in games, toys, and other objects a baby can handle helps stimulate his perceptual growth. So does a wide range of experiences and contacts with adults throughout the day.

If you love your child and spend considerable time with him, you may do many things to foster his intellectual development almost by instinct and without realizing precisely why. But parents of youngsters in culturally deprived homes are often absent, too busy, too burdened with economic problems, or too uninformed to make the effort to stimulate a child's growth. Even affluent parents, with the best of intentions, can be "time poor" and leave their child in a day-care center where staff members are more con-

cerned with keeping order than keeping children stimulated, or with an uncommunicative caregiver who watches TV
all day. The results show up markedly in kindergarten and
first grade.

"All later learning is likely to be influenced by the very basic
learning which has taken place by the age of five or six," emphasized one of the groundbreaking reports dealing with this
problem that was published by the University of Chicago.
There are large, measurable differences in development, the report noted, between youngsters who have had great opportunity to explore, to touch, to handle, to try, to play, to learn, and
to be with interested adults and those who have not.[6]

The opportunity to learn language skills also separates children who start school ready to succeed and those who seem
marked for failure, even at age six. A child's language development depends to a great extent on the adults around him in
his earliest years of life. Parents who are aware of a child's
learning needs encourage him to say words. They surround
him with talk, used freely and naturally. They cheer on his efforts to say the correct words, respond to him when he tries
and when he succeeds, read to him, and provide him with
what educators call "corrective feedback."

In this kind of rich verbal environment, a child's vocabulary
grows and his ability to use sentences develops. As he becomes
more skilled with words, he learns to put his emotions and intentions into language. He begins to compare and to differentiate and to express abstract ideas. He uses words as tools of
thought.

In homes where parents make great efforts to motivate a
child, reward him, and reinforce him, he "learns to learn," the
University of Chicago report noted. "He comes to view the
world as something he can master through a relatively enjoyable type of activity, a sort of game, which is learning." On the
other hand, the report warned, "If the home does not and cannot provide these basic developments, the child is likely to be

handicapped in much of his later learning and the prognosis of his educational development is poor."

Because the mounting evidence about the urgent importance of early learning has been so compelling, a wide variety of programs have been started by local, state, and federal governments, by public and private agencies, by universities, foundations, and churches to make learning opportunities available to young children from homes that appeared to be disadvantaged. Best known are the enormous collection of programs receiving federal money through Head Start.

Unfortunately, the kinds of learning opportunities many Head Start programs offer young children are too little and too late. A large percentage of them pay little attention to using new theories about how to foster intelligence. Most are modeled on traditional social-adjustment nursery schools, with an emphasis on group games and social activities. Many have to be so concerned about the youngsters' physical health and nutrition and about helping their families find essential social and community services that they cannot concentrate on encouraging mental development. And the children usually attend such nursery schools at the age of three or four for only two to three hours a day—sometimes for only a single summer. Often these programs are able to offer only a little compensation for an unstimulating home environment where the youngsters still spend most of their time.

Nevertheless, research shows that even a little attention to children's learning needs during the preschool years can help. Dozens of scientifically sound, long-term studies have now been completed that trace the results of Head Start and similar preschool learning programs over many years. Almost uniformly, they document significant gains for children in Head Start and other early-learning programs, especially when measured over several years.

The general pattern of such results is that the children show an immediate gain in achievement that usually persists

14

through the first two or three years of elementary school. Then the academic differences between the children who have had the advantage of being in a Head Start program gradually diminish and the gap between them and other youngsters gradually narrows. But subsequent testing at the junior high and high school levels once again shows considerable advantage for the Head Start children in terms of school grades and other measures of mental development.

Compilations of studies on Head Start children, for example, show that they had higher IQ scores than comparison youngsters—ranging from 7 to 10 points in several studies to as much as 30 points in one report. Far more of them were scoring at grade level in reading and math. Fewer had been flunked and needed to repeat a grade.

One long-term study even offers evidence that preschool education can also pay off in terms of lower costs to taxpayers in dealing with social problems. During the 1960s, the Ypsilanti Perry Preschool Project conducted by the High/Scope Educational Research Foundation of Ypsilanti, Michigan, began a study of 123 African-American preschoolers living in poverty and considered at risk for failing in school. Few of their parents had finished high school. Half the parents were on welfare and almost as many were single parents.

The children were randomly divided into two groups. One attended a high-quality preschool program five mornings a week, either for one year at age four or for two years when they were three and four. And a teacher came to each child's home for 90 minutes a week to work with a parent on early learning. The other group had no preschool experience and no efforts were made to help parents increase learning stimuli in the home.

Both groups have been followed and evaluated ever since. At the age of 19, those who had preschool experience were much more likely to have finished high school, to score average or above on competency tests, and to have a job or be enrolled in post–high school educational programs. By age 27, the preschool group had half as many arrests as the comparison group. Those who had attended preschool were also far more likely to own their own homes and to earn $2,000 or more a month and were less likely to have been on welfare or to have had children out of wedlock.

The money spent on providing the high-quality preschool program also paid substantial dividends for taxpayers—saving $7.16 in reduced welfare payments, court costs, and need for special-education programs for every dollar originally spent.[7]

Preschool early learning starts a "chain of cause and effect," the researchers suggested. Because they are more intellectually and socially competent, the youngsters do better in school. As a result, they are more likely to be graduated from high school, less likely to be involved in crime, and more likely to get a job. "These factors weave a pattern of life success that not only is more productive for children and their families but also produces substantial benefits to the society at large through reduction in taxpayer burden and improvement in the quality of community life," the report concluded.[8]

Another such study has demonstrated that intense, early intervention can raise children's IQ scores and rescue those who might have been termed mentally retarded. Known as the Abecedarian Project (*abecedarian* is Greek for "one who learns the alphabet"), the study involved more than 100 mostly African-American children in North Carolina considered at high risk of academic failure. Half attended a special day-care center with a rich educational curriculum five days a week from infancy to kindergarten. As babies, they were held, fed, talked to, and cared for all day. As toddlers, they could play in different "interest centers" dedicated to art, blocks, language skills, and prereading preparation. The other half of the children were placed in a control group that stayed home and got no special enrichment. By age two, the preschool group had IQ scores 15 points higher than those in the control group. By age

15, the IQ difference had slipped to 5 points—but the Abe-cedarian children still scored significantly higher in reading and math than did the control group. Fewer had been kept back a grade or assigned to special-education classes. Several of the control children had been labeled borderline mentally retarded.[9]

"Can intelligence be modified in the early years of life? We believe this crucial question has been settled scientifically. The answer is a resounding yes," declared Craig T. Ramey, a profes-sor of psychology, pediatrics, and neurobiology and director of the Civitan International Research Center at the University of Alabama at Birmingham who was one of the Abecedarian Project's creators.[10]

Evidence is overwhelming that opportunities for early learn-ing are critical—but they don't require a formal preschool pro-gram. By now, a substantial number of research projects have shown that young children can profit enormously when their parents are given some information and encouragement about early learning. For example, the New Parents as Teachers pro-gram has become a national model for assisting parents at home. Begun in four Missouri school districts in the early 1980s, the program involved 380 families from a broad cross-section of socioeconomic backgrounds. Even before a child's birth, specially trained educators made regular visits to each home, teaching parents how to help their offspring develop well. Mothers—and fathers—also met periodically in small groups at a nearby school.

Parents were given packets of learning materials, directions for simple learning games they could individualize for their own offspring, and detailed kits of information about every short phase of a child's development from birth to age three. They also got lots of encouragement ("This one will take an extra dose of patience on your part, but it's definitely worth it") and happy suggestions for ways to have fun in making learning a natural part of their home environment.

At age three, the youngsters—and a comparison group whose parents had not received training—were tested by independent evaluators. (Outside evaluators are rare in child-care research and give added substantiation to the findings.)[11]

"Children of parents participating in the New Parents as Teachers Project consistently scored significantly higher on all measures of intelligence, achievement, auditory comprehension, verbal ability and language ability than did comparison children," the report noted.

In the Missouri program, gains were chalked up by youngsters from homes with well-educated parents and above-average resources as well as by high-risk youngsters from poor families. Only about 10 percent of American families manage to give their children enough learning opportunities to get them, by age three, as well educated and developed as they should be, according to Dr. White, the senior consultant to the Missouri project.

It is now clear that there are no practical substitutes for involving parents in providing the kind of home life and stimulating experiences that encourage a child's mind to grow. Home and parents are so pervasive, so dominating in a child's life that parental participation in and understanding of early-learning techniques is essential—even when toddlers and preschoolers spend much of their time in day-care centers.

We now know that informed, caring parents—using many loving, happy, and easy ways—can do much to raise the level of intellectual functioning in their children and to help them realize to a greater extent their true intellectual potential. In fact, such stimulation may be necessary for the development of a "bright" or "gifted" young person, regardless of his innate potential.

"In no instance [where documentation exists] have I found any individual of high ability who did not experience intensive early stimulation as a central component of his development," pointed out Dr. William Fowler, professor of applied psychology at the Ontario Institute for Studies in Education and a former director of the Laboratory Nursery School at the University of Chicago. He also noted that deprivation is relative and should be measured against an individual child's ultimate potential.[12] "Deprivation may be just as extreme for the potentially bright who must endure average conditions as for the potentially average to live through conditions below the stimulation 'norms' of the affluent half of our society."

Large numbers of potentially superior, as well as average, achievers are probably lost to our society because of a lack of sufficient early stimulation, said Dr. Fowler.

Recent decades have seen a new and growing interest in children who are identified as "bright" or "gifted," probably for several reasons. Educators and parents are less reluctant to speak out for the needs of these exceptional youngsters, now that special programs are largely in place for children who need extra help. Research has shown conclusively that most bright children are emotionally healthy, socially adept, and usually delightful to know.

It has also become increasingly obvious that the United States' position in the free world depends on maintaining its leadership in the sciences and in technology and production. Yet evidence is growing that young people in other countries, particularly the Japanese, are ahead of American students academically.

Even though the average IQ of people throughout the industrialized nations has been rising sharply for years, the Japanese remain in the lead, according to a compilation of IQ studies made by British psychologist Dr. Richard Lynn. In one generation, the mean IQ of the Japanese jumped 7 points to be 11 points higher than the mean for the United States and other advanced Western nations.[13]

Among Americans and Europeans, said Dr. Lynn, only about 2 percent of the population have an IQ higher than 130. But 10 percent of the Japanese do. And 77 percent of Japanese do better on IQ tests than the average for Americans or Europeans.

IQ tests, of course, are a limited and controversial way to measure intelligence. There are many hazards to drawing conclusions from them about the comparative intelligence of different races and nationalities. But the tests used in these studies were designed to be culture free. Testing samples were carefully chosen to measure the same socioeconomic cross-sections of population as in the United States.

It's probably not heredity that accounts for this difference in intelligence, said Dr. Lynn, because the increase has been too rapid to reflect a change in the genetic makeup of the population. Because the increase in IQ can be found even among six-year-old Japanese, it's also not likely that what is boosting the IQ is the stiffly competitive atmosphere and rigorous workloads of Japanese schools. Instead, Dr. Lynn suggests, improvements in health and nutrition may be in part responsible.

But what almost certainly accounts, at least in part, for the fact that IQ is so much higher in Japan than elsewhere in the world by age six is probably the kinds of early-learning experiences that the Japanese are giving very young children. Japanese mothers are intensely involved in their children's education; in fact, they are often called *kyoiku-mama,* a name that translates as "education mama."

A major cross-cultural study made by the University of Michigan's Center for Human Growth also found that American children lag behind Japanese and Chinese youngsters in reading and math right from the beginning of first grade—and they stay behind, especially in math. Japanese children work much harder in school and spend much more time in class than do American children. But what accounts for the differences at age six is that Japanese and Chinese mothers and fathers use more of their time with their children for informal education, for providing opportunities to learn that are fun, and for showing enthusiasm about their offspring's achievements, according to Dr. Harold Stevenson, professor of psychology at the University of Michigan, who directed the study.[14]

The problem with American youngsters isn't working mothers, said Dr. Stevenson. Even employed parents have time in the evening and on weekends to be with their children. The critical element, he said, is that the time together be used for direct interaction.

It's one thing for the Japanese to build better cars and cameras and TVs. Or for the Chinese to make products for American markets more efficiently than American manufacturers can. But it's much more worrisome to educators and political leaders when the Japanese and Chinese seem to be building better brains—and making children's learning more successful.

There is also increasing public awareness that bright children are a major national asset and that they should be encouraged and cherished and their intellectual development fostered not only for their own benefit but for the public good as well.

Along with the new interest in the brightest children has come an enormous increase in special programs to identify them and provide them special educational opportunities. These now include everything from special summer camps to early admission to universities, Saturday programs in colleges for young teenagers, enrichment classes, honors academic tracks, individual tutorials, mentors, individualized learning, and many other strategies. (Chapter 12 has more information about bright and talented children.)

If you fill your child's life full of stimulation all of her early years, if you make your home what scientists call an enriched, "culturally abundant environment," if you use early-learning techniques we now know, you can do much to raise your youngster's intelligence. In such a home a child who would have grown up to be "average" will almost certainly become an "above-average" individual. And a youngster who would have been "above average" in normal circumstances will probably grow up to be "bright" or "gifted."

This doesn't mean that you must set up a school in your

family room and proceed to hold formal lessons for your three-year-old. It doesn't mean substituting the alphabet song for your baby's evening lullaby. It doesn't mean drilling a 4-year-old in number facts or showing flashcards with the names of dinosaurs to your 12-month-old baby, as one highly promoted "superbaby" program advocates. It doesn't mean pushing your three-year-old aggressively to get her into a particular nursery school that is reported to be a pipeline to Ivy League colleges. It doesn't even mean you must buy your child toys that are labeled "educational" or send him to a day-care center or nursery school that is promoted as "educational."

Your role may indeed occasionally be to teach your child directly, especially if he's asking questions or trying to master a task you can break down into small steps for him. But more often, you should function more as a scene setter who provides a loving atmosphere full of learning experiences your child can choose for himself and as a coach who cheers him on and shares the exhilaration of his accomplishments with him.

You can guard against any possibility you may be pushing your child undesirably by monitoring his reactions to the learning stimuli you give him. If he's not interested, there is no reason to push a learning activity on him. You should not insist that he stick to a task you have chosen if it's too difficult or he doesn't want to. You should never let him get the idea that you won't love him if he can't succeed in a task you've set. And you should remember that a major purpose of early learning is to make your child happy by fulfilling his brain's need for stimuli and to help him learn at his own individual pace and in his own individual way, as he will not be able to do once he enters school.

Using early-learning techniques with a young child can be just as simple and easy as this incident that occurred in a restaurant. A young couple brought their baby girl, about nine months old, with them and plopped her into a high chair at the table to wait for her dinner.

Looking around for something to do, the baby reached out and grasped a goblet with a single ice cube from the table and put it on the high chair tray. Her mother glanced at her, then resumed talking to the baby's father but kept her hand near enough to the tray to catch the goblet if necessary.

For 10 quiet, fascinated minutes, the baby was seriously absorbed in experimenting with the ice cube. She slipped it in and out of the goblet. She slid it around the tray. She tasted it, rubbed her nose with it, passed it from hand to hand. As it melted, she repeated the activity with the ice water.

Until her dinner came, the baby continued to fill her brain with information and stimuli. And because this filled a basic—although often unrecognized—need, she was happy and absorbed. As a fringe benefit, the baby's father and mother were free to talk together at an adult level, without constantly saying no and fussing at the youngster to "be good." It was far easier for them to use the early-learning technique of letting the baby explore a tiny portion of her environment, using every possible sensory organ, than it would have been had they acted as most parents, taking the goblet away and then having to cope with the crying of a bored and frustrated child.

Fathers and mothers who have tried using early-learning principles with their offspring are delighted not only with the intellectual progress of their children but also with the new and happy relationship that follows.

"I had no idea my daughter would be so interesting to me," commented a mother who had been teaching her four-year-old to read. "It's just like the way I felt the day she took her first steps toward me, only better." And because her four-year-old is seldom bored, she is seldom fussy, unhappy, angry, or defiant, unlike many four-year-olds.

You can help your child to become brighter, more intelligent, happier. There is no doubt about it. And in the process your offspring will have a more satisfying childhood, and you will enjoy him more. You don't have to pressure or push your child, and your efforts to help him learn will not hurt him in any way, unless you make your love for him contingent on his performance.

This is not just another job you have to do. It is a wholly new, exciting, wonderful way of looking at your child and your relationship with him during the first six years of his life.

Chapter 2 will explain the new psychological, neurological, and physiological concepts and research behind early learning. Succeeding chapters will give you more precise information about how and what you can do to foster the development of your child's intelligence.

2

Why You Can Raise
a Brighter Child

The excitement about early learning—with its promise that children of every level of ability and from every background can become more intelligent—is based on a convergence of discoveries in the fields of education; medicine; the behavioral sciences; and the new specialties of neurobiology, neuropsychology, and cognitive neurophysiology—in short, the neurosciences.

Scientists learned more about how the brain works and grows just in the 1990s than in all the preceding decades, and these discoveries have helped validate what psychologists and educators had been observing, independently, about how children learn. Together, all of this new evidence confirms the basic premise of this book: Parents can make a substantial difference in their child's mental ability by the kind of stimulating environment they provide during the earliest years of life.

Several important concepts provide the rationale for the suggestions made in later chapters of this book, showing specific ways in which you can help raise the level of intellectual and creative abilities of your youngster. These concepts also explain the scientific rationale behind this new philosophy of child rearing that is rapidly being put into practice. And they underscore why growing numbers of scientists, educators, and politicians feel such an urgent need to ensure that all children get the best possible start in life, before critical periods for learning have passed.

A knowledge of the new research will also help you as a parent to understand your child better and help to give him the mental stimulation he desperately needs. The major theories behind the emphasis on early learning include these:

1. Your child does not have a fixed intelligence or a predetermined rate of intellectual growth, contrary to widespread opinion in the past. His level of intelligence can be changed—for better or worse—by his environment, especially during the earliest years of his life.

It used to be assumed that every child had a preset level of intelligence that unfolded automatically at various stages of his development and had a lot to do with how smart his parents were. But the revolution in brain research has demonstrated conclusively that heredity is only part of the equation. Now, researchers know that genes provide the basic framework of the brain and that experiences—in the form of input from the environment—largely build the rest. To use a computer analogy, heredity furnishes the brain's hardware and experience provides the software programming.

At birth, your baby already has approximately 100 billion neurons—virtually all the brain cells she will ever have. Some of those neurons already are dedicated to controlling heartbeat, respiration, and other vital functions. But the rest are waiting to be wired into the complex tapestry that will form her working mind. Each neuron sends out branches called dendrites, which connect with the dendrites from other neurons and exchange information through connections called synapses. These connections form at an astonishing rate during the first few years of life—as many as 3 billion per second. By the time your baby is eight months old, she will already have about 1,000 trillion.

Most of these synapses form randomly in this frantic infant growth spurt. But they are activated and strengthened by sensory input from the outside world. Each new stimulus your baby receives sends tiny bursts of electricity shooting through her brain, building new synaptic bridges. The sight of a new colorful mobile over her crib stimulates neurons in her retina to make electrical connections in her visual cortex. Hearing a new lullaby sparks neurons in her ear to signal her auditory cortex. The touch of a soft stuffed animal or a father's scratchy beard sends similar signals flashing through her sensory motor cortex.

The more such input your baby has, the stronger and more elaborate her neurological connections become. Those, in turn, will determine how smoothly the electrochemical impulses of more complicated thoughts and emotions flow as she grows older. By giving her wide, open access to as many experiences as possible, you can actually improve her brain, raising her intelligence and her potential to keep learning all through her life. As Ronald Kotulak, the *Chicago Tribune*'s Pulitzer Prize–winning science writer, explained, "The outside world comes in through the senses—vision, hearing, smell, touch, taste—teaching the brain what to become."[1]

But this extraordinary growth spurt doesn't last forever. In landmark studies in the 1980s, Dr. Peter Huttenlocher, chief of pediatric neurology at the University of Chicago, studied brain tissue removed during autopsies and conducted the first actual synaptic census. He found that a young child's brain forms nearly twice as many synapses as it will ultimately use by roughly age two. That level remains fairly stable for the next few years, but after age 10 or so, the brain ruthlessly prunes the weakest synapses, those that have been least used. By age 16, the brain has only half as many connections as it did at age two, a level that stays steady until roughly age 70, when the number of synapses declines once again.[2]

This overabundance of synapses early in life ensures that the growing baby's brain can adapt to virtually any environment he finds himself in—a jungle, a desert, or an urban high-rise. The synapses that are stimulated early in life become part of the intricate web of the mind, and the more such connections there are, the greater the child's ability to learn and understand, to make sense of his surroundings and generate new ideas. Synapses that are not stimulated and used will dwindle and die. In fact, scientists estimate that the number of neural connections can easily go up or down by 25 percent or more, depending on whether a child grows up in an enriched environment or an impoverished one.

"If a child gets too little stimulation, play, affection, discovery, language, and person-to-person contact, development of the brain that depends on experience will be slowed down or will fail to progress," wrote Craig T. Ramey and Sharon L. Ramey, directors of the Civitan International Research Center at the University of Alabama at Birmingham, who have spent years studying early educational interventions. "The brain won't achieve its full potential for complex, streamlined, efficient, and flexible function. Specialized and higher-order brain processes, especially those associated with reasoning, language, and solving complex problems, may be permanently limited."[3]

Even when a normal, healthy child of average intelligence is placed in an institution such as a hospital or orphanage where she gets adequate physical care but little mental stimulation, she will become mentally duller in as little as three months. The longer she stays in a deprived environment, the greater the decline in her intelligence. Some of this loss is reversible, but much is not. This concept has long been accepted in the United States and is one reason why foster homes have been substituted for orphanages for children whose parents could not care for them.

One classic study that shows vividly what can happen to institutionalized children was made in 1960 by Dr. Wayne Dennis, then professor of psychology at Brooklyn College of the City University of New York, in three orphanages in Tehran.[4]

In the first institution, where most of the youngsters were admitted before the age of one month, the infants were confined almost continuously to their cribs, laying on their backs, with milk given in propped-up bottles. These babies had no toys. They were changed when necessary and bathed every other day. Four poorly paid attendants cared for a room of 32 infants, and Dr. Dennis noted that the supervisors cared more about the neatness of the room than the development of the babies. He also described seeing rows of older children who were able to sit up. They were seated on a bench with a bar across the front to prevent them from falling. They had nothing to do.

When these children were about three years old, they were transferred to a second orphanage where conditions were the same or worse. Overall, their development was severely delayed. Fewer than half of those between the ages of one and two could sit up by themselves. Only 15 percent of the three-year-olds had learned to walk.

Children in the third Tehran orphanage provided a dramatic contrast. Most of them had been transferred out of the first institution because they seemed to be more retarded than others. But in the third orphanage, they began to flourish. They had more contact with attendants, who were encouraged to mother them whenever possible. They were held during feedings and given toys to play with. As a result, most of these supposedly retarded children between the ages of one and two had progressed far more than the supposedly normal babies. All of the two-year-olds could sit up, creep, and walk holding on to a hand or chair.

In a later study in an orphanage in Beirut, Dr. Dennis demonstrated how even a little sensory stimulation could produce great gains in the development of babies. An experimental group of foundlings between the ages of seven months and one year, none of whom could sit up, were taken from their cribs into an adjoining room for an hour a day. Here they were propped up in low chairs or on a foam-rubber pad and given a variety of objects to look at and handle: fresh flowers, paper bags, bright jelly molds, multicolored plastic dishes, small plastic medicine bottles, metal ashtrays. No adults worked with the babies or helped them play with the objects.

All of the babies quickly learned to sit up independently, and after considerable hesitation by some, all delighted in playing with the objects. Dr. Dennis reported that during the experiment, these infants made four times the average gain in development, just as a result of the daily hour of stimulation.

More recently, studies of some of the over 100,000 Romanian children raised in state-run institutions during the regime of Nicolae Ceaușescu showed yet again that sensory deprivation early in life can have devastating effects on mental development. Some observers described these orphanages as "pediatric gulags" where children were simply warehoused, with minimal food, clothing, heat, activity, mental stimulation, or interaction with caregivers. Ratios of 1 caregiver to 20 infants were not unusual. In one study of 25 such orphans aged 23 to 50 months, nearly all were functioning at mental levels less than half their chronological age.[5] Another study found that even after being adopted by U.S. and Canadian families, children who had spent at least eight months in a Romanian orphanage had difficulty forming attachments, had behavior problems, and scored lower on IQ tests than those who were adopted sooner.[6]

Once you accept the theory that a child's intelligence can change and that it can be lowered by lack of stimulation during the earliest years of life, the next obvious question is this: What happens if you deliberately enrich a youngster's environment with intriguing, loving stimulation from birth on?

A growing number of behavioral scientists, delighted parents, and successful children have already demonstrated the answer: The child becomes brighter. Numerous studies since the 1960s have shown that exposing children to stimulating environments and quality preschool programs where they are given individual attention can raise their IQ's by as much as 20 or 30 points beyond those of children in control groups.[7]

It's even quite likely that we may eventually be able to raise the level of intelligence of our whole population as we understand better how to feed the innate learning abilities of small children. Understanding these principles "could mean the difference between a life in an institution for the feebleminded or a productive life in society," said Dr. Benjamin Bloom, a professor of education at the University of Chicago and a former president of the American Educational Research Association. "It could mean the difference between a professional career and an occupation which is at the semiskilled or unskilled level."[8]

These new understandings about the way the brain grows have effectively put to rest the old debate about whether nature or nurture is most important in human development. Clearly, they work together to determine each unique individual. The findings also shed new light on how the human race may have evolved over the years. After all, if heredity alone were responsible, humankind would not have changed much from apes. "The upright human, with free upper extremities, continuously sought new challenges, new enriched conditions and in turn, could alter the dimensions of his brain," wrote Marian Diamond, a professor of brain anatomy at the University of California at Berkeley. "It is the interaction of the environment with heredity which has changed the brain over millions of years."[9]

The genes that your youngster inherits lay the groundwork for his intelligence. They determine the basic quality of his brain. Clusters of genes probably give rise to special talents, particularly musical and mathematical abilities, which can be traced through families for generations. And genes help determine your offspring's basic body constitution.

But it is your child's environment that determines how much of his genetic potential will be realized—just like malnutrition or overeating can alter his body type. Even an Einstein, born with the intellectual capacity for genius, might have been classified as mentally retarded all of his life if he had been reared in an atmosphere like that of the Tehran orphanage.

You can't do anything to change your child's heredity, of course. But you can alter your offspring's environment in many ways, which will affect the development of his inherited potentialities—just as you can help your child develop the physique he inherits.

Is it possible to push a child too hard in hopes of raising her IQ to its maximum? At least one aggressively promoted program of baby stimulation has raised that question in the minds of some parents and early-childhood educators. But young children seem to have considerable built-in protection that should prevent mental overloading: They fuss, they turn off, they go to sleep, they run off, or they simply say "No more book" or refuse to cooperate.

The best gauge for using any early-learning ideas and stimulation with your child is simply to monitor her reactions. If she's interested, if she enjoys learning, if she's responsive, and if she seems generally happy, you are doing her good. But if she resists your efforts, squirms away, or won't pay attention for even a few seconds, you should reconsider whether the learning opportunities you are offering her are pushing her too fast—or perhaps whether they are stimulating enough.

2. Early stimulation can actually produce changes in the size, structure, and chemical functioning of the brain.

Thousands of experiments with dogs, cats, rats, mice, monkeys, guinea pigs—and even with chickens and fish—over the years have shown that when these animals are given stimulation in infancy, they develop at a more rapid rate and become more intelligent than others that are not stimulated. A rat, for example, that comes from a strain known to be dull will outperform a rat of similar age from a genetically bright strain if he is given extra stimulation as a baby that is not given to the supposedly born-bright rat. It even makes a demonstrable difference whether the early stimulation comes before or after weaning. The more stimulation and the earlier the rats receive it, the brighter they become.

Very young laboratory animals that are handled and stimulated as babies develop at a more rapid rate than those which are not. They open their eyes at an earlier age and show better motor coordination. They gain weight faster than do other animals in the same litter that are not stimulated—not because they eat more food but apparently because their bodies make more efficient use of what they do consume. They also seem more resistant to disease.

An enriched environment actually produces changes in the anatomy and chemical characteristics of rat brains. Back in the 1960s, psychologists at the University of California at Berkeley observed that rats raised in cages with simulating toys, colors, and obstacles developed brains that were heavier and had thicker cortexes, more complex dendrites, and more blood vessels than rats raised in ordinary cages. Interestingly, as they grew older, the enriched rats were able to tackle new challenges more deftly than were rats in the control group, suggesting that they had actually "learned to learn."[10]

We can't assume, of course, that the results of experiments with animals apply across the board to human infants too. And it is impossible to conduct the same type of controlled laboratory experiments with people. But evidence is rapidly accumulating that early experience not only is recorded in human neurons but also actually shapes and reshapes the brain into a more powerful organ.

Researchers at Baylor College of Medicine, for example, have found that babies that are rarely touched or played with develop brains that are 25 percent smaller than those of other babies.

Scientists in Germany used magnetic resonance imaging to study the brains of string-instrument players and found that the areas of the players' sensory cortex that govern movements of the thumb and fifth finger of the left hand were larger than the same area in nonplayers. Interestingly, how long the musicians practiced each day did not affect the area of the cortex—but the earlier in life the musicians started playing, the larger was the area of the cortex devoted to playing music.[11]

Arnold Scheibel and his students at the University of California at Los Angeles (UCLA) have looked at the brains of deceased adults and found fascinating correlations with their jobs and educational levels. People whose jobs demand dexterity—two typists, for example—had more extensive branching of the neural dendrites in the area of the cortex that governs hand and finger movements than did people in other occupations. UCLA researchers also looked at the area of the cortex responsible for understanding speech and found that the higher a person's educational level, the more dendrite branching the person had in that part of the brain.[12]

Neuroscientists are continually making more such discoveries about how experience physically shapes the brain, particularly now that the new imaging technology allows them to study the living brain in action. But it already seems abundantly clear that the more the brain is used, the more it grows and the more it is capable of doing.

* * *

3. Changes in mental capacity are greatest during the first few years of life, when the brain is growing most rapidly. The brain grows at a decelerating rate from birth on.

Educators—and parents—have long observed that young children absorb knowledge like sponges and that early learning experiences are the most indelible. Now, neuroscientists can provide a biological explanation.

In groundbreaking studies using positron emission tomography (PET) scans, Dr. Harry Chugani, chief of pediatric neurology at Children's Hospital of Michigan, Wayne State University, measured brain activity from infancy to adulthood by monitoring the brain's consumption of glucose. He found that a child's brain undergoes a great spurt of activity between the ages of 4 and 10, using more than twice as much energy as an adult's brain. This coincides quite neatly with the period of life in which the brain is rapidly absorbing information as it decides which neural connections to keep and strengthen and which to prune away. After age 10 or so, the brain's use of energy begins to trail off. By around age 16, it resembles an adult's.[13]

This cerebral building boom in the early years helps explain plasticity—the young brain's remarkable ability to reprogram itself even after serious injuries. In numerous cases, children who have lost entire hemispheres of their brains because of accidents or surgical interventions have been able to learn to talk or walk or write again through practice and therapy. Excess synapses in their brains are reassigned to compensate for the lost functions. Adults who have lost function because of strokes or other injuries can learn to reprogram their brains too, but with less success and far more difficulty.

In short, the brain is busily building itself in the years before age 10—evaluating what functions it will need to perform based on the information it receives and the challenges it is asked to meet. In effect, the brain is determining where the child wants to go and is laying down neural highways to take him there. What the child experiences and learns during this critical phase becomes part of that neural road system.

As a result, what is learned—or not learned—during these critical years "can completely change the way a person will turn out," Dr. Chugani said.

Educators and psychologists have noticed the same phenomenon from another perspective: a person's IQ score often varies considerably during the preschool years, then generally stabilizes at its adult level by age 17. Some studies show slight increases or decreases during the college-age years and afterward, but adult intelligence is generally considered to be a stable characteristic, just as adult height is.

Your child will continue to learn and acquire knowledge, of course, after age 17. He may use his mental capacity to a high degree in obtaining further knowledge and in productive work. Or he may waste it. But after 17, he can't change it to a significant degree. The opportunity to increase his basic intelligence will be almost completely gone by the time he is old enough to finish high school.[14]

The implications of these discoveries are both simple and profound: The stimuli you add to your child's environment will have the greatest results during the earliest years of his life. The same amount of input during his elementary or high school years won't result in nearly such large gains.

Yet the U.S. educational system hasn't caught up with this reality. American schools still tend to overlook the importance of intellectual development early on, and concentrate their most intense efforts in high school and college years, when the brain's biggest building period is over.

"Who's the idiot who decided that youngsters should [start to] learn a foreign language in high school?" asked Dr. Chugani. "We're not paying attention to the biological principles of education. The time to learn languages is when the brain is receptive to these kinds of things, and that's much earlier, in preschool or elementary school."

4. Critical periods exist in the life of every child in which the brain is being "hard-wired" for specific functions. Learning those skills is easiest during those key time periods—and far more difficult once those periods have passed.

Remember those old experiments in which a newborn duckling opens its eyes for the first time, sees a lab assistant, and forever afterward thinks the lab assistant is its mother? That phenomenon is called "imprinting" and it's a vivid example of how the brain is primed to absorb specific learning experiences at specific times. Once key information is recorded in the brain, it becomes almost impossible to erase.

Similarly, other studies have shown that if an animal misses a critical learning experience at a crucial time, the lesson can never be made up. Some birds that are isolated from birdsong during the early weeks of life, for example, never sing well, regardless of how much they are exposed to singing birds the rest of their lives. A newborn lamb, separated from its mother for a few days, never learns to follow the flock, no matter how many years it is kept with other sheep.

Neuroscientists now say that such "critical periods" exist in human development as well—just at the time that specific areas of the brain are getting organized. Given the right stimulus from the outside world, brain cells and the connections between them will become hard-wired to perform certain tasks. Without the proper input, those cells and synapses will go off and perform other duties or shrivel and die, leaving their original functions unfulfilled.

Scientists Torten Wiesel and David Hubel demonstrated this in the 1970s in a historic experiment with newborn kittens. They sewed one eye of each kitten shut and reopened it two weeks later. Even though the eyes were otherwise normal, the kittens were never able to see out of the eyes that had been closed. Without visual input, the connections that should have linked the eyes to the kitten's visual cortex never formed. Interestingly, when an adult cat's eye was sewn shut, the same phenomenon did not occur. The experiment provided vivid proof of a discovery that won Wiesel and Hubel the Nobel Prize: The brain needs the right kind of outside stimuli—at just the right time—to teach brain cells their jobs.

Armed with this fundamental information, neuroscientists are making fascinating discoveries about when and how critical periods exist for human learning. Dr. Chugani's PET scans have shed important new light here as well: Various areas of the brain undergo visible spurts of activity, in a precise sequence, just as the functions those brain areas govern are developing. When each part of the brain matures determines its critical period for learning.[15]

Sensory circuits mature in childhood. The brain's visual cortex, for example, has a growth spurt between two and four months of age—the period when your baby stares wide eyed at everything around her as if she is drinking in information visually. *She is.*

If babies, like kittens, miss out on this period of visual input, they never learn to see. That lesson was learned the hard way with babies born suffering from cataracts. Doctors once waited until the babies were older and stronger to remove the cataracts, but the children remained permanently blind. Now doctors remove cataracts as soon as possible, before the brain becomes hard-wired without learning the sense of sight.

Between age six months and one year, the parts of the brain's cortex that register and react to surroundings show maturation—just about the time that stranger anxiety reaches its peak.

The brain's auditory cortex, which processes sound, explodes with new connections from birth until about age 10, and it is closely linked to the ability to hear, speak, and learn languages. Children who have grown up in the wild without other human contact—so-called feral children—rarely learn to talk if they don't have exposure to language before they are 10 years old.

Neuroscientists are still just beginning to map out which regions of the brain become hard-wired, at what times, for more complex kinds of learning. But psychologists, behavior specialists, educators, and savvy parents have long observed that there are distinct periods in life when children seem particularly receptive to learning new skills.

For example, a growing body of evidence suggests that learning to play a musical instrument is easiest from about age 3 to age 10, and that children who learn to play during that period perform at a more advanced level than do those who start later. Very few musicians who reach concert level started playing as teenagers or later.

The late Japanese violin master Shin'ichi Suzuki believed that young children could learn music much earlier, the same way they learned language—through listening and repeating. He pioneered a method for teaching toddlers to play scaled-down musical instruments as soon as they could hold them. Parents participate actively in the Suzuki method, playing tapes of fine music in their baby's crib. Great emphasis is placed on playing by ear; children do not learn to read music until years later. The approach, first introduced in the 1950s, has its critics, but it has had a profound effect on music instruction. More than 300,000 youngsters in 34 countries are learning music with the Suzuki method, and it is now quite common to see children starting music lessons at age 3 or 4, whereas 10 or 12 was the norm in past decades.

Anecdotal evidence certainly backs up the notion that a critical period exists for music in the early years. Dr. Chugani began studying piano with his daughter when he was in his twenties and she was four years old. They took lessons at the same time, from the same teacher, and practiced the same amount. But she made much faster progress than he did, he observed. "Today, I play the guitar better than I play the piano," he said—even though he played the guitar only briefly as a youth and abandoned it for several decades. The ability to play guitar was wired in his brain when he was young, whereas playing the piano was not.

Can music make your child smarter in other ways? Gordon Shaw, a theoretical physicist at the University of California at Irvine, caused a brief stir with his theory that early music training enhances the brain's ability to form patterns and reason spatially—the so-called Mozart effect. Studies with college students found that those who listened to Mozart's Sonata for Two Pianos did better at solving paper-folding puzzles than did a control group, but the effect only lasted 10 minutes. A later experiment with three-year-olds showed that those who took piano lessons for six months did better at spatial reasoning than did three-year-olds who took computer lessons or three-year-olds who took neither.[16]

The idea became so trendy that in Georgia and Colorado, parents of newborns received classical tapes or CDs in their hospital goody bags as a start to a smarter future. Entrepreneurial "educators" have jumped in to market specially selected Mozart tracks promising to improve your baby's brain. But to date, there is less proof that listening to Mozart will make your baby smarter than there is evidence that starting music lessons early can make her a better musician later on.

Are there other critical periods for learning? Dr. Maria Montessori, the first woman ever to be graduated from a medical school in Italy and the founder of the Montessori method of teaching, observed that children develop a keen sense of order between the ages of 2½ and 3½. This is the age when your toddler insists on routine. He wants his teddy bear put precisely in place before he's willing to go to bed and only then provided the door is open just so many inches, the usual lullaby has been sung, and the blankets are adjusted just right. He insists on having the red boat, the blue submarine, the yellow bar of soap, and the white washcloth in his bathtub, or he refuses to get in. He demands his milk to be served only in his special glass (and he can tell one glass from another, even if you can't).

Most American parents consider this stage a dreadful nuisance and talk about the terrible twos. But researchers say it reflects a period of special sensitivity when a child's growing brain is trying to form generalizations from observations and formulate concepts from perceptions. Insisting on routine and ritual gives children a sense of order and continuity from which they can draw conclusions. You can use this special period to teach your child orderliness and good working habits, according to Dr. Montessori. Children in Montessori schools are taught to put away every item of equipment they use before starting a new activity. They are encouraged to see every task or game as having a beginning, a middle, and an end and to finish each cycle before starting another. These children take great pleasure in being able to control their environment by ordering it precisely and show great satisfaction in completing self-chosen projects before beginning new ones.

Dr. Montessori also concluded that the sensitive period for learning to read, write, and understand numbers is between the ages of four and five. The disadvantaged slum-area children she taught in Italy read and wrote beautiful script before they were five years old. Today, many four- and five-year-olds in Montessori schools learn both reading and writing as a free-choice activity, with great enthusiasm.[17]

You may see evidence that your three- or four-year-old is interested and eager to read and write. She may identify labels on cereal boxes in the supermarket because she has seen them on TV. She may pester you to teach her how to write her name, your name, and the names of her favorite toy animals. She may delight in having you identify words in the books you read to her.

In the past, parents have been told to ignore such signs and advised to tell a preschooler who asks questions about words that "you will learn all about that when you get to first grade." Parents have been warned not to teach a child the alphabet because they may do it wrong, because home learning will confuse the child when she gets to first grade, or because the youngster will be ahead of the group.

But research shows that these important signs of special sensitivity should not be ignored but observed and encouraged. The child who is eager and interested in reading and writing at four may already be past her optimum period for developing these skills by the time the school is ready to teach her at age six or later.

5. The critical period for learning language also comes early—and a child can learn a second or third language easier at that time than he ever will again.

Babies make all of the sounds of all of the languages on earth during the early months of their lives as they babble and experiment with making noises. But after they learn to talk, they gradually lose the ability to pronounce sounds that are not part of their native language and that they do not hear daily in the talk around them. For example, Japanese people raised in Japan have great difficulty distinguishing between the English *r* and the *l* sounds because they are nearly identical in the Japanese language. But Japanese-Americans, who hear English all their lives, have no such difficulty.

That sound-sorting process starts very early. Patricia Kuhl, a researcher at the University of Washington, found that Swedish babies just six months old preferred the *eu* vowel sound common to their native language, whereas American babies showed a preference for the *ee* sound heard more often in English. By the time a child is 12 months old, Kuhl says, his babbling has acquired the sound of his native tongue. By the time he is 15 years old, if he hasn't learned to speak another language, he will never be able to do so without an accent.[18]

That a child can learn something as complex as a language merely by hearing it is nothing short of miraculous, yet language learning follows the same path as does other early learning. Sounds are captured by receptors in the ear and converted to electrochemical signals that travel along nerves to specific parts of the brain, where they awaken neurons to their potential to process language. The more words the child hears, particularly with clues about their meaning, the stronger those neural connections become and the sooner he learns to speak in return.

As with so many other forms of learning, the more sensory input a baby receives, the more brain power he has. Psychologist Janellen Huttenlocher of the University of Chicago demonstrated that babies whose mothers talked to them more had larger vocabularies. At 20 months, they knew 131 more words than those with less talkative moms. At 24 months, the gap had grown to 295 words.[19]

These neural networks for language, connecting the brain's centers for hearing, speaking, and understanding, form at a furious pace during the first few years of life. The connections form the pathways that a child will use to process the words he hears, the thoughts he understands, and the words he speaks back—all the rest of his life.

When a child learns a second language early on, his brain can still form new neural pathways to process it. His fast-growing brain has dendrites and synapses to spare, and it can easily and automatically dedicate them to hearing, understanding, and speaking something even as complex as another language. But that excess capacity will have dwindled dramatically by the time he is 10 or 12 years old. Then, when he learns a new language, he must use the same sound-thought-speech pathway his brain built for his native tongue. He has to go through the mental process of translation, and he has only limited ability to form speech sounds he never heard when he was young.

"Instead of imitating the sounds of the new language, he tries to employ his own verbal units—his mother-tongue units—and so speaks with an accent and even rearranges the new words into a construction that is wrong," wrote Dr. Wilder Penfield, a pioneering neurosurgeon and longtime director of the Montreal Neurological Institute of McGill University who studied the bilingual children of Canada extensively. "This is a common enough experience. Even though they travel over the world, the Cockney and the Scot and the Irishman betray their origins all through life by a turn of tongue learned in childhood, to say nothing of the Canadian and the American."[20]

On the other hand, "A child who is exposed to two or three languages during the ideal period for language pronounces each with the accent of his teacher," Dr. Penfield wrote. "If he hears one language at home, another at school, and a third perhaps with a governess in the nursery, he is not aware that he is learning three languages at all. He is aware of the fact that to get what he wants with the governess he must speak one way and with his teacher he must speak in another way."

It is often argued that it is useless to expose a small child to a second language if she lives in an English-speaking community and will not continually hear and use these foreign words all the while she is growing up. But even if your child forgets the foreign words she has learned, if she studies that language or visits a country where it is spoken later in life, she will discover that the basic units of that speech are still stored in her brain.

Years ago, while Dr. Penfield studied in Madrid, his five-year-old son attended a Spanish school for three months. It was assumed that once the boy left Spain, he forgot any Spanish he had learned. But 25 years later, when the young man needed to learn Spanish for business purposes, he made very rapid progress. Forgotten pronunciations came flooding back and he was able to speak excellent Spanish without the usual Canadian accent. Dr. Penfield explained that units of understanding and pronunciation were hidden away in his son's brain but not completely lost.

The lesson is clear: Early exposure to a second language can give your child an invaluable boost in speaking and understanding it later on—even if he doesn't continue it through his school years.

There is also a valuable lesson in these findings for parents who entrust their young children for long periods of time to a non–English speaking caregiver: Use that second language as an extra learning opportunity, or it could be a major handicap. If your caregiver teaches your baby her own language, and they communicate with each other freely and often, your child very likely will learn a second language automatically, in addition to the English he will pick up naturally from you. But if your caregiver's language is a barrier to communicating with him in general, not only will your child have lost the chance to get an intellectual boost but he will also have lost irreplaceable ground in learning even his native tongue.

6. In assessing the intellectual capabilities of small children, we have failed to take into consideration the evidence of intelligence provided by the development of speech. Learning a language in all its complexities is one of the most challenging tasks an individual of any age ever undertakes—yet children master it as a matter of course before they reach age five.

"Grandma is coming to visit! Mommy telled me!" shouts Brian, age three. Daddy smiles indulgently at Mommy over his son's head and then explains to Brian that he should say *told*. It is just another charming childish mistake, his parents assume, and they think no more about it.

But *telled* is probably better proof of Brian's developing mental powers than *told* would have been. Brian didn't say *telled* because he was parroting an adult. What Brian did—although he probably wasn't aware of it—was to observe that the way in which we usually make a past tense in English is to add *ed* to a verb, and then he applied this general rule to the word *tell*. In this case, the English language makes an exception, of which Brian was not yet aware.

Four-year-old Avery also made a highly intelligent malaprop when she gave her stuffed bear a big hug and announced to her mother, "I love Teddy. He's so *have*." " 'Have'? What do you mean?" her mother asked. "You know, Mommy—you're always telling me to *be-have*. Teddy's always *have*."

Your child may say *mouses* instead of *mice*—not because she is slow or stupid but because she is highly intelligent. She has observed for herself that we usually form plurals by adding an *s* to root words, and she has applied this conclusion to a word that doesn't follow this general rule. *Mice* she could have learned by imitation or repetition. *Mouses* is evidence of important conceptual learning.

It's curious that young children seem to have no difficulty sorting out which words are verbs and which are nouns. They don't generally add *ed* to anything except verbs. Yet when they are 10 years older and learning grammar in school, many of them will have considerable trouble identifying the parts of speech.

It is this complex ability to observe language forms, draw conclusions from countless observations, and apply them to the construction of new sentences that makes it possible for small children to speak sentences they have never heard before. It also makes it possible for youngsters to use correctly all of the complicated parts of speech in the English language before they are old enough to go to school—without the help of teachers or textbooks and without the pressure of report cards or homework assignments or fear of punishment or failure.

David, in seventh grade, is having difficulty with homework in grammar. He can't seem to remember the rules about complex compound sentences, past-perfect participles, gerunds, and adverbial clauses. Yet he can use all of these forms correctly in sentences, and he can tell what is correct and incorrect "by the way it sounds." All this he learned for himself, without formal help, at the age of 3 or 4. Yet now, at 12, he can't understand the rules in school.

David's parents try to help him with the homework. But they have the same difficulty. They can use all the grammar rules correctly—because they learned to do so on their own as preschoolers. But they can't remember the rules either, which they were taught formally in junior high school.

Some early-learning experts say that because children are able to master language in all its complexities so early in life, there is ample evidence that they can also learn to read much earlier than most educators think, but that traditional preschool programs don't give young children nearly enough intellectual credit. "Between the ages of three and six, a period during which all normal children are completing their mastery of a complex system of symbols and completing it with little apparent effort and no formal assistance, our educational theorists consider the child capable of only finger-painting and playing musical chairs," commented reading expert George L. Stevens. "By not realizing that the very young child has the drive and the capacity for knowledge, educators have delayed the development of new and improved educational methods. The most damaging consequence of this educational philosophy has been the ruling idea that reading should not be taught to the very young child."[21]

7. Just as a child's neural circuits for intelligence are hardwired at a very early age, so are her emotional circuits—in ways that will affect her temperament and her ability to learn the rest of her life.

Psychologists have long observed that infants who are deprived of loving human contact grow up withdrawn, apathetic, slow to learn, and with serious behavioral problems. Now, researchers are beginning to understand how abuse and neglect can actually change the biochemistry of a child's developing brain.

Forming emotional attachments is among the first and most essential jobs of a baby's life, and she uses all her developing senses to complete the task. Studies show that an infant just hours old will visually track a shape resembling a human face while ignoring other drawings, and she prefers her mother's smell over any others. As she gazes into her parents' faces, memorizing their voices, shapes, and smells, a baby is strengthening the neural pathways that subconsciously tell her she is safe and loved and cared for, a security that appears to be a prerequisite for much of the rest of her learning. "If you have an abnormality in attachment experience in the first year, you will forever have abnormalities in the way that part of the brain functions," explained Dr. Bruce Perry, chief of child psychiatry at the Texas Children's Hospital in Houston and a researcher at the Baylor College of Medicine. "If during the first years of life a child is neglected emotionally, that's almost impossible to erase."[22]

Babies learn the language of attachment much like they learn other languages: through continual give and take, according to Dr. Perry. In fact, experts say the single most important thing an infant needs is at least one person who is *crazy* about him—and willing to interact with him, respond to him, talk to him, return his smile, and share his delight at each new discovery and cheer each new milestone. Each time a baby gets such feedback, his neural circuits register happiness and pleasure, reinforcing his desire to learn and interact again.

Some experts believe that a child's most basic learning instincts come from such emotional conditioning. "Emotion and learning are closely intertwined, because behaviors that elicit positive emotional responses are repeated and learned," wrote Dr. Lewis P. Lipsitt, a Brown University psychologist. A positive or negative response "is the sine qua non of learning," according to Dr. Lipsitt. "Those behaviors that are followed by a satisfying state of affairs will be repeated when the occasion arises again, whereas those behaviors that are followed by annoyance or pain will occur less frequently and may result in long-term exclusion from the behavioral repertoire."[23]

If a baby's smiles and steps and explorations are consistently met with indifference or anger, those emotional circuits can fail to develop or register the wrong message. Psychologist Geraldine Dawson at the University of Washington monitored brain-wave patterns of infants born to mothers with severe depression and found that their brains showed far less activity in the left frontal lobes—the area that serves as a center for joy and happiness—than did the brains of the babies of nondepressed mothers. By age three, the babies' brains still showed adverse effects. What mattered most was the quality of their interactions. The depressed mothers who managed to respond with at least some pleasure and encouraging feedback had happier babies.[24]

A child who grows up in an atmosphere of violence and abuse can actually be wired for fear, some researchers think. The emotional circuits are centered in the amygdala, an almond-shaped structure deep in the brain that governs the body's primitive fight-or-flight response. The amygdala evaluates incoming sights and sounds for danger even before they register in the neocortex, which governs more rational thought. Sights and sounds that have proved painful before—such as a beating by an abusive parent or caregiver—can trigger a powerful stress reaction. Later, the mere sight of that caregiver can induce fear.

Researchers say that children who have been abused often stay on mental high alert for days, constantly on guard for signs of more abuse, and they may misinterpret actions of others. A touch meant to be comforting, for example, can be seen as a threat. It's little wonder, then, that some abused and neglected children develop attachment disorders and are unable to trust or interact with others even years after the danger has passed.

Researchers have seen such reactions in Romanian orphans who have been adopted by loving families in the West. Several studies found that when faced with danger or frustration, some of these children would draw up into fetal position and rock on their hands and knees rather than seek comfort from an adoptive parent. Dr. Chugani has done PET scans studies of some Romanian orphans and seen abnormalities in the superoanterior temporal pole—a part of the brain involved in early bonding. Mary Carlson, a researcher at Harvard Medical School, did saliva tests on orphans still remaining in Romanian institutions and found that they had abnormal levels of cortisol, a stress hormone that affects growth, blood pressure, heart rate, memory, and anxiety.[25]

Still more studies of animals and human babies show that contact with a sensitive and responsive caregiver can buffer the effects of powerful stress hormones. Babies left with cold, distant baby-sitters, for example, had elevated levels of cortisol. Those left with friendly, playful sitters did not. The babies with the highest levels of cortisol were those who had stopped seeking attention from the distant baby-sitters, stopped crying, stopped playing, and appeared to fall asleep.[26]

Scientists are still just beginning to understand how the brain can be damaged by negative experiences early in life. But already, some think that aggression, violence, and criminal behavior may be rooted in the brain's biological reaction to violence and stressful experiences—in short, that crime may begin in the cradle. There is even early evidence that bad experiences can affect genes, switching them on or off at the wrong times, and short-circuiting brain connections, leading to seizures, manic-depressive episodes, and other mental problems. The National Institute of Mental Health is so intrigued by these findings that it has refocused its goals to study how the brain interacts with the environment during critical periods of development.

Meanwhile, researchers are fascinated by the fact that some children who grow up abused, neglected, or otherwise at risk for emotional and behavioral problems remain resilient to such hazards and are able to succeed despite the odds. The consensus is that most such children have at least one person in their lives with whom they are able to form an emotional bond.

8. A child has a built-in drive to explore, to investigate, to seek excitement and novelty, to learn by using every one of his senses, to satisfy his boundless curiosity. And this drive is just as innate as hunger, thirst, the avoidance of pain, and other drives previously identified by psychologists as primary.

Because of failure to recognize curiosity as a basic drive, much behavior among small children has been misinterpreted and labeled "naughtiness." Toddlers and preschoolers are frequently punished for "getting into everything" because their urgent need for mental stimulation isn't recognized and they aren't helped to find outlets for this basic drive that are better than emptying dresser drawers or seeing what happens when a box of detergent is flushed down the toilet.

Bright youngsters with an abundance of curiosity are often considered troublemakers in schools that fail to understand their great need for learning stimulation.

"Most of us have the spirit of scientific inquiry spanked out of us by the time we are twelve years old," a research chemist commented.

Today, however, psychologists and biologists are finding ample evidence of curiosity as a basic drive—not only in children but also in laboratory animals. Monkeys, for example, will work for long periods of time on mechanical puzzles, even when there is no reward involved—apparently just out of curiosity. Rats prefer to take a long but interesting route to reach their food rather than a short, quick one. Many laboratory animals can be motivated to perform tasks by the reward of a view out an open window, from which they can see activity outside their cage.

Even in newborn infants, behavior can be triggered by what psychologists call perceptual novelty. For example, when researchers show a two- or three-day-old baby in a hospital nursery a simple, bright-colored object, such as a red ball or a red circle on a white card, his eyes can be seen to focus on it and his whole body seems to become alert. The next time he sees the same object, the infant pays the same alert, interested attention. But after a while, the novelty begins to wear off. And the baby will give more attention to a second, different shape than he will to the first one.

Much behavior that we have considered childish or immature may actually be a sign of this primary drive in operation. For example, we know that a small child has a very short attention span and have assumed it was because her brain was capable of learning only in small amounts. However, it is more likely, in view of the new research, that a youngster can concentrate on one thing for only a brief span because of her brain's urgent need for more stimulation—because of her great drive to pay attention to many things.

When parents find a better means of helping a youngster satisfy her urgent need to explore, to look, to experiment, to try, not only will she learn but she will be much more content. The baby who is dry, fed, neither too hot nor too cold nor ill, and is still fussing in her crib or playpen has an unsatisfied basic need—the need for new sensory stimuli.

9. Your child has a built-in drive for competency, an inborn desire to do and learn how to do. He manipulates, handles, tries, repeats, investigates, and seeks to master as much of his environment as he can, primarily for the pleasure of such activity.

If you observe your baby's action closely, as Swiss epistemologist Dr. Jean Piaget did with his own youngsters, you can see this basic drive at work. Dr. Piaget, for example, described his own son Laurent, at the age of 3 months 10 days, lying in a bassinet. Over the baby, Dr. Piaget hung a rattle with a string attached. One end of the string he placed in Laurent's hand. Soon, by a chance movement, Laurent pulled the string to produce a noise. For the next 15 minutes, the baby delighted in tugging the string and listening to the rattle, laughing with obvious joy.

Three days later, Laurent again by chance pulled the string and set off the rattle. This time he obviously experimented with the effects of pulling the string. He swung it gently, tugged at it, shook it, listening to the different sounds produced from the rattle and laughing exuberantly.[27]

Your baby may drop his rattle over the side of his high chair and howl for you to retrieve it. Then he drops it again. And again. And again, as long as you are willing to fetch it for him. If you see his actions as purposeless behavior or as an attempt by your baby to control you, you'll probably become annoyed and cross with him. But if you understand that your youngster is trying to learn all he can about grasping and releasing, about falling objects, gravity, and impact noises, you'll find it much easier to be patient and understanding and to help him with his enormous learning task. The perceptual observations your baby gains from this repeated experiment are nothing he can put into words. But they will be stored away in his brain, where they can help him later in forming concepts and in developing intelligent behavior.

This drive for competency is easier to see in somewhat older youngsters. A toddler will often delight in spending half an hour climbing up and down the same three front steps. A three-year-old discovering how to zip her jacket will insist on zipping it and unzipping it a dozen times before she is willing to hang it away in the closet. A five-year-old will draw the same picture of a ship again and again for days.

Just how strong this drive is, any parent knows who has tried to do something for a child that the youngster is determined to do all by himself. No matter how difficult the task or how frustrating the failure, a two- or three-year-old will often persist to the point of exhaustion in his efforts to master his self-selected task. Emily spent much of her second year of life insisting that she be allowed to do things "Emmy-self!" Mindy's fiercest tantrum came when she, at 2½, insisted on scrubbing the kitchen floor, by herself, far into the night.

Such determination has a great underlying purpose in human development, suggested psychologist Dr. Robert W. White. He said that all human beings have an innate biological need for myriad perceptual and motor experiences to fill up the large, underdeveloped cortex area of the brain. A human infant is born so ill equipped to function in the world and has so much to learn before he is able to care for himself that this drive for learning—for competency—is essential for survival. He has to spend the earliest years of his life filling his brain with information and perceptions or he will not be able to act intelligently when he is older.[28]

Once a baby has had the opportunity to store up in her brain all of these many perceptions and experiences—to program her brain with information—then subsequent learning can be swift and complex, Dr. White explained. This conclusion, although it comes from psychological theory and research in the 1950s, is quite similar to what neuroscientists in the 1990s concluded after watching the brain at work via modern imaging technology.

This same need of a small child to develop competence was also observed by Dr. Montessori in her studies of preschool youngsters. She deliberately designed learning frames to help her tiny pupils develop competency in buttoning, buckling, tying, and lacing, for example. And she demonstrated how a young child can be helped to learn to carry out many of the simple operations of a household if taught in very simple, logical, programmed ways. The great joy this feeling of competency, or control over the environment, gives to children is the basis of her teaching methods.

10. Learning can be intrinsically enjoyable, and small children learn voluntarily when their efforts are not distorted by pressure, competition, extrinsic rewards, punishments, or fear. The more new things your child has seen and heard, the more new things he wants to experience.

Long before a child is ready for first grade, he's well aware that you don't go to school for fun. He knows you have to go. He hears older boys and girls talking about the strict teacher or the hard assignments or the confining rules. His mother tells him that he has to do what the teacher tells him. He learns to stand in line, to keep quiet, to do what the group does, no matter how much it bores him.

By the time he's in high school, his interest in learning is so distorted by worry about grades, by competition, by the need to win the teacher's approval, by homework assignments, and by pressures that he has almost given up expecting learning to be a joy. Even if he is lucky enough to encounter a class or a textbook or a teacher he finds fascinating, he knows it isn't socially acceptable to admit it.

But in his beginning, it was not so. Because of his innate drive toward competency, because of his inborn curiosity, learning was originally a pleasure. He worked almost constantly at learning during his waking hours—by looking intently at everything around him, by touching, tasting, listening, practicing sounds, exploring, trying, falling down, trying again. He enjoyed the process of learning and he enjoyed practicing again and again what he had learned.

A parent who remembers that learning should be intrinsically pleasurable for a small child has a good guide in planning mentally stimulating activities that aren't too immature or too advanced, too easy or too difficult. The purpose of these activities isn't to push the youngster or pressure him or make him compete with the neighbor's child or perform like a puppet to show off but to make the youngster happy himself.

3

How the Atmosphere in Your Home Can Foster Intelligence

The emotional climate you create in your home can do much to stimulate your child to learn, to foster his growing mental abilities. Or it can stunt his developing mind and dull his innate creative feelings. Your relationship with him as a parent, coupled with his inborn traits and temperament, will largely determine how he goes about learning for the rest of his life.

It's impossible to blueprint precisely the ideal home in which maximum learning can take place—and have it fit every individual youngster. Children differ too much. So do parents and family circumstances. But recent research suggests many important guidelines you can use to make your home a creative, stimulating environment for your child.

Many long-term research projects show that your youngster's intelligence will develop to a higher degree if the attitude in your home toward him is warm and democratic rather than cold and authoritarian. In one study, for example, the IQ of small children living in homes where parents were neglectful or hostile or restrictive actually decreased slightly over a three-year period. But in homes where parents were warm and loving, where they took time to explain their actions, let children participate in decisions, tried to answer questions, and were concerned about excellence of performance, there was an average increase in IQ of about eight points.

This doesn't mean that you should be completely permissive or let your youngster run wild or interfere with the rights and possessions of others. It doesn't mean giving her a vote equal to her father's in a council that makes all the family decisions. Nor does it mean that your home must be child centered.

It does mean that you should love your child wholeheartedly and enthusiastically and be sure that she knows it. (If a youngster thinks her own parents don't love her or approve of her, how can she face her teacher or her friends with self-confidence enough to keep trying?)

Sometimes it even helps to point out to a three- or four- or five-year-old just how many different ways you do show your love for him, especially if you work full time away from home or if you have a younger baby. Often an older child, who equates love only with hugging and cuddling, may think that the baby is getting the bigger share.

"I show Lisa I love her by cuddling her and rocking her and changing her diapers," you can tell your firstborn. "But you certainly don't want diapers anymore, and you like to be rocked just once in a while, when you've hurt yourself or you are very tired. So I show you how much I love you in ways you enjoy better now—like inviting your friend Michael to go to the beach with us and reading to you and fixing the pedal on your trike and taking you to the park to swing. I even show you that I love you by not letting you play in the street, because I don't want you to get hurt."

A warm and democratic home also means that you plan your family's activities to take into consideration your child's needs to grow and develop as an individual and that you give him as much voice in decisions involving him as he can handle. Your goal is to develop a thinking individual who can evaluate a situation and act appropriately—not a trained animal who obeys without question.

Even a two-year-old can be given choices, when you intend to abide by what she decides: "Do you want to wear the blue shirt or the green one today?" "Would you like to have your milk warm or cold this morning?" "Shall we have peas or carrots for dinner this evening?" "It's almost bedtime; shall we finish the puzzle or shall we stop now so there will be time for a story?"

It helps, too, if you explain the why behind the rules you set up and the decisions you enforce on your child—not in tiresome detail, not as an apology, not at a level above her understanding, but as a teaching device. Your child will learn, gradually, to evaluate alternatives. She will slowly begin to accumulate information upon which she can make good decisions. And she will realize, increasingly, that the rules you set up and the discipline you enforce are based on reasons and love and wisdom—not caprice or arbitrary or dictatorial power that she will sometimes feel compelled to challenge.

There is a happy by-product of this strategy, too. A two-year-old who is permitted some choices of his own isn't quite so negativistic and zealous of his independence as is a child who is struggling for some beginning recognition of his developing self. An older child, who has learned that his parents set up rules and make decisions for him only when it is necessary, isn't nearly so apt to rebel as a youngster whose mother or father expects him to obey "because I say so."

"The intellectual tasks involved in the process of socialization are formidable," pointed out Dr. Kenneth Wann and his associates at Teachers College, Columbia University. "It is all too easy to come to see only the overtly behavioral aspect of social development. When this happens, then the job of the child is seen as simply that of conforming to the do's and don'ts of behavior codes. The role of the adult, then, is viewed as primarily that of restraining the changing, overt behavior. This, of course, is not an adequate concept of the child's task or the adult's role. Such activity is part of the socialization process, but only a small part. The major task is intellectual. It consists of understanding and conceptualizing the demands of social living so that one can respond to the complex stimuli of continually varying situations with appropriate, adequate behavior. This is a giant of a task. And young children work hard at it."[1]

Parents, said Dr. Wann, should do whatever they can to help children with this intellectual task of learning how to get along in the world. Within a warm and understanding home, you should see yourself not only as a parent but also as your child's first, best, and most successful teacher.

Teacher doesn't imply that you help your child by means of structured, formal lessons. Your role is much more informal: to teach by example, by creating a stimulating environment, by talking to your youngster, by listening to her seriously, by loving her, by letting her teach herself with your guidance, by introducing her to the fascinations of the world you know, by taking advantage of every opportunity for learning in your life with her.

Just as you are not a formal teacher, so your preschooler is not a pupil in the sit-down-and-be-still-while-you-learn image of the word. Most youngsters can't sit quietly for very long before the age of six; that's one reason why it's often been assumed they aren't ready to learn. Most preschool learning takes place on the go, along with much motor activity.

Many factors interlace to make most homes a good place to learn and most parents ideal teachers. At home, a youngster can learn at his own pace. He needn't wait in fidgety boredom for two dozen other pupils to catch up, or he needn't continually drag behind because he can't maintain a grade-level pace or has somehow missed out on grasping some essentials. He faces no competition. No academic pressures. No formal timetable for learning. No tests. No fear of humiliating public mistakes. At home, a youngster can receive immediate feedback of praise or correction, which is considered by many researchers to be of major importance in the learning process and which is difficult for a teacher to provide for large groups of children.

At home, before age six, a youngster's growing brain makes her hungry for learning and uniquely easy to teach. During the preschool years, too, most children are eager to imitate and emulate their parents—to a degree seldom experienced by teachers or by parents themselves at other stages in their offspring's life.

These are positive strengths and great advantages that parents possess in their role as teachers. Almost always they outweigh parents' lack of special training and formal educational skills in dealing with their own youngster.

"But I have a job and a house and a whole family to take care of; I haven't time to be a teacher, too," some parents object. Yet it takes no longer to think of your child in terms of helping him learn than it does to function chiefly as his caretaker, and it certainly makes both of you happier in your relationship.

A case in point: A trip to the shoe store. Often you see a mother with her fidgety preschooler waiting for a salesperson. The mother is bored, cross, impatient. The youngster is bored, restless, whining. He begins pulling shoes off of a display counter. The mother watches him idly for a few minutes, then scolds him to stop. He doesn't. She jerks him away. He pulls back. She hoists him back on his chair, scolding, "No, no, no." As soon as she lets go of his arm, he goes back to messing up the shoes. This time she yanks him away. He cries. She slams him down on the seat in exasperation. He slides off defiantly and sits on the floor.

It's so easy to do it differently. The mother might have anticipated a wait in the store and brought along a book to read to her youngster. Then she'd have found 10 bonus minutes the two of them could have enjoyed together. They could have played a beginning reading game or a guessing game. The mother might have a small pad of paper in her purse so she and her son could have drawn pictures for each other. They could have walked about the store together, talking quietly about the kinds of shoes they saw and guessing what kind of people would buy them or how women's shoes differ from those for men. The mother might have shown the youngster how shoe sizes are marked or how laces go.

Almost anything the mother wanted to do to help the youngster learn or satisfy his curiosity or direct his restless energy toward acquiring information or sensory experiences would have kept him intrigued and interested—and better behaved—for the waiting period. The mother had to spend the time with the child anyway and whatever effort she put into reading or talking would have been less than the strain of scolding him or trying to deal with his unpleasant behavior in public.

A child's attention span is usually short. You needn't hunt for big blocks of time in your day to help him learn. You can play word games with a child while you are doing almost anything else around the house, for example. You can count red cars or white trucks or out-of-state license plates while you're driving. You can keep a mental file of ideas handy for all the times you wait with your child—for the doctor, the barber, the salesperson, the bus, or the checker in the supermarket. Even if you invest only the usual quota of scolding-whining-fussing time in learning, it will pay dividends for your child later on and make your relationship much happier now.

As a parent, you have the time and the opportunity to study your child as an individual, not just as a member of a class or an age-stage group. Better than any teacher ever could, you know how she learns best, what encourages her to try, when she needs a touch of humor and when a bit of firmness, how much challenge spurs her on and how much blunts her interest. You can observe her responses and understand her feelings and shape the learning environment in your home so it is uniquely right for your child.

Another way to foster your child's mental development is to make encouragement, love, and praise your chief methods of discipline. These techniques work most effectively in helping your child grow not only socially and emotionally but intellectually, too.

Christopher, five, attended a four-family picnic one evening and was introduced to the architect husband of one of his mother's friends. Although he had not yet been taught to do so, Christopher happened to stick out his hand for the man to shake at the introduction. Later that evening, the architect remarked to Christopher's mother what a fine impression the boy had created with this simple courtesy and how well the gesture reflected on the whole family.

That night, when his mother tucked Christopher into bed, she repeated what the architect had said, and she thanked him for helping to make a friend for all the family. Christopher glowed at her praise. Never once afterward has he failed to offer his hand promptly, courteously, confidently, and without a reminder when he is introduced to an adult.

It isn't always so easy to reinforce a desirable response in a small child, of course. But it does help to be alert to opportunities to give your youngster legitimate praise. False compliments ring phony even to a small child. But no matter how dull or slow or troublesome the child, you can always find a few opportune moments to praise him justly for something he is doing right or well or thoughtfully. If you emphasize what he has done right rather than scold him for what he has done wrong, you'll teach him to work from strength, not from weakness and discouragement.

Sometimes you can even create situations that will give your child small successes and you opportunities for praise. Some parents set their standards so high, in an attempt to keep their child striving toward major goals, that he never can satisfy them. But it's much more likely that the youngster will become discouraged, feel inadequate, and stop trying if you continually point out where he has fallen short.

It helps if you let your child know that you have confidence in his abilities so he will have enough self-confidence in himself to keep trying. Your youngster has enormous respect for your judgment. If you tell him he's "stupid" or "never will amount to anything" or that he's the "naughtiest boy in the neighborhood" or that he "won't get into college" the way he's doing now, he's almost certain to believe you and quite likely to give up trying.

Because a child does believe almost any label a parent hangs on him, you can use this technique to foster a self-image that will enable the youngster to learn easily and without dragging self-doubts. You might tell him, for example, "This is hard, but you are the kind of boy who enjoys tackling difficult things. I can remember how hard you worked at learning to walk, how you never stopped trying, no matter how many times you fell down or how many black-and-blue bruises you got."

"I enjoy reading to you because you always listen so closely," you could tell a child. Or "It makes me feel proud to take you to the supermarket with me because you behave so well and you help me find the groceries I need." Or "I know I can always count on you to be gentle with your baby sister; it's no wonder she loves you so."

Don't use fear—of failure, of scolding, of disappointing you, of physical punishment, of the withdrawal of your love, of ridicule, or of unmentioned consequences in the future—to motivate your child. Most parents do use fear of one kind or another as a handle to control a youngster, without intending to or even being aware that they are doing it. It may take time and practice to get out of the habit—but your child will learn more readily if you do, and your relationship with him will be more pleasant and comfortable.

Do encourage your child to feel that it's all right to try, that failure isn't a crime, and that a mistake can be one way of learning. Many youngsters spend so much energy worrying and trying to keep out of trouble and avoiding mistakes that their ability to learn is stifled.

Your child will make mistakes, of course. Everyone does. It will encourage her to keep on learning if you teach her how to handle her mistakes. Spilled milk, for example, is just that, not evidence that your offspring is hopelessly clumsy or naughty. All you need to do is show your youngster how to wipe it up and get herself another glass. If she accidentally breaks another child's toy, help her to apologize, work with her to make a plan for seeing that the toy is replaced, and then talk with her a bit about why some toys break and how they can be safeguarded.

This doesn't mean, of course, that you immediately absolve your youngster of responsibility when accidents or mistakes occur. You should help her try to understand what went wrong and how it can be prevented. But you can do it in an objective way that promotes learning rather than discourages your youngster from trying.

Every child develops a lifestyle or "learning style" that determines how he reacts to his environment, to people he encounters, to new experiences like school. "Learning style is the way individuals concentrate on, absorb, and retain new or difficult information or skills," explained Dr. Rita Dunn, professor at the Center for the Study of Learning and Teaching Styles at St. John's University. "It is not the materials, methods, or strategies that people use to learn; those are the resources that complement each person's style. Style comprises a combination of environmental, emotional, sociological, physical, and psychological elements that permit individuals to receive, store, and use knowledge or abilities."[2]

This learning style is shaped in part by constitutional factors with which he was born and to a larger extent by his experiences from infancy on. The older a child grows, the harder it is to change his learning style.

Many parents, inadvertently, encourage a child to develop a lifestyle that hampers learning. For example, Jeremy's parents seem to show their love for him only when he is quiet, clean, and undemanding. Their house is full of no-no's that Jeremy mustn't touch. His mother insists on feeding him because "he makes such a mess of things if he holds the spoon." She runs to catch him every time he tries to take a step on his own, because he might fall. And she keeps him in the playpen most of the day so he won't be spoiled by too much attention and get into everything.

Jill's mother is making exciting progress in her career in business management. She is efficient, hard working, well paid, and so busy and highly organized that she tries to schedule her time with her daughter down to the minute. Jill has learned that her mother seems to love her best when she plays by herself, never asks questions, and keeps out of the way. Jill's mother assures everyone it's easy to juggle both parenthood and career. But the sitter who is with Jill all day while her mother is away also makes it clear she likes Jill best when she's undemanding and quiet. Eventually, the behavior style Jill is being pressured to develop will hamper her learning and perhaps her eventual level of intelligence.

When both parents work full time, or in a single-parent home, it's particularly important that whoever takes care of the child during the day—sitter or staffer in a day-care center or parent who runs a day-care home—understands the importance of encouraging the child's mental ability and won't insist on behavior that hampers learning and the development of an effective learning style.

Sometimes the youngest child in a family finds it rewarding to develop a lifestyle of being babyish and depending on others. Or a boy may discover he gets more of the attention he needs by clowning than by serious achievement. Or a little girl may be subtly encouraged to smile and wheedle rather than to put forth learning effort. Parents must be alert to such situations and make sure their offspring gets attention when he is behaving constructively in ways that foster learning rather than when he is being a problem.

One major way in which you shape your child's learning style is by your use of language with him. How you talk to your preschool child and the verbal method you use to control him have an enormous effect on encouraging—or discouraging—the growth of his intelligence.

After studying groups of mothers and children from different social, economic, and occupational backgrounds, Dr. Robert D. Hess, a professor of psychology and education at Stanford University, and his associates concluded that a major difference between disadvantaged youngsters and others is not basic intelligence or emotional relationships or pressures to achieve but the way in which parents use language with the youngsters.[3]

Language largely determines what and how a child learns from his environment, and it sets limits within which future learning may take place, Dr. Hess pointed out. It can encourage—or discourage—thinking.

For example, a small child is playing noisily with pots and pans in the kitchen. The telephone rings. In one type of home, the mother says, "Be quiet" or "Shut up." In another, the mother tells the youngster, "Would you keep quiet for a minute? I want to talk on the phone."

In the first instance, explained Dr. Hess, the child has only to obey a command. In the second, the youngster has to follow two or three ideas. He has to relate his behavior to a time dimension. He must think of the effect of his actions on another person. His mind receives more stimulation from the more elaborate and complex verbal communication.

The command "Be quiet" cuts off thought and offers little

opportunity for the child to relate information to the context in which behavior occurs. The second type of communication helps the child to link his behavior to his environment and may encourage him to seek the whys in future situations.

If incidents like this continue to occur during the early years in the lives of the two children and if they continue to receive quite different learning stimuli, their verbal and intellectual abilities will be significantly different by the time they are ready for school, Dr. Hess observed.

Communication from parent to child that is stereotyped, limited, and lacking in specific information curtails a youngster's learning, emphasized Dr. Hess. Such language patterns are characterized by short, simple, and often unfinished sentences, clichés, and generalities, such as "You must do this because I say so" and "Girls don't act like that."

But by using words to relate your child's behavior to his surroundings, to the future, and to possible consequences, you are teaching your child problem-solving strategies that will be useful in other situations, suggested Dr. Hess. You are encouraging a wider and more complex range of thought. You are stimulating your child to learn and you are laying the foundation for learning in the future.

Dr. Ellen Sheiner Moss of McGill University in Montreal found the same sort of differences in teaching style between parents of gifted preschoolers and parents of children of the same age who were tested as average. She videotaped the interactions of mothers and children as each parent helped her preschooler with three different problem-solving activities: a puzzle, a peg game, and a block design task. And she found that the mothers of the gifted youngsters spent more time helping their youngsters understand the goal of each activity, gave them more cues as to the concepts involved, and offered them more encouraging feedback. They did more to suggest that the children anticipate the consequences of the actions they were planning and encouraged them to monitor their own thinking processes than did the mothers whose young-sters tested out as average.[4]

Everyone learns by all of the sensory pathways that relay information to the brain. But almost everyone—children as well as adults—learns more easily and efficiently by some sensory pathways than others. Some adults know, for example, that they grasp material better if they hear it in a lecture or a conversation than if they read it. Others learn better by reading. Some adults know that if they want to remember, say, a telephone number or a name, they must write it down and read it so they can learn it visually. Others learn just as easily by hearing it.

These physically based learning abilities vary at different stages of life, said Dr. Dunn, and are still developing during the preschool years. Kindergarteners, for example, don't have as much ability to learn by either auditory or visual means as do older school children, several studies show. But preschoolers are strongly tactile and kinesthetic in style, she pointed out, and "they find it easiest to learn by manipulating resources and actually experiencing through activities." She suggested helping young children find as many ways as possible to learn through their sense of touch and by means of physical games, acting out situations and real-life experiences. She also emphasized that young children cannot sit still for more than a short period, if that long, and need opportunities to learn on the move.

It's estimated that the average young person has watched TV and listened to the radio and to CDs for a total of almost 20,000 hours by the time he reaches age 18—probably twice as much time as he spends in school. Some of these hours yield high dividends in terms of learning. Much more of it is wasted on mindless programs, irrelevant commercials, and brain-numbing time-passing.

One of the greatest gifts you can give your child is the habit of watching television wisely. You should help her learn to choose what she sees deliberately, not merely look at whatever is on the screen. You should encourage her to evaluate her choices in comparison with other uses she could make of the time. And you should reinforce what she does learn from television with books, discussions, and other activities.

Television programs and videotapes can be marvelous aids for children who are just learning to read. (*Sesame Street* does it deliberately, for example. Commercials, by showing a few words clearly on the screen while they are being spoken, often teach reading inadvertently.) TV shows can expose young children to wonders and places and ideas and events impossible for them to experience otherwise. But because they have no background for understanding what they see or for putting it into realistic perspective, they need a great amount of parental help.

It's also essential that parents realize they are setting a powerful example for their children in the use of TV. Those who keep a TV set turned on regardless of what's on view or who watch randomly or excessively have little chance of teaching their offspring to do otherwise. Those who demonstrate that they often prefer to read a book or pursue a hobby or enjoy an in-depth conversation have at least a chance of convincing their children that there may be better uses for at least some of those 20,000 hours.

As you begin to understand and better satisfy your child's urgent need to learn, to experiment, to try, to explore, to handle, to touch, to see, to understand, you'll find she is much happier. She is easier to manage. She presents fewer discipline problems because her inner needs come closer to being fulfilled and she has an outlet for her restless curiosity.

Much of the typical preschooler's time is spent in activities that bore him and his parents and in matters of discipline. Parents who use early-learning principles with their youngsters report they cut down drastically on the frequency with which they say "Don't!" and "No!" and on the amount of "What can I do now?" whining.

In assessing how much your child is interested in learning and knowing about before he's old enough to start first grade, you're much more likely to err by underestimating than over-estimating. Almost everyone does—including educators.

For example, three members of a research team from Teachers College, Columbia University, along with the staffs of five schools for three-, four-, and five-year-olds in the New York City area, made a detailed study of preschoolers' learning activities. The 319 youngsters observed came from a wide range of home backgrounds—poor, immigrant, middle class, upper income, foreign-language speaking, city, and suburbs.

At the beginning of the study, reported Dr. Wann and his associate, "No one would have denied that young children know and think. We had worked with children too long to be that naive. We also had the benefit of the work of other people before us who have studied young children. None of us, not even the most sophisticated of our group, however, was prepared for what was found. The depth and extent of the information and understanding of three-, four-, and five-year-old children was much greater than we had anticipated."[5]

For a brief time, the team kept anecdotal records of the children's activities and comments. In the first 600 such notes, the youngsters covered a total of 609 topics, and they were far more interested in questions of how and why than merely what, observed Dr. Wann. "We found children attempting to understand people, places, and events remote in time and space from their own immediate surroundings. We found children struggling to understand phenomena in their environment. We found children developing confused and inaccurate concepts. We found children indulging in animism and the enjoyment of fantasy as they viewed their immediate world. More frequently, however, we found them seeking to understand the causes of the phenomena they observed and to test their own thinking about these phenomena."

Parents and teachers need to realize that not only do children crave great amounts of knowledge but they also enjoy having information and using it, said Dr. Wann. They often relay facts to another child, starting out, "Guess what!" And they frequently make a game out of testing their own or other children's information. "Probably the greatest resource for young children, in this respect, is adults who listen to children, who talk with them about their ideas and who provide experiences for developing further understanding," Dr. Wann noted.

He suggested that adults should take preschoolers on more trips—to museums, zoos, and other places of interest—visit people working at interesting occupations. They can tactfully and encouragingly help children correct some of their misconceptions. Not only can they furnish children with stimulating sensory material, but they can assist children in sorting it out and making sense out of their observations. One of the happiest and most successful ways to stimulate your child's mental development is to let him share your own interests and activities.

It's easiest, of course, for parents who aren't holding a job outside the home to use these ideas. They can most often take advantage of the unpredictable, teachable moments and have more time and energy to interact with their children. But current reality is that more than half of the mothers of babies under the age of one year hold jobs away from home. The percentage goes up for toddlers and preschoolers. Many families need two incomes to have an acceptable standard of living. Single mothers may have to work; others are being forced off of welfare into jobs. Highly educated women aiming for top-level careers often find that peak demands on their time and energy—a hospital residency, for example, or competition for a law-firm partnership or academic tenure—coincide with the years when the needs of their children are most urgent. Even the most caring, interested, and involved fathers face similar pressures.

Some strategies do help. Flexible hours, shared jobs,

telecommuting options, and high-level part-time options may all help give parents more time with young children. Harried parents are pushing employers to be more "family friendly," and many corporations are responding in limited ways. But the "mommy track" can mean a job that requires 40 or 45 hours a week instead of 60 or 70 and still costs a woman her place on the career ladder. The average work week has been lengthening, especially for those in administrative jobs. Commuting time is also growing. And despite company policies, workers are often given to understand that if they spend more time away from the workplace with their children, they won't be considered to be serious about their jobs.

Increasingly then, young children—sometimes starting at the age of just six weeks—are spending large chunks of time with parent substitutes, at home with sitters or nannies or in a day-care center, in family day care, or with a neighbor or relative. Parents who do choose alternative care for their offspring should not only measure their choices in terms of cost and convenience but also look for caregivers who understand the importance of early mental stimulation and make such opportunities routinely available or who are willing to follow parents' guidelines about learning activities. It's not easy.

A few high-income parents even hire a teacher with a degree in early-childhood education to be a nanny for their child. Such care is enormously expensive and hard to find and not an option most families would even consider. An experienced nanny who is tuned into the idea of early learning and has time and energy to spend on an individual basis with a child is another good choice. But that, too, is beyond the means of most families. What's worst is hiring someone—say, a neighbor or relative—to simply "watch" a child while parents are working. This is more affordable and should keep the youngster physically safe. But "watching a child" can translate into keeping a baby in a crib most of the day or plopping a toddler down in front of the television for hours, wasting irreplaceable opportunities for mental development. A grandmother or aunt who can be turned on to the concept of early learning and will use some of these ideas might work out well, if available.

Many parents have only a limited choice of group care—either a day care or family day care. Day-care centers differ widely. Some are nonprofit, often housed in local synagogues, mosques, or church Sunday school rooms; in community centers; or even in facilities provided and subsidized by an employer. Others are part of national for-profit chains. Before you enroll your child, you should check not only state accreditation, safety inspections, and policies about sick children but also staff credentials and staff–child ratios. In many centers, teacher turnover can be as high as 50 to 70 percent a year. You should spend time observing in the center, evaluating how much real learning is going on and how much time children spend in aimless wandering and traditional bead-stringing activities and how alert staffers are to the mental needs of their charges. As interest in early learning has increased, some day-care centers have adopted names like "wee learners" or "preschool academy" while doing little or nothing to incorporate new ideas into their programs.

What seems to be a sizable assortment of toys for a room full of toddlers, for example, may not keep them stimulated and learning week after week, cooped up in the same room or two. Staffers may have to spend more time diapering and toileting and setting up juice breaks than in reading books. Strictly enforced schedules over an eight-hour day—juice, lunch, nap, TV—may be hard for your independent two-year-old to take and he may turn off part of his eagerness to learn. Four-year-olds may be bored by another year in the same setting, with the same equipment and same learning possibilities they also had at age three. (By that age, you should consider sending your child to a nursery school. In contrast to day care, which is intended to serve parents' needs by relieving them of child care for many hours, nursery schools are designed specifically to benefit young children, with trained teachers and half-day sessions, a comfortable time frame for preschoolers to be away from home.)

Long-term studies about the effects of day care generally suggest that high-quality centers may have some positive benefit for young children, particularly if their own homes are not particularly stimulating. The catch is that only about 10 percent of day-care situations are rated as quality. Most are considered by researchers to be poor to mediocre. Stacks of studies made by government agencies, child-advocate organizations, foundations, and even corporations conclude there is reason for serious concern about the care young children are getting when their parents are at work.

A major problem is that most working parents cannot afford what high-quality day care usually costs. Day care work is the second lowest paid job in the United States; most staffers make little more than minimum wage and have few if any benefits. So it is difficult to recruit and keep caregivers who love small children, have infinite patience, and know how to help them learn.

Family day care can be better—or worse. Typically, a mother who is at home with her own child or children needs to earn money and takes on other youngsters, too. Her arrangement may be an informal, nonlicensed setup, or she could have training and approval from the state, often depending on where she lives. In theory, family day care could offer your child the loving, low-key learning routine of his own home, provided the mother actually spends her time interacting with the youngsters and understands ideas about mental stimulation. But it's also possible the mother will plop the youngsters in front of the TV while she does her housework or takes care of her own children. One analyst of a major study called the situation "dismaying."

A parent who provides family day care should take on no

more than six youngsters, including her own, unless she has a full-time helper—and fewer if she is caring for babies or toddlers. If you decide on family day care, you should visit several times before enrolling your child and often afterward to be sure he is not only safe but happy and learning.

It's not easy to find an adequate substitute for a parent's personal care of a baby or young child. But millions of mothers and fathers find it necessary to do so. Research studies show that even babies remain clearly bonded to their parents, even if a majority of their waking hours are spent with others. But encouraging mental development in out-of-home care can be challenging unless you can find an ideal situation. Even so, a majority of child-care experts still have concerns about putting babies and toddlers into full-day care and urge parents to find some other solution, if possible.

If you must use full-day out-of-home care for your young child, it's even more important to use the time you do have with him in ways that will encourage his mental development.

In studying the home backgrounds and child-rearing practices that produced famous twentieth-century men and women, authors Victor and Mildred Goertzel observed that parents who raise distinguished offspring themselves tend to be curious, experimental, restless, and seeking. The common ground for the highly diverse types of families that produce outstanding sons and daughters—as well as many other highly competent and successful children not quite so famous—is a driving need to be going, doing, learning, striving, involved in activities and concerned about ideas.[6]

Family value systems have the strongest impact on these children, rather than schools or teachers, reported the Goertzels. Parents help their children build on personal strengths, talents, and aims. They are usually so interested and interesting themselves that their youngsters eagerly tag along to share the excitement.

Parents who set high standards of excellence for their children and who are warm and positive about their abilities and accomplishments usually find that their youngsters live up to their expectations, researchers who have studied gifted preschoolers have found.

"Parents who explain their requests, consult with their children, and give reasons for discipline have higher achievers," noted Dr. Merle B. Karnes, who studied gifted and talented preschoolers attending a special program at the University of Illinois. "In general, the attitudes, values, and expectations of the parents influenced the child's behavior and aspirations. Finally, the parents' acceptance of the child had a definite effect on the child's self-concept. In other words, children who perceive that their parents think highly of them are likely to feel good about themselves.[7]

"If the child is not challenged and if expectations are not compatible with his or her abilities, motivation to learn may be dulled and the child may join the ranks of the underachievers," continued Dr. Karnes. Preventing gifted youngsters from becoming underachievers and wasting their abilities and talent is a strong argument for the involvement of parents in early learning.

In an unusual kind of investigation into the environment in which great talent and ability develop, Dr. Bloom and a team of researchers picked out 25 individuals who had made world-class achievements before the age of 35 in each of six fields: research mathematics, research neurology, concert piano, sculpture, Olympic swimming, and tennis. Then they interviewed these outstanding individuals, their parents, and some of their teachers to learn more about their characteristics, the influences in their environment, motivation, training, and learning stages.[8]

What Dr. Bloom called "the most striking finding" is the "very active role" of the family, selected teachers, and sometimes a peer group in helping these young people develop into world-class stars. "The old saw that 'genius will out' in spite of circumstances is not supported by this study of talent development," said Dr. Bloom. "Whatever the individuals' original 'gifts' or special early abilities, skill, and achievements, without extremely favorable supporting and teaching circumstances over more than a decade, they would not have been likely to reach the levels of attainment for which they were selected in this study."

Dr. Bloom and the researchers had expected to find that these outstanding individuals showed extraordinary gifts and abilities early in life and as a result were given special instruction, attention, and encouragement. But instead, they discovered that the encouragement and instruction came first, and then later on, the youngsters were identified as being unusual.

Typically, these children grew up in homes where their parents were keenly interested in the field in which they later excelled, although the mothers and fathers themselves were usually not outstanding. The pianists, for example, were surrounded by music from babyhood on. The swimmers were at ease in the water and enjoyed water activities as early as the age of three or four. The mathematicians were remembered as asking questions and trying to sort the answers out into logical relationships.

But these characteristics aren't extraordinary in young children, Dr. Bloom noted. When they are introduced to water and to swimming by a good teacher, almost all preschoolers enjoy the experience and learn to swim quite quickly. "Under the proper circumstances virtually all children should quickly become at ease in the water, learn to swim in a very natural way, and enjoy swimming and play in the water," he said. "Ideally, all humans should possess this 'gift,' were it not for poor instruction, inept teachers of swimming, and very late introduction to swimming."

Similarly, parents of the world-class pianists recalled that as babies, their offspring had appeared to be listening to music that was being played in their hearing and that they moved in rhythm to the sounds. But "child specialists as well as musical specialists note that some early sensitivity to music is displayed by virtually all children in most cultures of the world," pointed out Dr. Bloom. "Responses by infants to music, rhythms, and other sound patterns are universal, even though what is responded to and found to be pleasant differs from culture to culture."

Most three- and four-year-olds ask questions by the dozens, although the future mathematicians may have done so with more purposefulness than other youngsters. "Whether most children would ask such questions if encouraged by adults is not clear," said Dr. Bloom. "Perhaps the important point is that the curiosity represented by this questioning was taken seriously by the parents, who took the time to answer these questions in a truthful and relatively sophisticated way. Such responses by the parents encouraged the child to ask further questions as the need arose. This type of question-raising in other forms characterized these individuals over the years and eventually became central in their field of interest—research mathematics."

Whether the highly talented adults studied by Dr. Bloom and his researchers really had unusual aptitudes, traits, or other qualities as young children isn't at all clear, he pointed out. What is important is that their parents thought that they did and treated them as having great potential, providing them with an unusual amount of learning opportunities and making clear they appreciated and valued the early signs of talent.

Dr. Bloom added, "It should be noted that children have many qualities and characteristics which may or may not be special and distinctive. It is in part the values and interests of the parents which determine which qualities they will or will not note and mark as special and worthy of further attention and cultivation. Girls were, in the past, rarely noted as having special gifts in mathematics and science by parents, while a boy with similar attributes and interests might be much encouraged. Similarly, in the musicians' homes, athletic abilities and interests were rarely noted or encouraged. . . . The values and interests of the parents determine which traits and qualities will be given great encouragement and further cultivation and which traits and qualities will be ignored."

Because parents thought these youngsters had special abilities, they encouraged them, provided them with opportunities to learn and, often, special teachers. They helped their youngsters practice for lessons, paid attention to them, and led them to understand that they were expected to work hard and to achieve. When the children did work hard and perform well, their teachers began to give them extra attention and praise and they soon became "star pupils," winning prizes and still more attention and praise.

As the children's abilities continued to develop, parents invested even more in their training, with special equipment, special schools, special summer experiences, advanced teachers—even freedom from the usual chores and duties expected of other youngsters. The children enjoyed the rewards of their talent as well as the activity itself, liked to please their parents and teachers with their successes, and flourished in the close attention their families gave them.

The continued development of great talent in older children and adolescents is beyond the age limits of this book. But briefly, the cycle of special attention, special teaching, high achievement, and resulting praise and rewards goes on. At a point somewhere between the age of 10 and early adolescence, it becomes evident that these young people do indeed have extraordinary potential. By their own choice, they begin devoting more time and effort to their training, even at the cost of slighting other areas in their lives. The commitment of family resources to the pursuit of high achievement becomes greater. And as a final stage, a master teacher or coach is found who spurs the teenagers to outstanding achievement and opens the way into the top ranks in their field.

The point of citing Dr. Bloom's research here is not to advocate that parents set out to develop future Olympians or scientific geniuses but to demonstrate once again the enormous influence parents and the home environment they create have on young children. And it's to remind parents that the mothers and fathers of these extraordinarily talented young adults motivated them to learn as children, not by pressure or fear but by sharing their own interests and by praise and attention.

There is much to be said for considering your preschooler as a gifted child, even though there is little reason to have him formally tested and labeled and most tests for giftedness are designed for school-age youngsters. But if you see your child as needing special and ample opportunities to learn, you'll be more likely to fulfill his needs and to appreciate his accomplishments more. Many of the signs of giftedness are quite similar to characteristics of young children who haven't yet been pushed into learning conformity. And if you cherish these traits and help your youngsters to develop them, chances are good he will be considered gifted when he's older.

For example, one list of the behaviors of a young child who could be considered gifted, which was compiled by Dr. Margie Kitano, an early-childhood education specialist at New Mexico State University, included the following:[9]

- Has a high level of curiosity
- Is alert and attentive
- Learns rapidly
- Shows early interest in books and reading
- Retains information
- Has a large vocabulary for his age
- Likes new and challenging experiences
- Enjoys being with older children
- Asks many questions

- Experiments with materials around him
- Produces original ideas
- Likes to do things in his own way
- Adapts easily to new situations
- May prefer to work alone
- Has a good imagination
- May give unexpected, smart-aleck answers

Dr. Kitano made several suggestions for fostering the development of bright children that are useful for parents, although they are intended primarily for teachers in preschool programs where there are gifted youngsters. For example:

- Give your youngster opportunities to think creatively. You can make a game of asking him questions that have many possible answers instead of only one correct response. For example, "How many ways can you use a wagon?" (There are many more examples of this strategy in Chapter 8.)

- Plan activities that encourage him to stretch his mind and to do some in-depth thinking. For example, instead of just letting your youngster scribble with a crayon or splash paint on poster paper, talk with him about colors, how they can be mixed to form other hues, what emotions his artworks suggest, why he made the artistic choices that he did.

- Involve your child in planning and decision making and encourage him to talk about his ideas, feelings, and thinking processes.

- Provide things he can do that encourage the orderly process of scientific thinking. (Chapter 6 explains this strategy in detail.)

- Help your child to develop moral concepts and apply them to specific situations. (Chapter 6 also details how parents can help in this regard.)

Whether your youngster is formally identified as a gifted child isn't important at this age. What is essential is that you make sure she has enough mental challenge and stimulation in her life and the kind of atmosphere in her home that encourages mental development. Not only will your child be happier if the needs of her fast-growing brain are satisfied but you will enjoy your youngster more. Parents can't help enjoying their offspring's excitement and delight in learning, just as they shared the joy of her beginning to walk and talk.

That early learning should be a happy experience for a child needs to be emphasized again. New research about the marvelous abilities of very young children to absorb new information and about brain growth during these early years has tempted a few teachers and parents to subject toddlers and preschoolers to intensive, rigid programs that bombard them with unrelated facts. These programs have once again aroused some opposition to early learning, on the grounds that it creates undesirable pressures on youngsters and may turn them off from learning in the future.

This kind of mental force-feeding is not at all what this book advocates. There are three ways to make sure you are not "pushing" your youngster in a harmful way, even inadvertently. First, you should not suggest in any way to your child that your love for her is contingent on her intellectual performance, that you are disappointed in her, for example, if she forgets a word you are trying to teach her to read or isn't using a grammatical form correctly.

Second, you should let her reactions to the early-learning experiences you give her be your guide in helping her learn. If she seems interested and eager most of the time, you are on the right track; if she balks, refuses to pay attention, or indicates in other ways she doesn't want to do what you are suggesting, don't try to force her.

And third, if what you are doing seems to make your child happy, then you almost certainly are not pushing her. Your purpose is to provide the nourishment her brain needs, not to force-feed her mind.

An emotional relationship between you and your child in which you act as guide and teacher and fellow explorer in a fascinating world—rather than as judge, jury, examiner, therapist, or boss—is one that grows well with time. Your child will feel less need to rebel against you when she is an adolescent and less of a sense that she must make a clean break with you to be independent when she is a young adult.

4

How to Raise
a Brighter Baby:
The First Year of Life

When you bring a newborn baby home from the hospital, many of his needs are obvious. He must be fed, burped, changed, bathed, protected, loved. Dozens of pamphlets, hundreds of baby books, and millions of grandmothers can tell you precisely how. But because the needs of a baby's fast-growing brain are not so obvious, they have usually been overlooked or misinterpreted or left to chance. Many of the ways in which we usually go about caring for babies may actually be limiting the growth of their intelligence.

During the first few years of his life, your baby's brain will triple in size. Even before he is ready to be born, all of the approximately 100 billion nerve cells he will ever possess have already been formed. But the connecting links between these special cells grow at a tremendous rate during early childhood, and their growth appears to be stimulated, at least in part, by the activity of the nerve pathways leading to the brain.

"The brain's growth spurt of the last fetal trimester and the first three months postnatally will never be matched again in the child's life," noted Brown University's Dr. Lipsitt. "We cannot help being awestruck by the phenomenon." And like the growth of the brain itself, the rate at which babies learn is also "phenomenal," he pointed out.[1]

"All of the developmental milestones involve an immense input and appreciation by the baby of sensory stimulation, the registration of that stimulation in memory and the alteration of behavior style as a function of that experimental input," he added. "This is the stuff of which learning is made."

In a very real physical sense, your baby's early environment and the amount of sensory stimulus he receives will build his brain and foster the growth of his mental capacity.

This "developmental explosion" in the early years of your baby's life does not happen by chance or by a predetermined process, noted Dr. Leon Eisenberg, of Harvard Medical School. "How fast it happens and how far it goes are, within limits, a direct function of the amount and variety of patterned stimulation supplied by the environment."[2]

Your infant's brain is actively learning from the very first hours of her life, chiefly by means of sensory stimulation and motor activity. But because she has such limited means of communication, because she can't talk or walk, the importance of early input into her brain has been largely overlooked.

An enormous amount of sensory stimulation is necessary to give a baby's brain basic information to use in functioning and in forming concepts. It is during the earliest years of life that the brain is best able to record sensory experiences, researchers have discovered. That's why parents should give a baby all possible opportunities, within the limits of safety and common sense, to learn through a wide variety of sensory stimuli. Your baby needs vast experience in hearing, seeing, touching, moving—and to a lesser extent, in tasting and smelling.

But your newborn's brain isn't just a blank computer disk on which you can write any program or store any data that you choose. The genes she has inherited and the experiences of her prenatal life interact even before her birth to form the basis of an innate temperament and personality that will, in part, determine how and how well she will learn. Part of the art and science of parenting is to shape learning opportunities so they work best for your individual child.

Just how much difference the environment you create for your baby does make can be seen from research Dr. Burton White and his colleagues did years ago at Harvard University's Laboratory of Human Development.

Dr. White and his associates made intensive studies of babies between birth and the age of six months, trying to pinpoint how much of their development is an automatic result of age and growth, how much can be changed by the way in which they are handled, and how much they are influenced by their surroundings.

Because home environments vary so much and are difficult to measure precisely, Dr. White did his research in a Massachusetts hospital, where infants awaiting adoption lived in a special wing for several weeks or months (a practice that fortunately has since been replaced by speeding up adoption procedures or by placing babies in individual foster homes within a few days of their birth). At that time, all of the babies were exposed to the same environment, which the researchers then enriched in different but measurable ways.

First, the researchers observed a control group of infants carefully, for long periods of time, charting what the babies did every minute they were awake. They developed complicated devices for measuring the infants' abilities to focus their eyes and to follow moving objects visually and for recording blink reactions to approaching objects.

All of the babies in Dr. White's studies were physically and mentally normal. Like infants in some private homes, those in the control group were kept in cribs lined with solid white bumpers. They lay on their backs; they were changed when necessary, picked up for feedings at four-hour intervals, and bathed daily by nurses who were devoted and kind—but very busy.

As newborns, these infants were visually alert—that is, paying obvious attention with their eyes—only about 3 percent of the daylight hours, Dr. White discovered. Gradually, during the first few weeks of life, they began to pay more attention to the world around them with their eyes. At an average of 50 days of age, they discovered their hands with their eyes. Fascinated by their fingers, they increased their visual attention sharply, to about 35 percent of daylight hours by the age of 60 days. For the next few weeks, these babies spent much of their waking time watching what their fists and fingers were doing.

Hand watching tapered off a little between the ages of 13 and 15 weeks for the babies in Dr. White's control group. But another spurt in visual activity occurred at 105 days to 120 days, when the infants were put into open-sided cribs where they had more chance to look out. About this time, their visual attention jumped to 50 percent of daytime hours.

Dr. White also studied the abilities of infants to follow an object with their eyes as it approached or receded. Until the babies were about 30 days old, Dr. White found, they could focus on and track a moving target only at one specific distance—usually about 7½ inches from their eyes. But by the time they were 45 days old, their visual accommodation had improved. At 4 months, the babies had visual accommodation skills comparable to those of normal adults.

The precise steps by which an infant learns to coordinate the movements of his hands and eyes, so that he can reach out accurately and grasp what his eyes are seeing, were also studied.

Typically, at about the age of 2 months, the babies in Dr. White's control group began to swipe haphazardly at objects with their hands. By about 78 days, they could raise one hand deliberately and a few days later, both hands. Soon after they were 3 months old, they could bring both hands together in front of them to clasp an object they were offered.

At 15 weeks of age, these babies learned to turn toward an object they could see. At 18 weeks, they could grasp by moving one hand toward the object, glancing back and forth from the object to the approaching hand before making contact. What Dr. White called "top-level reach," or skilled one-handed grasping directed by the eyes, was achieved at about 150 days of age.

Yet this normal pattern of eye–hand development, so enormously important between the ages of 45 days and 5 months, is "remarkably plastic," according to Dr. White. It can be speeded up considerably by enriching the baby's environment.

For example, after he had recorded developmental data for babies as they were normally cared for in the hospital, Dr. White began to change and enrich their surroundings. First, he arranged for nurses to have time to give one group of babies 20 minutes of extra handling every day when they were between the ages of 6 and 36 days. After this period, these babies were more visually active than the control group—but their developmental timetable stayed about the same.

Next, Dr. White added more stimuli to the environment of another group of infants. The white padded bumpers on their cribs were replaced by bumpers and sheets with a multicolored, printed design, starting when the babies were 37 days old. After each daytime feeding, the bumpers were removed from the cribs and the babies were placed on their stomachs so they could see the activities of the hospital ward around them. A special stabile was erected over each crib to give the babies something colorful to look at.

The stabile, which Dr. White designed, contained a small mirror in which the baby could see his face, two rattles low enough for him to grasp, a rubber squeeze toy that made a noise, and a gaily colored paper decoration at the top. These objects were mounted on a red-and-white-checkered pole at various distances from the infant's eyes and the entire stabile was suspended above his head, where he could easily see it.

The babies in this enriched environment were a few days slower in beginning to observe the motions of their own hands and not quite so visually alert at the start of the experimental period. But soon they became much more attentive and active than the control babies. In less than one month, they learned how to reach out and grasp accurately—a skill that took the control babies 3 months to develop. They reached the stage of top-level grasping at about 90 days of age—about 2 months sooner than the infants in the standard environment.

For a third group of infants Dr. White tried a modified environment. This time, instead of adding the bright stabile to the crib on the thirty-seventh day of each baby's life, he mounted a pacifier against a red-and-white-patterned background on each side of the crib rails at an easy distance from the infant's eyes. Then, on the sixty-eighth day of life, he replaced these with the stabile.

These infants made the fastest gains of all, apparently because the stimuli in their environment were better matched to their basic needs. They were much more visually alert and active than the other groups of babies. They began swiping at objects several days earlier than control babies. They started guiding their hand visually toward an object at about the sixty-fifth day of life—20 days earlier than babies in the normal environment. They reached top-level grasping at the eighty-ninth day of life, in contrast to 150 days for the infants in the standard environment.

Dr. White's experiments showed to what a great extent "developmental landmarks" in early childhood can be speeded up by changes in the environment. And they demonstrated what major gains can be achieved by relatively small changes in an infant's surroundings.

Dr. White called these changes "of striking magnitude." For when an infant is able to reach and grasp and learn from his sense of touch at the age of three months, he can learn more—and wants to learn more—from his environment than does a baby who doesn't develop this skill until he is six months old. The infant who is paying attention visually 45 percent of the day learns more than the one who is attentive only 20 percent of the time.

You will see a great variety of learning activities occurring in your own infant, if you watch for them—and if you give her enough learning opportunities. Following are guidelines suggesting what you can expect as your baby grows and how you can foster her learning. But your best guide will be the reactions of your child. Watch her. Learn from her, even as she is learning from you.

(These age-level divisions aren't sharply defined stages. Some babies develop more quickly. Some go more slowly. Most grow and learn unevenly, by jumps and spurts, with plateaus and even some backtracking. If you begin providing your child with extra stimulation early in her life, you'll probably need to read ahead of these general age classifications to find ideas for her.)

Birth to 6 Months

The moment of birth thrusts your baby out of a warm, watery, sheltering, dark, cramped environment into a new world of lights, sounds, smells, human contact, and somewhat frightening freedom to move about. He may be exhausted and a bit battered by the long process of birth, and he must cope with the instant need to breathe and survive on his own, separated for the first time from the support system of his mother's body.

Yet he is already learning—from the moment he is gently laid on his mother's abdomen and nuzzles his way to her breast, where he may begin nursing with a little help. If researchers test him during the first day of his life, or the next few days following, he will show them that he can focus his eyes on shapes and patterns and register obvious enjoyment at looking at them. He will prove that he is learning by beginning to act bored after he has looked awhile and by showing preference for more complicated patterns over simple shapes and by paying more attention to a new design than one he has been shown repeatedly.

Babies as young as 12 hours can detect differences in odors and will indicate by their facial expressions which ones they like and which ones they don't. Newborns not even a full day old generally indicate that they enjoy the smells of banana, vanilla, and strawberry. But they dislike the offensive odors of rotten eggs and fish, experimenters have found. By the time they are one to six days old, infants are able to determine where an unpleasant odor is coming from and will turn away from it.

Infants will pucker up their lips if a drop of lemon juice is placed on their tongue but will indicate an obvious liking for a drop of sugar water. Given different concentrations of sugar water, they show they can tell the difference by sucking the hardest when offered the sweetest liquid. By the age of 12 days, babies are able to do something as complicated as imitate an adult sticking out his tongue; if a baby has a pacifier in her mouth so she can't stick out her tongue, she can remember what she wants to do and will stick it out when an adult removes the pacifier.

Newborns also show emotions from the minute they are born, researchers point out. And they are capable of forming give-and-take relationships with other people from the first day of their life. They have been practicing their hearing skills before birth and, after they are born, will move their eyes in a way that indicates they can tell where sound is coming from. They also make it clear that they prefer the human voice to any other sound.

In fact, the more researchers study newborn babies, the more competent they find the babies to be. In the past, scientists have grossly underestimated newborn competence, Dr. Lipsitt said. He described a newborn as a "complex biological system, shaped by its evolutionary history to solve problems in a complex environment."

It's easy to forget your baby's need for sensory stimulation when you first begin taking care of him after his birth. You're tired. He is still recovering from the trauma of birth. His sleep patterns don't match yours. Just the unfamiliar actions of handling him still make you feel awkward and anxious. His breathing patterns may seem irregular and worrisome. And even the healthiest infants with the most experienced mothers can still scream with colic for hours a day until they outgrow it at about the age of three months.

But it's worth the effort to be sure your infant is getting at least adequate sensory stimulation right from the beginning— because like satisfying his intense need for food, satisfying your baby's mental hunger will make him happier and easier to care for.

It isn't as difficult to begin filling your infant's life with appropriate sensory stimulation as it may sound. You can easily tell when a stimulus is effective, or when your infant is too sleepy or too hungry to care, or whether she's just not interested. Your baby will concentrate intently on sights and sounds and movements that interest her. And she'll fuss and cry when she's bored. When she's fed, changed, burped, and not too hot or too cold but is still crying, you can often quiet her by giving her something fascinating to look at, to feel, or to hear, or by rhythmic motor activity.

As you come to know her better, you can also tell by her reactions the infrequent times when she's had enough stimulation—it's usually when she's been tickled or jiggled—and needs to be rocked or nursed or back-rubbed or soothed to sleep. But too much stimulation is comparatively rare and almost all babies don't receive nearly enough.

From the first day of his life, your baby will enjoy having something interesting to look at. You can hang a bright shape or colorful mobile over his bed, make it move whenever you are in the room, and get him a new one every few days. (They are easy to construct yourself, using photographs or paper shapes—and the variety will be more interesting to your baby than an expensive store-bought mobile he stares at for months.) You can use bright colors in his room wherever possible, instead of hospital white or wishy-washy pink. You can tack or tape bright pictures on his wall. You can carry him from room to room with you and encourage him to look at objects in your home and outside of the window. You can put him in a safe, padded spot in the kitchen where he can watch you preparing meals and listen while you talk to him.

During the first few weeks of life, if your infant is crying and you pick him up and put him on your shoulder, he will usually stop crying and start looking around—at least for a short time. This visual alertness can be of major importance in your baby's very early learning, research at Stanford University School of Medicine suggests. This particular combination of a parent's soothing along with an opportunity to look about seems to be ideal for learning in very young infants, according to the Stanford study.[3]

Toting your baby with you in a canvas sling that holds him cuddled against your chest or, when he can manage his head better, lets him ride on your back, gives him a wealth of sensory stimulation. It's effective even if you just pack him around the house with you occasionally, but even better when you can take him outside for a fresh rush of stimuli. For longer jaunts, a stroller that allows your baby to face forward, rather than at you or up at the sky, will give him a better view of the passing world and all its fascinations.

A playpen and an infant's seat make more sense during the first few months of your baby's life than they do later on. At this age, your aim should be to give your baby a chance to see as much as possible, and both playpen and seat are better than bassinet, crib, or baby carriage for this purpose. It's when a playpen is used to restrain a crawling child from physically exploring his environment that it begins to limit development.

The foundation of language is laid during the earliest weeks of life, too. You should begin talking to your baby from the very first time you hold her. You should vary your tone of voice as you greet her in the morning, change her, feed her, put her to bed. Take her attempts to communicate with you seriously and respond—for even in the first weeks of life she'll learn how to tell you by her cry when she is hungry, hurt, colicky, or bored.

Soon, your baby will begin babbling, practicing vowels, consonants, syllables, sounds of every type. But eventually, she will discard those which are not part of the language she hears in her home. As an adult, she'll never again be able to make some of these sounds, even if she studies a language in which they are used.

Do listen interestedly when your baby babbles at you. When he stops, talk back to him. This will help him get the idea of what language is all about. When he makes the same sound consistently and deliberately, you can repeat it to him. But generally, you should avoid baby talk because your infant needs your example to learn correctly. Sing to your baby, too, and play music for him—of all kinds. Your baby will enjoy hearing and learning from your old rock-and-roll tapes just as much as from classical music or collections specially marketed for babies.

Physical movement is another major way in which your baby develops his intelligence. There is considerable evidence that the tactile-kinesthetic sense is the basic avenue of very early learning. Movements generate a great number and variety of sensory stimuli and sensory information, which is stored in the brain, accumulating and becoming interrelated until the baby has an organized body of information learned from movement exploration.

To this basic tactile-kinesthetic information, a baby then relates the stimuli he gains through his eyes, his ears, his nose, and his taste buds. A newborn probably learns to recognize his mother by the sensory stimulus of being cuddled close against her and to anticipate feeding by the bodily position in which he is being held and the feeling of the nipple against his lips. But soon, he will associate the visual stimuli of seeing his mother and hearing her voice with the tactile-kinesthetic information he has already acquired.

Later on, as his brain accumulates more information gained from movement and touch and he has had a chance to receive much more visual stimuli, your baby will begin to rely more on seeing than on touching. Eventually, he will learn primarily by means of his eyes. But even as a two- or three-year-old, he will still feel a great need to touch new objects, to verify the visual stimuli, to learn through more than one sensory route. Adults do the same thing when they finger a fabric they consider buying or handle a dish as they browse around a china shop.

To build up this basic body of sensory information obtained from movement, your baby needs great freedom and opportunity to touch, to move about, to manipulate objects, to reach, to grasp, to learn to release. She also should have as much freedom as possible—consistent with her safety and health—from constricting clothing and from a confining bassinet.

How a baby's environment can inadvertently retard development is illustrated by an observation Dr. Piaget related about his three youngsters. Both Laurent and Lucienne reached the stage at which they could follow the movements of their hands with their eyes shortly after they were two months old. But Jacqueline didn't until the age of six months. The reason for the delay in development, suggested Dr. Piaget, was that she was born in the winter. So that she could be kept outside in the sun as much as possible, which her parents thought desirable at the time, her hands were usually mittened and her arms tucked under blankets.

During the first months of your baby's life, you can help him pour tactile-kinesthetic stimuli into his growing brain in many ways. You can give him opportunity during his waking hours to lie on a pad on the floor, where he can move his arms and legs freely without hitting the sides of a bassinet. You can put him on his stomach on a hard surface so he can eventually learn to roll himself over. You can hang a plastic ball or bell on the side of his crib for him to bat. You can suspend a simple toy from a piece of elastic so he can watch it move and learn to pull on it.

Most important, you can remember that your baby isn't an invalid who needs to live in bed and to be quiet almost all of the time, but a living, growing child who needs activity, exercise, and stimulation.

You can give your infant interesting textures to grasp: swatches of material like velvet, silk, wool, burlap, and satin; small blocks of foam rubber; a piece of sponge; tissue paper that crinkles with a fascinating sound; simple wooden toys. (Do remember that she'll try to put almost everything in her mouth, so make sure that the materials are too big to swallow and watch her carefully.) You can touch her fingers gently with an ice cube and with a just-warm trickle of water. You can play nursery rhyme games that involve counting fingers and toes or touching eyelids, ears, nose, and mouth.

As your infant begins to coordinate her hands and eye muscles, you can encourage her to reach out for objects, and when she has grasped them, let her experiment freely in banging, testing, shaking, and using them in any exploratory way that is safe. Peekaboo, with a handkerchief laid across your baby's eyes, makes a delightful game as soon as you are sure that your baby can grasp the cloth and pull it away.

If you observe closely during the third, fourth, and fifth months of your baby's life, you'll probably notice that he likes repetition. He makes the same movements again and again. He may spend a surprising amount of time handling and looking at an object that intrigues him or repeating the motions of his hands. If you rock him or bounce him on your knee and then stop, he'll often try to imitate the motion to get you to repeat your activity. If you do, he'll smile and laugh delightedly.

This experimentation with familiar activity is based on preliminary months of absorbing a great variety of sensory stimulation, both Dr. Piaget and Dr. Hunt have noted. In turn, repetition of familiar patterns leads into the next stage—that of fascination and curiosity in exploring new objects and activities. Dr. Hunt, of the University of Illinois, said that "the more different visual and auditory changes the child encounters during the first stage, the more of these will he recognize with interest during the second stage. The more he recognizes during the second stage, the more of these will provide novel features to attract him during the third stage."[4]

These changes in your baby's basic motivation for learning, Dr. Hunt suggested, explain what Dr. Piaget meant by his statement that the more a child has seen and heard, the more he wants to see and hear.

As Dr. Lipsitt put it, a baby is born with sensory systems immediately ready for learning. At the same time, these systems are immature and that tends to canalize infant experiences in particular directions and to put some limitations on what he can learn. As a result of this sensory learning made possible by his environment, his brain continues to develop and to become more capable, and he becomes better prepared to cope with the development tasks of later childhood.

It's also critical that you develop a warm, loving, personal relationship with your baby, in which you learn from each other and each of you shapes the other's behavior. Your baby learns much by discovering how to please you and how to fit into the environment you have created for him. And you learn from his responses and actions how best to be his parent.

As you get to know your baby better during these early months of her life, you can begin to shape her learning experiences to take into account her innate temperament. As child psychologists use the term, temperament includes such characteristics as your youngster's general level of activity (Is she constantly busy, restless even in her sleep?), her sociability (Does she smile and laugh easily and seem to enjoy being with people?), the ease with which she fits into a daily rhythm of activities, soothability (Is she easy to comfort when she's unhappy and irritable?), ability to concentrate, and the way she deals with frustration (Does she persist or shift her attention to something else?).

If you understand, for example, that your child is slow to warm up to new stimuli and often reacts first with fear instead of interest, you can plan to give her extra emotional support until she's comfortable in new situations. If you know that your youngster gets frustrated and angry when she can't master a new challenge quickly, you can figure out how to break the activity into smaller steps that make quick success much more likely.

Your child also needs some basic sense of order and consistency in your parenting, so she can build up what psychologists call "cognitive operating systems." She needs to know what kind of behavior you will allow, what makes you respond happily to her, that her home life is stable and predictable enough so that she can draw reliable conclusions from what she is experiencing.

Six to 12 Months

By the time your baby can sit up by himself, he'll be enormously fascinated with looking at and handling objects of every kind, and he needs great opportunity to do so. By this age, too, he's ready to do more than just look and touch and record these sensory stimuli in his brain. He's beginning to make some primitive experiments with cause and effect. He'll pick up a small block and drop it again, testing repeatedly just what relationship there is between the movement of his fingers and the bang on the floor.

In fact, the force of gravity is the one constant point around which a baby systematizes all the spatial relationships he is working out for himself during his early sensorimotor stage of life, suggested Dr. Newell C. Kephart, when he was director of the Achievement Center for Children, Purdue University.[5] (This *may* make you feel a little bit better about picking up your baby's toys for the eighty-seventh time in a morning.)

At this stage, you can stimulate your baby's mental development by providing him with a changing variety of objects to touch, taste, bang, throw, grasp, and shake. Toys with safe, moving parts that can be attached to playpen bars and plastic blocks with bells inside make stimulating toys. So does an unbreakable mirror with hard-rubber edging. Sponge toys, floating animals, boats, and pouring utensils encourage him to experiment with water in his bathtub. He'll want one or two cuddly stuffed animals with interesting textures, especially for going to sleep.

But you needn't spend much money to buy toys for your baby. He can find great delight and learning stimuli in a block put into a small kettle, in a nest of lightweight plastic bowls, in a small cardboard box with a piece of tissue paper inside, and in scores of simple objects already in your home.

As soon as your baby is ready to begin moving forward with a crawling motion, she needs to be put on a clean floor where she can propel herself along. If you have carried and held your baby almost constantly during her first few months of life, it may be difficult for you to break the habit. But remind yourself that she needs the chance to explore and stretch her growing physical abilities. You can encourage her to start crawling by putting toys just out of her reach and by cheering her on.

The best learning stimuli you can provide for a crawling baby is a big room with a clean floor, where she is free to move about safely and freely for a large part of her waking hours. The room should be kept warm enough for your baby to be barefoot, and she should be dressed in overalls with padded knees, if possible. Everything that can be broken, toppled, swallowed, pulled over, or tripped on should be removed from the room, and all exits and stairs gated and locked. Electrical outlets should be capped, and electrical cords should be put well out of reach, where your baby can't pull or chew on them.

The point is that your baby should be free to explore and manipulate without discouraging and frustrating no's and don'ts from adults—although she does need your watchful, interested supervision. If you continually snatch objects out of her hands, slap her fingers, and scold her, she'll be apt to get the idea that it's wrong to be curious and naughty to investigate.

You will, of course, eventually need to teach your youngster not to touch objects that don't belong to him and to have respect for the property of others. But he is too young now for you to be sure he will heed and remember your prohibitions, although he will sometimes. Your baby will learn more easily and obey with less fuss in a few more months if he is getting ample sensory stimuli and your no's don't frustrate his learning attempts completely.

The room in which your baby does his crawling should contain at least one low shelf of toys and objects your baby can handle. A shallow box can also be used, but the usual toy box is too deep to be effective and produces only confusing clutter. A pot and pan cupboard offers delightful sight, sound, and touch stimuli for a crawling baby, if you can arrange your kitchen so he can explore safely. But he shouldn't be permitted in the kitchen unsupervised, particularly after he is able to pull himself up on his feet.

If the weather is suitable and you can supervise him closely, you can let your baby crawl outdoors on the grass. Opportunity to crawl on carpet, on wooden floors, and on linoleum and vinyl flooring can also vary the stimuli your baby's physical activity is sending to his brain.

The first day your baby crawls an inch, you need to safety-check every place in your house your baby can possibly go. It's almost impossible to overestimate the speed with which a crawling baby can pull a tablecloth off a just-set table. Or reach a hand up to pat a hot electric burner. Or locate a poisonous household cleaner under your kitchen sink and swallow a dangerous dose. Or pick up a pin or a button you had no idea had fallen on the rug.

It's estimated that there are well over a quarter of a million household products on the market today that could kill a baby if swallowed. Some of these carry a poison warning. Most do not. No cleaning agent of any kind, no detergent, furniture polish, or bleach should be kept where a baby could possibly get it. If you've been in the habit of leaving medicine on a night table or on a kitchen counter, change now. Many drugs can be lethal to a baby. Aspirin is the greatest single cause of death by poison in small children and even the pleasant-flavored baby aspirin can be fatal in large enough quantities. Babies can die from drinking whiskey or other liquor stored where they can reach it.

It will disrupt your household considerably more to construct a home environment that gives a crawling baby optimum opportunity for learning, rather than one designed primarily for the convenience of adults and the protection of their possessions. But it is tremendously important for your baby during this early sensorimotor period.

During the second half of his first year of life, your baby will be making greater progress in matching up stimuli from all his senses. He can now anticipate your coming by the sound of your footsteps—and differentiate between those of his father and his mother. He may discover how to make the TV louder by touching a particular button. And he will start crawling toward the cookie box if you mention the word.

He'll also be learning more about space and time, about cause and effect, and about the sequence of activities. He'll scream now when you take him into the pediatrician's waiting room because he can remember that the last visit included an injection. He may cry when he sees a baby-sitter coming into the house, not because he dislikes her, but because he knows that her presence means his parents will go away.

Your baby is now beginning to associate words with objects, although she won't be able to form most of the words herself for several more months. You can encourage her development of language by naming an object she is looking at or holding: "cup," "cookie," "toast," "block." You can put her actions into words for her: "Now we're putting on your shirt" and "Sit on my lap and we'll rock." In addition to this simple labeling, you should continue to talk with her conversationally whenever you are with her and, in turn, listen seriously to her vocalizations.

When your baby makes a sound like "Mama" or "Dada" by accident, you can react with obvious delight; you'll want to, anyway, and it will help your baby understand that she can make noises that have meaning. At this age, it can be helpful if you recognize and use her first few approximations of words—perhaps "wawa" for *water* or "Nana" for *grandmother*.

When Diane, for example, began to make the sound "baba" rather consistently in her babbling, her mother told her three-year-old that his little sister was trying to say "brother." Paul puffed up with pride and joy to discover that the baby's first word meant him. He responded eagerly and lovingly whenever Diane said "baba," and the baby quickly learned to associate the sound with him. The family used the syllables until Diane was able to say "Paul" properly.

Once your baby has grasped the idea that things and people have names and that she can form the names herself, it's better to shift to correct pronunciations for every word. Your child's speech will progress more rapidly and efficiently if you do.

You should begin reading to your baby from children's books by the time he's six months old. Find a quiet place and time, when your baby isn't engrossed in crawling or trying to pull himself up on his feet, and cuddle him close as you read. Picture books that show familiar objects are good. So are simple stories. Encourage your baby to look at the pictures and to attempt to turn the pages. A few excellent books for very young children also involve the sense of touch by including sandpaper whiskers on a daddy's face to rub or a ring-shaped cutout in the page to slip a finger through or a cotton-soft bunny to feel.

Your baby won't understand every word that you read to him at this age, of course. But he will grasp more than most parents realize. And he will enjoy the cuddling and the sound of your voice and begin to associate books with pleasant feelings.

Your baby's experiments with banging, dropping, throwing, picking up and releasing, poking, pushing, and pulling will continue at this age. But if you observe closely, you'll see more purpose in what he is doing and more serious concentration on the results of his actions in contrast to the random behavior of a few months earlier. He now gets enormous delight from his increasing skill in coordinating thumb and forefinger to grasp and let go of small objects. He enjoys pursuing crumbs around the tray of his high chair and has great fun with small toys and objects of all kinds. (Do remember they'll still go into his mouth and must still be large enough to be safe.)

The amount of sensory stimuli and motor activity your baby has had during the first half of his first year of life will already be reflected in his learning behavior, as Dr. Piaget pointed out. The more stimuli he has been able to store away in his brain and the more points of reference he now has for new objects in his environment, the more curious he will be and the more eagerly he will go about exploring his surroundings, instead of reacting with fear or indifference to new sights and new experiences.

5

The Insatiable Drive
to Learn: Ages One
to Three Years

The years between your child's first and third birthdays may well be the most critical of her life. Never again will she change so fast, learn so much, or accomplish such a formidable intellectual task as learning his native language.

During these two years, your youngster will change from a baby into a child. She will gain enough control over her growing body that she can walk, climb, jump, run, and manipulate without having to pay attention to making her brain and muscles work together. She will learn to use language to communicate, question, joke, demand, seek help, and learn. Her learning style will become more evident. Her personality will be crystallizing, reflecting not only her innate temperament and heredity, but her environment and parenting. By three, it will be apparent, as it was not at one, how competent she is likely to be later on. Critical differences among three-year-olds that will foreshadow their future will be obvious.

A child's home environment and her relationships with her

parents are particularly crucial during these two years, as new studies make clear. Yet one researcher estimated that perhaps only about 10 percent of families give their toddlers optimum rearing during this vital stage—in part because they are busy with other demands in their own busy lives and in part because knowledge about what young children need during these years has not yet been widely reported.

Once your child has discovered how to pull herself up into a standing position and to take a few staggering steps while hanging on to a low coffee table or chair and finally to walk independently, she'll begin to get a fresh perspective on old, familiar territory and her intense interest in exploration will increase. Her curiosity now seems insatiable. She can push, pull, climb, grab, pick up the tiniest objects, and move about with surprising speed. Her attention span is short. Her energy seems triple that of adults caring for her. And her ability to get into everything will exhaust her parents long before she is ready to stop and nap.

How parents and other caregivers react to a toddler's insistent, persistent eagerness to learn and the kind of learning environment they provide for her will be a significant factor in the lifelong level of her intelligence and her attitude toward learning and new experiences.

The more research educators and child development experts do on children between the ages of one and three, the more convinced they become that these may be the two most critical years in a child's life. By age three, there are many measurable, important differences between children that predict with considerable accuracy how well they will do later on in school and how successful they will be interacting with their environment and with other people. The most crucial requirements for the development of competent, intelligent children, researchers have found, are freedom to explore in a safe environment and encouragement and help in learning language.

One of the first and most important of these studies was made by the long-term Harvard Preschool Project, which was designed to gain basic, accurate knowledge about how young children develop ideally and why there are such great differences in the abilities of six-year-old children. These differences have become a major national problem because of the difficulties they create in schooling and because it seems to be almost impossible for the least competent youngsters to overcome their handicaps.

One of the first things the Harvard researchers, headed by Dr. White, did was to define precisely what the results of ideal rearing during the first six years of life should be. What is a competent, successful six-year-old?

The Harvard researchers began by studying hundreds of preschool children with a great variety of educational, ethnic, and socioeconomic backgrounds. They talked to teachers, parents, pediatricians. They gave tests. They observed youngsters carefully at home, at school, on playgrounds, in supermarkets. Then they chose two groups of children. Half of these youngsters were rated high in overall competence, "able to cope in superior fashion with anything they met, day in and day out." The other half had no physical or mental abnormalities but were "generally of very low competence."

Next, the researchers set out to analyze exactly what the differences between the competent and incompetent six-year-olds were. They observed the children carefully over an eight-month period, often recording their activities with minute-by-minute evaluations. The researchers didn't find much difference between the first graders in physical skills and abilities. But they did pinpoint several abilities that distinguished the competent six-year-olds from those who had poor ability to cope with their surroundings.

These are the characteristics that mark a competent six-year-old, according to the Harvard researchers:

- He is able to get and hold the attention of adults in socially acceptable ways, such as talking to them, showing them something, moving toward them, or touching them.

- He can use adults as resources when a task is clearly too difficult. He can get information or assistance in a variety of acceptable ways, without trying to get an adult to take over the task.

- He can lead and also follow other children his age in a variety of activities. He can give suggestions, direct play, act as a model for others to imitate, and follow the suggestions of others.

- He is able to compete with other children his age.

- He can take pride in his own achievements, in something he has created, possesses, or is doing.

- He can playact an adult role or adult activity or talk about what he wants to do when he grows up.

- He can make good use of language and grammar and has a good vocabulary for his age.

- He is aware of discrepancies, inconsistencies, and other kinds of irregularities in the environment and can talk about them and can occasionally act on these inconsistencies appropriately.

- He can anticipate consequences and act on them or talk about them.

- He can use abstract concepts and symbols, such as numbers, letters, and rules, in an organized way.

- He can put himself in someone else's place and can show an understanding of how things look to another person.

- He can make interesting associations, relating scenes, objects, or discussions to past experiences.

- He has the executive ability to plan and carry out activities that involve several steps.

- He can use resources effectively, choosing and organizing people and/or materials to solve problems.
- He can do two things at once, or concentrate on one activity and still keep track of what is going on around him.

Once the Harvard researchers had a working definition of a competent six-year-old, their next step was to trace how children acquire these abilities and what factors in their home life favor the development of these traits. As a beginning, they analyzed their massive records, which covered the development of more than 100 preschool youngsters whom they had studied for more than two years, again sorting out the competent and the incompetent children. These studies turned up an unexpected finding: The competent three-year-olds had already developed most of the abilities that marked the competent six-year-olds. It was immediately obvious that the study needed to shift to an earlier age level.

Next, the Harvard researchers determined that there seemed to be very little difference at age one between those children who later turned out to be most competent and those who turned out to be least so. It was what had happened in the home when the youngsters were between the ages of one and three years that accounted for most of the crucial differences that were detectable by age three and almost impossible to change by age six, the Harvard researchers concluded.

In further studies, the Harvard group sought out families that had already produced highly competent or markedly incompetent children and that also had another child who was a year old or younger. With parents' permission, the Harvard researchers observed these babies and toddlers carefully for up to two years, correlating the degree of competence they developed with the child-care practices in their homes.

Harvard researchers then identified two areas of particular importance during the critical two years between ages one and three: freedom to move about in a stimulating environment and the use of language.

In the first months after he learns to walk, about the time of his first birthday, a toddler's newfound ability to move around—combined with his innate curiosity—produces a great amount of work and stress for his mother or whoever is taking care of him. How his parents respond to this insatiable into-everything activity of their toddler helps determine whether he will be highly competent or incompetent by the time he is three years old—and as a first grader.

Parents who raise the least competent children use playpens and gates to restrict their children's freedom to explore and move around much more frequently than do those whose youngsters are rated as highly competent, according to the Harvard findings. More effective parents arrange their homes so that their children are protected from dangers in the house—and the houses are safe from damage by the youngsters. Then, they give their toddlers free access to roam and explore. These parents in particular make the kitchen safe and useful and provide kitchen cabinet space and safe utensils for their children's play, according to Dr. White.

Regardless of how successfully they are developing, one- and two-year-olds spend much more of their time interacting with objects than they do with people, according to the Harvard findings. One-year-olds average 86 percent of their time with objects and 12 percent with people; two-year-olds, 81 and 19 percent, respectively. Most, but not all, of the objects that hold the attention of toddlers are small and can be easily carried about.

Toddlers between the ages of 12 and 15 months spend much of their time looking intently at objects (an activity the Harvard group labeled "gain information—visual") or simply exploring the qualities of these objects. But gradually, children begin to devote more time to mastering simple skills. The toddlers who turn out to be most competent later on put in more time mastering easy tasks during this age period than do the less competent youngsters. Poorly developing toddlers tend to spend far more time in idleness than do other children; these statistics Dr. White called "an index of emptiness."

The other major factor in how well a young child develops is the kind and amount of language his parents and the rest of his family give him, according to the Harvard studies. Talk between toddler and parent is often very brief, usually no more than a few words. Frequently the words come in direct response to what a youngster is doing or in answer to a short question from him, an interchange lasting no more than 10 to 30 seconds. But because the language relates so directly to what the child is doing, because it comes when he is most open to learning, such talk is a powerful teaching device.

"The mother's direct and indirect actions with regard to her one- to three-year-old children are, in my opinion, the most powerful formative factors in the development of the preschool children," said Dr. White. "I would expect that much of the basic quality of the entire life of an individual is determined by the mother's actions during these two years."

What makes an ideal parent for a one- to three-year-old? "Our most effective mothers do not devote the bulk of their day to rearing their children; most of them are far too busy to do so. Many of them, in fact, have part-time jobs," Dr. White noted.

"What they seem to do, often without knowing exactly why, is to perform excellently the functions of designer and consultant," he added. "They design a physical world, mainly in the home, that is beautifully suited to nurturing the burgeoning curiosity of the one- to three-year-old." Such a home is full of "small, manipulable, visually detailed objects" and of opportunities to move about and climb, according to Dr. White.

"These effective mothers talk a great deal to their infants and very often at a level the child can handle," Dr. White continued. In talking to their offspring, these parents "consider the baby's purpose of the moment" and use language that is "at or slightly above his level of comprehension" and "do not prolong the exchange longer than the baby wants."

Dr. White also noted that "though loving and encouraging and free with praise, these mothers are firm. They set clear limits. They speak a disciplinary language the baby can understand. They don't overintellectualize or expect the baby to do more than he is capable of."

Said Dr. White: "Effective mothers seem to be people with high levels of energy. The work of a young mother, without household help, is, in spite of modern appliances, very time- and energy-consuming. Yet we have families subsisting at a welfare level of income, with as many as three closely spaced children, that are doing as good a job in child rearing during the early years as the most advantaged families."

If you've ever doubted that small children have an urgent, insatiable drive to learn, just watch a youngster in the running-climbing-questioning-chattering-getting-into-everything months between the ages of one and three. A two- or three-year-old can outexercise a professional athlete, outtalk a radio disc jockey, outrun most parents in active training, and still have energy enough to fight going to bed. You're lucky if you can persuade your wiggler to sit still long enough to eat.

The years between one and three also include the four- to six-month stage called the "terrible twos." This is the frantic period—usually around 2½—when almost every toddler is in active rebellion against the restrictions placed on her free exploration by no-ing adults and when she is most frustrated by her inability to become more independent and to "do it all by myself."

If you give your youngster more opportunity to learn and to satisfy her curiosity and to become more competent, she'll be far easier to live with. If she has fascinating, challenging learning materials to play with and ample opportunities to exercise her exploding interest in language, she'll not be as likely to empty the wastebasket into the goldfish bowl or crayon the walls or flush socks down the toilet. And if you can help her learn to develop some degree of control over the everyday objects in her immediate environment, she won't experience nearly as much frustration.

During this 12- to 36-month period, your child still needs great opportunity to learn through sensorimotor activity, just as she did in the earlier stages of her life. The more stimuli she can pour into her brain through looking, listening, tasting, smelling, and touching, the more intelligent she will become.

But now, as she changes from a baby into a preschooler, she needs more than just a variety of sensory activities. These experiences must be integrated into patterns that help her understand relationships and form concepts. She is better able now to think, to reason, to draw conclusions, to use objects as symbols for ideas and activities. The great surge of language that comes between the ages of 1½ and 4 years not only helps her to express her thoughts, but also to formulate them.

During this period, too, your youngster's learning style begins to crystallize, and this will influence the way in which she goes about learning and her reactions to new experiences all the rest of her life. Your offspring's learning style is based partly on individual constitutional factors—whether she's quick or placid, impatient or relaxed, independent or clinging, happy-go-lucky or a born perfectionist. But it's determined to a greater degree by whether her attempts to learn at this age meet with enthusiasm and help from her parents or whether the attempts are constantly frustrated, punished, or minimized.

How can you arrange a rich, stimulating learning environment for a youngster between 12 and 36 months of age—in view of today's expanding knowledge about how the brain develops? It isn't as big a job as it sounds.

Basically, you'll discover that your youngster gives you many useful clues to what his growing brain needs. You don't have to impose learning on him or try to teach him facts by rote, as a few misguided early-learning programs have prescribed. You don't have to try to force him to sit still to learn or even program ahead of time what he should be learning. Your job, generally, is to see that he has opportunity and encouragement to teach himself.

In the months after your toddler's first birthday, you can help increase his mental abilities by enlarging the environment in which he is permitted to play freely and safely. You can begin teaching him how to handle possible hazards—how to slide off an adult bed safely, feet first, and how to go up and down stairs sitting down, for example—so that he can be allowed more freedom.

When it's warm and dry outside, you can fence off a sizable portion of your yard, make sure it contains no hazards, and let your toddler explore freely. Or tote him to the nearest park to let him roam. You will need to watch him closely until he's outgrown the habit of putting everything new and interesting into his mouth.

To help make this greater freedom possible, you will need to teach your toddler the meaning of *no*. But it is important that you do not say no too often or too harshly, or your toddler may get the idea that you love him better when he isn't trying to explore and learn.

You need not resort to slapping a toddler's hands or spanking him to teach him to respect the rights and property of other people. Slapping hands to discourage active exploration usually teaches a child to slap back or to hit other, smaller children. Spanking carries a feeling of humiliation that isn't necessary in helping youngsters learn to behave properly. Spanking should be used rarely, if at all, only with toddlers too young to understand your words and only when they are in immediate danger—reaching up to touch a hot stove burner, for example, or darting into the street.

For some adaptable, easygoing toddlers, it's enough to say

no in a quiet, firm, disapproving voice, pointing out what is forbidden and offering a substitute object or activity. But most toddlers are more determined.

One good way to teach your toddler "No" without curtailing his exploratory drives or resorting to slapping or spanking is this: First, be quite clear in your own mind what objects you don't want your child to touch or what you don't want him to do. Keep this list as short as possible. Whenever your youngster reaches out to touch one of these objects or to do something you are forbidding, sit down in front of him and hold him securely by his forearms, so that his hands press against his cheeks and you can turn his head to face you squarely. Now he has to listen to you. Keep him facing you for about half a minute, saying firmly, "No" and "Don't touch."

When you let your toddler go, give him a hug. This method compels him to pay attention to you and lets him know that you mean what you are saying, but it avoids the idea of punishment. A toddler who is trying to fill his brain's urgent need for stimuli should not be punished; he merely needs to learn a lesson about the property rights of others and the dangers inherent in this fascinating world.

You'll probably have to repeat this strategem a few times. But after that, your child should understand the meaning of *no* and be convinced that you mean what you are saying. But you will have to be consistent. A little later, you can begin adding a short reason to the no's you give your child: "No, that will burn you." "No, that is Daddy's." "No, that will break." This gives your child information he can apply in other situations (you are trying to raise a thinking, reasoning, independent adult— not obedience-train a puppy), and it will help convince him you aren't arbitrary and mean.

If you are giving your toddler plenty of opportunity to explore and fill his brain with sensory information, if you love him and he knows it, he'll accept your no's in good grace— most of the time. If you begin this way, if you are warm and loving, if you understand your child's real needs, you'll find you almost never have any need to punish him and discipline is just not a problem in your house.

Once your toddler has his walking well under control and can get where he wants to go without paying attention to his feet, his interest shifts to talking.

In the six months after his first birthday, your youngster will probably add only about two dozen words to his speaking vocabulary. But his understanding of what you are saying will increase enormously. You should talk to him whenever you are with him—when you dress him, while he's eating, while you're doing housework and cooking, when you take him on an outing, when you rock him. Asking him to carry out very simple directions can turn into a happy learning game in which he takes great delight, especially if you praise him and hug him when he's successful. The more language your child hears now, the larger and richer will be his vocabulary when he begins talking explosively, about the time of his second birthday.

By the time your toddler is 2, you probably won't be able to total up his vocabulary. By 2½ he'll hold up his end of a conversation quite effectively, even if he has to invent a string of nonwords to do so. And by age 3, you'll be wishing that he'd stop talking for a few minutes so you can have some peace.

A great many parents do a superb job of helping their youngster acquire the mechanics of language—simply by filling the child's environment with good language models, by matter-of-factly correcting his mistakes, and by responding to and praising his efforts. The child delights in his increasing competence with words and in the power that words give him to function in his world. Parents usually enjoy his learning so much that they can't resist quoting him to any adult who will listen.

So receptive is a child of this age to the language he hears about him that he learns to speak it precisely as he hears it, whether it is French, Hebrew, Chinese, Bostonian English,

Southern drawl, or slum patois. In homes where parents are too busy, too unschooled, too ignorant, or too uninterested to provide good models of language for their young children to absorb, the loss is almost impossible to make up later on without enormous effort. The lack of opportunity to learn correct language easily and naturally during the first few years of life is probably the major factor that depresses the learning abilities of disadvantaged children.

The sooner your child learns to talk well enough to communicate her needs and feelings, the happier she will be and the easier she will be to live with. Many of the frustrations and tantrums of the "terrible twos" are triggered by a toddler's inability to let her parents know what she wants. Hillary, 2½, spent much of a long car ride wailing in her car seat when she suddenly stopped crying and declared to her family: "There are three things! I'm tired. I'm hungry. And I'm mad that Emily got another piece of cake and I didn't!" Stifling astonished chuckles, her parents were able to respond to each of Hillary's complaints and she spent the rest of the ride contented.

You don't need to teach your child to talk by drilling her on syllables, of course. But you can help her absorb the words she needs most by talking to her casually whenever you are together. For example, you can name the part of her body she may not have learned yet as you bathe her—shoulders, heels, thighs, chest, chin. Then, when she knows them, let her tell you in what order she wants to be scrubbed. You can describe each article of clothing as you dress her—white undershirt, blue overalls, red sweater. Then, as she learns to say these words, you can give her some choice about which clothes she'll wear. In the supermarket, you can ask her to bring you products she knows and to put them in your cart—crackers, paper napkins, bread, cake mix, salt.

You should not put words into your toddler's mouth before he has a chance to say them. (Sometimes when a two- or three-year-old is unusually slow to talk, it's discovered that his mother—or perhaps an older sibling—is anticipating his needs so completely that the child feels no compelling urge to speak up himself and doesn't.) But there are tactful ways in which you can supply him with the words he needs but doesn't know.

For example, Stephen's ball is stuck so far under the chair he can't reach it. He tries to explain the situation to his mother and asks her to get it out. But his vocabulary is so limited he can't make her understand and he's getting so angry and frustrated he's about to cry.

Tactfully, his mother can hold out her hand and suggest, "Show me what you want me to do." When she sees the ball, she can remark in a friendly fashion, "Oh, your ball is stuck under the chair. I'll pull it out for you." Or she can say, "Let's get the yardstick to push it out." This sort of conversation supplies a small child with words he needs and helps him discover for himself how he can use language effectively.

Just by carrying on friendly conversations with your toddler, you can supply him with words he needs to describe his activities, his feelings, his experiences. "Daddy's chin feels scratchy when he needs a shave," you can comment. "The dog is making tracks on the kitchen floor because his feet are wet." "I like the way this sprig of pine smells when you hold it in your hand."

Even at the age of 18 months, when a youngster can say only a few words himself, it's not too soon to begin using language as a way of encouraging him to think, to see relationships, and to formulate concepts.

This doesn't mean that you should start lecturing him or going into long explanations for everything you do. But in simple ways you can help him see cause and effect. ("If you turn the faucet just a little way, the water won't splash on you.") You can suggest time relationships. ("We're going to the grocery store now so we'll have hamburger to cook for dinner.") And you can supply facts that help him draw his own conclusions. ("This knife I am using is sharp, so I must be careful; scissors are sharp, too.")

Most parents help toddlers learn language so naturally that they may not be aware of how much verbal stimulation they are providing. For example, Ernst L. Moerk, a psychologist at California State University, Fresno, tape-recorded talk between a mother and a toddler named Eve for hour-long periods of time when the little girl was between the ages of 18 and 28 months. Analyzing this casual talk, he discovered that Eve's mother was actually giving her daughter 600 to 1,700 bits of "linguistically instructional input" per hour—an incredible 3.5 million bits of vocabulary and grammar a year. And Eve's mother was casually structuring her talk to reinforce what Eve was doing at the moment, to supply her new words and grammatical constructions, and to restate or rephrase ideas Eve appeared not to understand.[1]

As a parent, you should be teaching your child about the relationships between her actions and possible accidents by the time she is 18 months old, according to the American Academy of Pediatrics (AAP). "During this period, the child is learning the relationship between cause and effect," the pediatricians' organization pointed out. "In particular, he is learning that what happens may be the result of something he has done." Furthermore:

When minor accidents do occur—and they will—the child should be helped to understand the extent to which something he did caused the accident. In teaching the child the dangers of his environment and why he must avoid them, it is of little help to blame inanimate objects. If we say, "Oh, did the bad stove burn your hand?" we fail to show the youngster the true relationship between cause and effect, namely that the stove is hot, he placed his hand on it, and the hand was burned.

Compensating minor accidents with cookies, excitement,

or gifts only convinces the child of his innocence. A careful, patient explanation, along with appropriate sympathy for the injury, will help teach the child about cause and effect and about his responsibility to be alert to dangers and obedient to parental rules.

At this age the child is learning obedience, which in some cases must be absolute. He should know and respond to the command, "No." But it should not be overused or it rapidly loses its effectiveness, or worse yet, stops the child from any investigation or experimentation. Its uses should be limited to situations that cannot be converted into learning situations.[2]

The whole area of discipline becomes simpler, too, when your child can understand language well enough that you can explain rules and safety regulations to him, instead of enforcing them by physically removing him or preventing him from hurting himself.

Although it's estimated that about 90 percent of parents occasionally use spanking as a means of discipline, it's not really necessary and there are more effective ways of helping a child learn how to behave. The American Academy of Pediatrics has spoken out against spanking, pointing out that it teaches children that aggressive behavior is a solution to conflict and is associated with increased aggression in preschool and school-age youngsters. Although spanking may immediately reduce or stop an undesired behavior, it loses its effectiveness with repeated use, and it can worsen relationships between parent and child. Better methods of discipline include time-outs and loss of privileges, says the AAP.[3]

Parents can often avoid incidents of undesirable behavior by helping their youngster use words to express their feelings, by helping them understand the consequences of their behavior, and by maintaining a warm and positive relationship with them. For example, instead of issuing orders to your child and demanding obedience, you can add a few words of explanation to what you tell him, so he understands you are not merely being arbitrary and he gets information he can apply in other incidents.

As your two-year-old becomes able to use words, you can begin playing word games with her. An easy one to start with is "I'm thinking of something in this room that is red; what is it?" You can play it with shapes and sizes and other variations—and while you're doing dishes, cleaning house, or even driving the car. As soon as your toddler can talk well enough, let her take a turn quizzing you.

By the time your child is 2½, you can change the game to "Can you think of something that starts with the same sound as *Timmy*?" Or "Can you think of a word that has the same sound at the end as *cat*?" Games of this type sharpen a child's ear for the sounds that make up our language and provide her with an excellent foundation for learning to read.

Variations of the "silence game" used in Montessori schools can delight 2½- and 3-year-olds and provide them excellent training in auditory perception. You play it, basically, by encouraging your child to remain just as quiet as she possibly can—for the purpose of hearing and identifying a sound. Perhaps it's a train or a plane or a siren in the distance, or water swishing through the dishwasher, or a key turning in a lock, or pudding just starting to bubble in a pot, or a bird outside the window.

Or ask your child to play the silence game with her eyes shut and to guess what sound you make. Possibilities: a spoon striking a glass of water, keys jangling on a key ring, your hands clapping twice. Or have her play the silence game and listen carefully until she hears you whisper a simple direction she is to follow or tell her about a small surprise.

When she becomes adept at these games, set a time limit of one or two minutes and see which one of you can hear and identify the most sounds during this interval.

These games make excellent antidotes for parents who feel like they are screaming to attract their child's attention and for the youngster who has learned to tune his parents out so often he seldom hears them at all. They are also good ways to help a busy, active youngster make a tearless transition to bedtime, bathtime, or meals.

Between 18 and 36 months, your child's pleasure in books and in reading will grow enormously with even the slightest encouragement from you. If you haven't already, begin the practice of reading to him regularly. If you make it just before bedtime, it helps him relax, gets him into bed happily in anticipation of the treat ahead, and establishes the habit of a quiet evening talking time that you'll find invaluable at less communicative ages—such as 7, 11, and 13.

You should let your two-year-old buy books of his own whenever you can afford it, even if they are just inexpensive paperbacks from the supermarket. Some PTA (National Parent–Teacher Association) and library groups put on used-book sales as fund-raising projects, and here you can usually find stacks of hardcover children's books donated by parents whose youngsters have outgrown them; most are priced at only a fraction of their original cost. By now, your youngster should be making some of his own choices in library books as well. Toddlers often enjoy looking through magazines with you as you point out the babies, the toys, the chairs, an apple, a horse, a dog, a cat. Most toddlers like to have a stack of old magazines of their own that they can look at by themselves.

At this age, most youngsters prefer simple, factual stories about other small children, about animals, about what adults do, and about the world with which they are familiar. Their lives are already full of so much wonder and magic—at the world outdoors getting a shower when it rains, at the light switch that can chase away the night in a second, at water that gushes out of a faucet at a wrist's twist—that they don't appreciate fairy godmothers and magic lamps as much as six-, seven-, and eight-year-olds do. Two- and three-year-olds are still greatly intrigued with absorbing information about the world around them and forming concepts about it and their relationships to it. Some of the best-loved books of two- and three-year-olds tell what parents do at work each day, about what they were like as small babies, or about a child's pride in learning a new skill.

Because two- and three-year-olds are so sensitive to language, most of them are fascinated by poetry. Even traditional nursery rhymes—most of which are actually old English political satires that have no meaning for today's children—interest them because of their sound patterns.

But parents who make the effort to find meaningful poetry to read to their children find that they enjoy it far more than "Baa, Baa, Black Sheep" and "Little Miss Muffet."

More contemporary poems about funny situations or common emotions also resonate better with today's two- and three-year-olds than nonsense like Jack and Jill or the old woman who lived in a shoe. For example, there's Jack Prelutsky's "My Sister Is a Sissy":[4]

> My sister is a sissy,
> she's afraid of dogs and cats,
> a toad can give her tantrums,
> and she's terrified of rats,
> she screams at things with stingers,
> things that buzz, and things that crawl,
> just the shadow of a spider
> sends my sister up the wall.
>
> A lizard makes her shiver,
> and a turtle makes her squirm,
> she positively cringes
> at the prospect of a worm,
> she's afraid of things with feathers,
> she's afraid of things with fur.

She's afraid of almost everything—
how come I'm scared of her?

Two- and three-year-olds find great delight in classic poems about real-life experiences like Robert Lewis Stevenson's "The Swing."[5]

> How do you like to go up in a swing,
>   Up in the air so blue?
> Oh, I do think it the pleasantest thing
>   Ever a child can do!
>
> Up in the air and over the wall,
>   Till I can see so wide,
> Rivers and trees and cattle and all
>   Over the countryside—
>
> Till I look down on the garden green,
>   Down on the roof so brown—
> Up in the air I go flying again,
>   Up in the air and down!

You can find collections of many such intriguing poems for young children in almost every library and bookstore, and a poetry anthology is a good Christmas or birthday gift for any child of two or older. There's nothing wrong with teaching your child nursery rhymes, of course, and most parents do simply because it's easy. There's nothing wrong with nonsense, either. But this is all that most preschool children are given for poetry. Your child will absorb more and enjoy rhymes more if they have meanings that fascinate him as much as the sounds do.

You will find your child wanting you to read the same poem or story 17 times, even though both of you know it by heart. This is a characteristic need of children at this age level, and such repetition is important for them to gain mastery of the ideas and language patterns. It is not time wasted.

You can begin now to introduce your two-year-old to the idea that reading is just another form of language, that writing is just talk written down. You can show him what his name looks like in print. You can suggest that he dictate short notes to you to send to his grandparents or to his friends. You can point out the titles on books, the names on records, and the labels on grocery boxes. You can write memos to him, pin them on his bulletin board or tape them on his mirror, and read them to him the next day. You can answer any questions he asks about words. (If these steps make him eager to learn more, you may want to read ahead in Chapter 7 about teaching a preschooler to read, even before your child reaches his third birthday.)

When should you introduce your child to computers? Software manufacturers have seized on the growing interest in early learning and flooded the market with programs that purport to help children as young as nine months develop mouse skills, get to know the keyboard, and identify shapes, numbers, and colors. One popular program is aimed even at six-month-olds—an age when some babies still aren't sitting up. Several programs recommend covering the keyboard with a plastic protector, to keep baby drool from gumming up the keys.

Experts can't agree on a minimum age to expose children to such technology. Some argue that using a computer is basically like reading to a young child—only better—since the pictures move, make sounds, and sometimes respond to the child's actions. Others argue that until age three or so, the best benefit from so-called lapware is the lap—that is, the opportunity to snuggle with a parent and focus on something together. Critics have also dubbed software for very young children "guiltware," believing that some manufacturers are playing on parents' fears that their offspring could fall behind in the race to master technology.

As always, the best guide is to observe your child. Does she clamber into the desk chair with you, eager to bang on the computer keys and see what happens on the screen? Or does she just want to sit in your lap and bang on the table? Would she have just as much fun if the computer was turned off?

Other questions to ask yourself about all software products: What is this program teaching? Can my child learn it just as well from a book or a real-life experience? Familiarity with computers, the Internet, and software of all kinds will be crucial to your child's success in school and ability to communicate in the twenty-first century. But so will talking and walking, and there is time to master those first.

Indeed, a toddler still does a great part of his learning via sensorimotor activities. He still needs great freedom and opportunity to touch, to manipulate, push, pull, put together, take apart, group, rearrange, throw, and explore. He still must learn by doing as well as by listening and looking.

This is not learning that you can impose upon him or lecture into him. It's learning he acquires on his own, by exploration and experimentation, by trying and sometimes failing. (Remember this if you find yourself tempted to push him a little or pressure him into learning.)

This need for constant, reliable perception from which a child can draw conclusions about the world around him is probably a major reason why youngsters at about 24 and 36 months of age are so insistent upon routine and repetition. How can Johnny be sure just how far down a step is until he tries it over and over again? How can Jennifer learn that the same words written in her book always say the same thing unless she hears you read them in exactly the same way two dozen times? How can Tommy feel assured that the night will safely pass unless his frayed pink blanket and his teddy bear and his night-light are all precisely in place?

A scientist's efforts to control conditions in his laboratory and to repeat experiments so he can test a theory are respected by his colleagues. Small children need the same respect and patience and understanding from adults in their absorbing efforts to control conditions and test out conclusions—even though they can't explain what they are trying to do, as the scientist can.

Of course you can't let your pint-size Galileo test the law of falling bodies by dropping eggs from the top of your kitchen counter. Nor can he experiment with the principles of aerodynamics by throwing rocks at the neighbors' windows. But understanding more about the needs of his growing brain may help you to be more patient when your youngster demands the same bedtime story 13 nights in a row or if he cries when you let the water out of the bathtub instead of waiting until he decides to do it.

Instead of being annoyed at your toddler's insistence on routine and repetition, you can take advantage of it to help him acquire habits of neatness and order and independence in personal care, as Dr. Montessori suggested decades ago and is done, for reasons of learning, in Montessori schools today.

A parent who uses Montessori techniques at home keeps her child's toys on low, open shelves where he can reach them easily and choose freely what he wishes to use. Each toy and learning material has its own specific location and the youngster is encouraged to return it to this spot before he begins playing with something else. A small basket or box is used to keep parts of games together. A parent marks items that should be shelved together with bits of bright-colored tape. All the pieces of one wooden puzzle are identified with a smidgin of red tape on the back, for example; all the parts of another with green; all the equipment for a game is tagged with blue and kept in an open basket that is also marked with blue.

A low clothes rod and low pegs in his closet help make it possible for a small child to be orderly about his possessions. At this age, a youngster wants fiercely to become as independent as possible about his own dressing and undressing, as you know if you've ever seen a 2½-year-old on the verge of a tantrum because he can't button his shirt and won't give in and let his mother do it for him.

A small child who can manage his dressing and undressing—because of the tactful, behind-scenes planning of his parents—develops a great feeling of pride and competency. He has control of a particular part of his environment, which gives him pleasure. And he has become independent of adult assistance in at least one area of great importance to him, at a stage in his life when he values this freedom enormously. If parents let a child grow past this sensitive period without helping him develop habits of orderliness, they often find themselves nagging at him for years about the state of his room and his belongings—with little observable results.

More than just neatness about possessions is involved in this sensitive period, according to Dr. Montessori. She felt that this stage of childhood could also be used profitably by parents to teach a youngster that tasks have a beginning and an end, that jobs begun should be finished, and that mental processes, as well as physical surroundings, should be controlled and orderly.

A child's desire to be competent, to master as much of himself and his environment as possible, is particularly urgent when he is between 24 and 36 months old. If you take the time and effort to show a child how to perform easy tasks, he will usually learn with great concentration, interest, and obvious satisfaction. In the long run, it will take less of your time and energy to help him learn than it will to cope with his negative behavior and to try to amuse him and keep him out of trouble.

But few parents bother to think through how and what they try to teach a small child—whether it's to wash hands, tie shoes, button a shirt, or set the table. Adults usually work too fast, too automatically, for a child to follow and imitate. Dr. Montessori urged that an adult seeking to help a child learn should break down the activity into its component parts—the same technique modern educators call "programmed learning."

What precise steps are involved in buttoning a button? Adults do it so often without conscious thought that most of them can't describe the process without deliberately slowing down and thinking it through. But if you do break up the task of buttoning into its small component steps and show your child clearly what these steps are, he will learn with delight and pride.

By using these steps, a child can learn how to perform a necessary skill—washing his hands, for example—successfully by himself at an age when it gives him pleasure to do so. The alternatives are for the mother to continue to do it for him, which usually makes him impatient and rebellious. Or he can do it inefficiently and unsuccessfully, which means his mother will nag, criticize, or send him back to try it again. The child need not continue to wash his hands in precisely the same way all the time, of course. The procedure will become automatic, and he will vary it as circumstances suggest. But he will be able to do it—at an age when he most wants to. Furthermore, the youngster learns a major lesson in how to go about learning. He discovers that there is a logical way to go about controlling his environment and accomplishing what he wants.

To help children isolate and practice the skills involved in dressing themselves, Dr. Montessori devised simple "dressing frames," which have since been updated for contemporary clothing design. Each square frame holds two pieces of cloth that can be fastened together in the center—by a series of buttons, snaps, ties, buckles, or laces or by a zipper. Three-year-olds in Montessori schools often spend 30 to 45 concentrated minutes snapping and unsnapping, buckling and unbuckling—by their own free choice. These frames can now be purchased from several sources, or they can easily be made at home. (One point: In constructing a frame to teach tying, when your child is three or four years old, make the left-hand ties one color and the right-hand ties another. This makes it easier for a small child to follow the tying action.)

Using programmed learning techniques, you can help your two- or three-year-old learn many household tasks that will give him immense satisfaction, such as polishing furniture, scrubbing a tabletop, washing plastic dishes, or setting a low table.

It's important to remember that you are making it possible for your child to learn these skills because she wants to become more independent and because it gives her satisfaction. When she scrubs or polishes, she will do it because the performance gives her pleasure. So discipline yourself to let her polish and repolish, scrub and rescrub, as long as she wishes. Do respect her work; if you must redo something, never do it over in her presence.

To avoid putting undesirable pressure on a child to learn what she is not yet ready to learn, all of these activities should be completely free choice. Ask your youngster, "Would you like to have me show you how to button the button?" If she says no, don't pressure or push or urge or coax or show any disappointment. Just change the subject and offer the suggestion again in two or three weeks. If your youngster is the kind who routinely says no to everything, you may change the question to a more positive, "Here, I'll show you how." But stop if she resists or isn't interested. And do it in a friendly manner.

Whenever your toddler begins to lose interest in a learning demonstration or wiggles away or says she's tired of it, stop. Put the material away and offer it again days later. Not only will this technique protect your child from pressures but it will help to avoid her developing a resistance to your teaching attempts.

Teaching the very young with real things, as Rousseau urged

long ago, is still a cardinal rule in helping toddlers to learn. Your house is full of utensils and equipment your child can learn to use effectively with a little help. And most of it is easier for small hands to manipulate than the cheap, flimsy miniatures made as toys.

But toys can, of course, be a delightful way to help feed your youngster's great need for varied sensory stimulation and motor activity during these vital years.

Look for toys that will give your child practice with concepts like "in" and "out" and "inside" and "on top" and "larger" and "smaller." Nesting blocks or cups make good toys for year-old children. So do small boxes with lids. Stacking cones with wooden rings that fit around a central core intrigue toddlers. Other possibilities: wooden blocks they can line up to make a simple train or pile into a tower; simple form boards containing a solid-color wooden triangle, square, and circle; a mailbox with geometric shapes to deposit and pull out below.

By the time he's walking, your toddler is ready for push-and-pull toys of every variety. Bright balloons are inexpensive playthings that help him absorb basic information about air and gravity (but don't let him bite or suck on one). He'll have great fun with a large cardboard packing box that's big enough for him to crawl inside, or with a sheet draped over a card table for a tent or cave. You can save milk cartons, wash and dry them thoroughly, and cover them with foil or bright contact paper to make easy-to-handle blocks.

Stairs hold great interest for a toddler. If you live in an apartment or ranch-type house, where your youngster has no opportunity to practice, you'll find him fascinated with stairs you encounter on shopping trips or on visits to other homes. Some toy stores sell sturdy, three-step wooden stairs that intrigue one- and two-year-olds.

Water play (which must still be well supervised at this

age) delights a toddler. Sponge toys to squeeze, sailboats, floating animals, and pouring utensils increase his pleasure in the bathtub—or outdoors in a clean, shallow, plastic pool.

Simple games of hide-and-seek played with familiar objects appeal to almost every young toddler and help him form concepts about the permanence of objects not immediately in his sight. When he is very young, you'll have to hide the objects while he's watching. But even then, he'll laugh with joy when he discovers them.

Toys serve many other purposes in a small child's life. There are toys to love (the soft, cuddly, feels-good-to-touch stuffed animals and dolls that are always there when a parent turns out the light and goes away, that always listen when things go wrong). There are toys to trigger the imagination (paints, paper, dolls, dollhouse, sand, puppets—the more simple and less structured, the more creatively they can be used). There are toys to help a child try out the idea of being a grown-up (realistic dolls and their miniature paraphernalia, housekeeping toys, garden tools, doctor kits, costumes, trucks, trains, farmyard sets). There are toys to help a child find the action (tricycle, scooter, wagon, anything with wheels; swing, glider, climbing bars, a tire on a rope hung from a tree, slide, sled, small trampoline, rocking horse, balls of every variety, any equipment that moves and encourages a child to run or chase or sway or swoop or bounce). Even though some of these toys seem chiefly to foster the development of a child physically, socially, or emotionally, they also encourage his mental growth, for there is an intellectual component in all of these areas.

There are also toys that are primarily for intellectual learning, even if they are not so labeled. These are often the toys with which you are most apt to get your money's worth in terms of hours-of-play value per dollar.

In addition to the general categories of toys already listed, your youngster can learn much and have fun with playthings like these:

- Kindergarten blocks, in as large an assortment as you can afford, made of smooth, accurately cut, natural wood in squares, oblongs, diagonals, triangles, curves, half-circles, and pillars

- Flashlight

- Inlaid puzzles of wood or hard rubber (some have pieces that can be removed and used as toys)

- Indoor slide, with ladder

- Simple rhythm instruments—bells, triangle, tambourine, drum, wrist bells, finger cymbals, small xylophone

- Take-apart trucks and toys

- Collection of hats for playing different pretend roles

- Inlaid form board containing simple geometric shapes

- Giant magnet (be sure to keep this away from TVs and computers)

- Unstructured playhouse

- Counting toys and number puzzles

- Cassette player simple enough for a small child to operate himself. There are many excellent tapes available for very young children—and many toddlers recognize and enjoy a few musical comedy songs and folk tunes

- Beanbags and baskets for targets

- Large wooden beads to string or fasten together

- Simple lotto games

Art and craft materials and projects suitable for youngsters older than two are described in Chapter 8. Some of the Montessori techniques and equipment listed in

Chapter 9 can be effective with children younger than age three.

Taking your toddler on a variety of very short trips is one of the happiest and most effective ways of increasing the amount of stimuli she receives. Even a walk around the block can be a good learning experience, if you take the time to let her watch the ants hurrying in and out of an anthill and poke her finger into a puddle and scuff in the leaves and go up and down every step that beckons.

When you are outdoors with your toddler, you can encourage her to feel the rough bark of a tree, the prickliness of fresh-cut grass, the softness of a flower petal, the fur of the neighbor's friendly cat, the brittleness of an autumn leaf, the tickle of snow, the gooiness of mud.

Even your trips to the supermarket can provide opportunities for sensory stimuli. You can buy a box of cookies and let your toddler sample one. Let her try to drink from the cold arc bubbling out of the water fountain. Give her an orange to put in and out of a small paper bag. Let her feel the cold frozen-food package, a heavy bag of sugar, the softness of a loaf of bread. None of this will take any longer than scolding her to sit still or trying to prevent her from wriggling out of the shopping-cart seat in boredom.

A zoo and a farm and a pet store are all full of delightful learning possibilities for a two-year-old. If you can arrange it, let her have a chance to pat a horse, sit on its back, listen to it, and watch it eat—to learn about it through three or four of her senses. Then talk about the experience afterward and encourage her to put her feelings into words. She'll learn more this way than if you plop her into a stroller and try to cover the whole zoo in one afternoon.

Other good expeditions for two-year-olds include a short trip on a bus; a train ride between two or three commuter stations; a visit to a bakery, a fire station, a shoe-repair shop; a trip to the beach and to as many different neighborhood parks as possible; an expedition to a fast-food drive-in, a greenhouse, an apple orchard.

The transition from this stage into the preschool period of three to six isn't a definite line that children cross in a birthday month. By about 30 months, a few youngsters will be ready for some of the activities listed in the next chapter, particularly if their parents have been enriching their environment since the earliest months of life, so you will probably want to read ahead in the sections about language, science, math, and perception before your child is fully three years old.

6

How to Stimulate
Intellectual Growth
in Three- to Six-Year-Olds

Peter, just six, is entering first grade this fall, already able to read independently and with great delight, at about third-grade level. He can count as far as he wants to; do simple addition, subtraction, and division; and has a good grasp of what numerical symbols mean. His vocabulary is probably about twenty-five thousand words, and he has developed many sound concepts about the natural and social sciences. He is eager, curious, fascinated by the world around him, responsive to adults, and happy. And because he is also self-confident, outgoing, and energetic, he finds it easy to make friends with other children.

But for Ted, also six, first grade is a threat. He can't talk well enough to make the teacher understand him. He has had no experience in interpreting even the pictures in his preprimer, let alone the more complicated symbolism of the obscure black marks underneath the illustrations. It seems easier to Ted to withdraw, to look out the window, to keep quiet, rather than to try. Ted already feels that he is a failure, and he shows it in the classroom and on the playground.

Yet Peter and Ted started life—just a few miles apart in the same large city—with far less difference in innate mental ability than these first-grade contrasts show. If they had been given an infant IQ test, they would both have scored in the same general range. They never will again. The differences between them now will almost certainly be self-perpetuating and will probably increase.

Peter, obviously, will be classified as a bright or gifted child. He will go immediately into the top reading group in his class. His eagerness to learn and his quick successes will delight his teachers. He will bask in their approval, and this, plus the joy he has already experienced from learning, will motivate him to keep trying and prevent him from being too discouraged if he draws a poor teacher or dull assignments.

It won't be long before Ted's teachers will stop expecting him to succeed. Even a patient, understanding teacher will find it hard not to become discouraged with Ted's obvious lack of effort and interest. Because of his lack of readiness and his deficiencies in language, Ted will be slow in learning to read and thereby handicapped in all of his other schoolwork. A sad, familiar cycle will probably begin. Because he can't keep up, Ted will begin to fail. Because he fails, he'll tend to stop trying. The less he tries, the less he will learn. He may have to repeat the year. Despite automatic promotions after that, he may be only a high school freshman or a sophomore before he is legally able to drop out of school and does so.

The contrast between Peter and Ted is not an exaggeration. There are hundreds of thousands of Peters in our first grades today, the product of stimulating homes, of Montessori schools, of laboratory schools in university settings, of preschools where teachers practice early-learning principles. Happily, children like Peter are increasing rapidly.

Boys and girls like Ted, however, can also be counted by the hundreds of thousands. Most come from poor homes, often with only a single parent. But some of the Teds also belong to affluent families where parents are too busy or too uninformed or too uninterested in seeing that their children get the mental nourishment they need.

In between the Peters and the Teds are millions of other youngsters whose minds have not been stunted as much as Ted's nor stimulated as much as Peter's. What they bring to first grade they have learned chiefly by osmosis in homes where they are loved and cared for physically but where their urgent need for mental stimulation has not been fully recognized.

What can you give your child between the ages of three and six to boost his mental abilities and start him off to first grade confident and destined for success?

No preset curriculum can be devised that will fit all preschoolers, all homes, and all parents with their varying talents, responsibilities, and available time. Even if such a curriculum could be devised by extensive research, it would not be desirable. Youngsters are so active physically and mentally that no preplanned pattern of experience can take advantage of the opportunities for learning that constantly occur.

A small child's mind works so fast and reaches out in so many unexpected directions that you'd miss great teaching opportunities if you tried to stick to a prescribed, formal lesson pattern. One of the great advantages of preschool learning at home is that you can adapt it to the needs and immediate interests of each individual child—an opportunity for personalized learning that rarely occurs throughout your youngster's years of formal schooling until graduate level.

Here are general guidelines for the major areas you'll want to cover during the years between three and six. Like any good teacher, you'll improvise and adapt the suggestions for your own child. How fast he will go in which areas will depend on how much time you spend with him, his own individual speed and way of learning, how much early stimulation he has had before age three, and whether he attends a nursery school or day-care center that actively fosters intellectual development. That's why these guidelines are not grouped more specifically by age levels.

These suggestions are not a checklist or a curriculum that a parent needs to follow. They are simply ideas that even a busy mother or father can use to encourage a child's mental development and their mutual enjoyment in whatever time they have together.

Language

Between the ages of three and six, your child's vocabulary will grow explosively and excitingly—and in imitation of yours. If you speak English correctly, so will your child by the end of this period. She will also pick up your swear words and pet expressions. One of the most important aids you can give your preschool child—and one that a disadvantaged youngster is most apt to lack—is a good language model to copy.

This doesn't mean that you have to speak copybook English with complete sentences every time you talk. But it does mean that you should use a full range of tenses, subordinate clauses, pronouns, adjectives, and adverbs for your child to absorb. She'll discover—without apparent effort—how to form tenses, plurals, and clauses without overt assistance from you, if you provide the example. Her ability to do so is greater when she's a preschooler than it will ever be again.

Don't be afraid to use words your child doesn't understand. She'll absorb them and gradually decipher their meaning. That's how she learned to talk originally. It's easy to underestimate a youngster's comprehension vocabulary because, like almost all adults, she understands a far larger number of words than she uses.

Sometimes, for the delight of it, you can deliberately teach your child big words. Four- and five-year-olds often enjoy learning the precise names of various types of dinosaurs, automobile parts, or flowers, for example. *Tyrannosaur, brontosaur, carburetor,* and *philodendron* are great fun for a child to roll off her tongue, especially when she knows what they really mean.

Almost all preschoolers go through a stage in speech development when they seem to stutter. This may occur simply because their thinking outraces their vocabulary. "I don't have enough words for my thoughts," one three-year-old told his mother in a worried voice.

Regardless of the cause, the type of normal stuttering that occurs in most children between the ages of 2½ and 4 should be ignored. These "disfluencies," as speech experts call them, almost always disappear as a child's skill in using words increases (or perhaps as the speech center in her brain becomes better established).

But a parent who calls a child's attention to her hesitancies and disfluencies may, with the best of intentions, turn her youngster into a persistent stutterer, some speech experts warn. There is risk, they caution, not only in telling your child not to stutter, but also in even suggesting that she pause and think, or take a deep breath, before she talks. This tends to make the youngster so conscious of the mechanisms of speech that the hesitancies and disfluencies increase and turn into habit.

One way you can help is this: Give your preschooler the courtesy of listening to her with as much respect and attention as you'd give an adult guest in your home. If your youngster feels that you are really listening to her, she won't try to rush through what she's saying, and there's less danger that she will stumble over sounds or skip syllables. This courtesy will also increase her feelings of self-confidence and personal worth and make her less inclined to whine for your attention.

Most youngsters continue to mispronounce one or two speech sounds even until kindergarten or first grade, speech therapists say. Unless your child's speech is almost impossible for others to understand after about her fourth birthday, you needn't be concerned about a few mispronunciations until school age.

As your child begins to acquire a beginning command of the mechanics of language, you'll want to help her learn how to use this marvelous tool. Language is so closely related to thought that some theorists even consider them almost synonymous.

During your child's irreplaceable years between three and six, you can help her learn to use language to foster thinking. When you talk to your child, you can encourage her to plan ahead ("When you have helped me put away the dishes, we can read a story together"). And to consider alternatives ("Should we make cookies or would you rather go to the playground?"). And to avoid mistakes ("If you move your glass of milk toward the center of the table, you won't knock it over with your elbow").

Helping your preschooler learn to put her feelings into words makes life easier for everyone in your family. If your youngster knows she can make you understand what she is feeling with words, she won't be so likely to whine or sulk or throw things or have a tantrum or pat the baby too hard.

You can also use words to help your preschooler understand the feelings of others and begin to act accordingly. "I know you are angry because the baby grabbed your toy car," you might say. "But you see, the baby admires you so and she is trying to do everything you are doing. She wants to grow up and be just like you. Will you help me teach her how to become as fine a person as you are?"

You can make it become a fascinating game if you sometimes ask your preschooler to choose precisely the right words to describe a cloud, a feeling, the taste of a new food, the touch of a fabric, the beauty of a flower. She'll delight in these verbal treasure hunts if you let her know you enjoy the aptness of her choices and join in the game, too.

A parent who listens with respect and interest and without

being condescending or all-knowing can have delightful conversations with a preschooler. If you make it a happy habit to converse with your child (not talking down to him or issuing orders or preaching at him) when you're driving in the car, riding the bus, tucking him into bed, doing the dishes, or whenever you can find time, not only will you stimulate his mental development but you'll keep open lines of communication with him that are invaluable later on in his life.

It will help your child's vocabulary to grow and his skill in using language to flourish if you give him something interesting to talk about. A trip, a visit to a museum or zoo, a shopping expedition, or a kitchen-sink science experiment not only provides a child with new words to use but also spurs his desire to try them out. Another incentive is for each member of the family to take turns telling the others what he did that day.

Television can be turned into a stimulus for your child's vocabulary development, too, especially if you encourage him to discuss programs he's seen with you. This gives you a good opportunity to help him sort out fact from fiction—often very difficult for preschool TV viewers—and to clear up misunderstandings he may have about what he has seen. Television can also whet a thirst for more information about a subject—space travel, rockets, airplanes, a foreign country, the ocean, the presidency—which you can help him find in a library, newspaper, or encyclopedia. These conversations can aid your youngster in developing critical judgment about television, and he'll be less inclined to watch indiscriminately when he is older.

Good parent–child talk is often silly, funny, absurd talk, as any parent knows whose youngster has twisted Pooh Bear's "Help, help, a heffalump, a horrible heffalump" around and around on his tongue with delight. A quick, happy sense of humor is one of the most common characteristics of gifted children, research shows. And the more your child enjoys the fun of jokes, riddles, verbal puzzles, puns, silly rhymes, and absurdities, the brighter he probably is. The more you join in his fun, the more he'll come to enjoy words and the more open he will be to learning through language.

You can build on this interest by suggesting games to heighten your child's awareness of sounds and sound patterns—a fundamental step in learning to read. You can help him recognize similarities and differences in beginning sounds by asking him to see how many words he can think of that begin with the same sound as *Maggie* or *book*. Or you can take turns thinking of all the words you can that end the same way as *Sam* or *Dad* or *pop*.

Skill with language involves listening and understanding, as well as talking, and there are many happy games you can play with your child to help him sharpen his listening ability. Simon Says is a good game for three-year-olds. May I? is fun for children old enough to count to 10. I Packed My Sister's Suitcase appeals to four- and five-year-olds.

Reading to your child should continue to be a shared pleasure, even after he is old enough to read easy books for himself and well into the early elementary school years. A child's level of comprehension is much higher than his reading level for many years and he needs to have you read to him to sustain his interest in books and to provide him with mental nourishment until he can find enough for himself.

Regular trips to the children's room of the nearest library should be a routine part of your offspring's life, starting no later than the age of three. As a special treat, he should be permitted to choose books to own on gift occasions, or whenever you can afford it. Books, generally, cost less than many toys, especially when figured on a dollar-per-hour-of-pleasure basis. Providing your child with his own special bookshelf or bookcase or bookends—and with inexpensive bookplates that carry his name—will also increase his interest in books.

It is important to keep reading a pleasure, not a task or a lesson. For example, you can show your preschooler how much fun it is to spread out a blanket under a shady tree on a summer afternoon and read together. Or let him cuddle up in bed with you on a stormy night while you read to him. Or let him substitute a story session for a nap on a day it's too hot for sleep. You can suggest that he help you in the kitchen, then reward him with a story. You can encourage him to avoid boredom by reading a book when he must wait for the dentist or for the next motel with a "vacancy" sign on a vacation trip.

"When I was about four years old, I used to get these awful earaches," recalled a teenage boy. "I'd wake up in the night crying because it hurt so much. My mom would get up and give me the medicine the doctor sent, and then she'd sit beside my bed and read to me all sorts of good stuff, until the hurt let up. She told me that reading couldn't kill the pain but that it would fill up such a big part of my brain I wouldn't pay so much attention to the hurting. Sometimes reading still makes me feel good, like it did then."

You should make certain your child realizes that reading is also an adult activity you enjoy independently of him. You should let him see you read often for pleasure and for information. You should make your trips to the library a time for you to select adult books, too. You can request books as gifts for yourself (a paperback is one of the least expensive material presents a child can choose). And you can comment often on what you do read. A youngster who grows up seeing his parents get most of their information and entertainment from television is quite likely to do likewise and may never become happily addicted to reading.

Your child's interests and responses will be your best guide to the type of books you choose to read to him. As they did at the age of two, many preschoolers still prefer factual books that explain the world around them and books about children much like themselves to fairy tales. A book about thunder and lightning can seem just as wondrous to a four-year-old as a story about fire-breathing dragons, yet it gives him information he craves about a familiar phenomenon. Given a choice, he'll usually take reality, at least until he's a little older.

Often a book for small children that is considered cute or charming by an adult will have almost no appeal for a four- or five-year-old. Some books for preschoolers are condescending in tone and far too limited in vocabulary and content.

In helping your child select books, a guiding principle should be that it's better to challenge his mind than to bore him. Your youngster's response to books will be a clear guide to his level of comprehension—far more accurate than any prepared book list (although you might consult one as a starter). If a book matches your child's mental development, he'll probably ask you to read it to him again and again, and he'll listen quietly and carefully. If it's too easy or too difficult, he'll probably wiggle away and begin to play with something else.

Good poetry stirs great interest in three- to six-year-olds, and you should continue to read poems to him all during this preschool period. Encourage him to memorize those he especially enjoys—not so he can recite them for your friends, but so he will have them in his mind for his own pleasure.

Your reading to your child shouldn't be limited to books, of course. You can also stimulate his interest in printed symbols by reading to him traffic signs, labels, historic markers that you encounter on vacation, menus when you go out to dinner, directions that come with toys and games, words that flash on the TV screen, signs that help him tell the difference between the "men's room" and the "ladies' room," reminders that you chalk on your kitchen blackboard for yourself and for other family members—anything that helps him to understand that printed letters make words that have meanings.

Reading

If you've been following the suggestions in this book, your youngster will probably be showing clear signs of interest to learn to read sometime between her third and fourth birthdays. She'll be fascinated by books, questioning you about the meanings of signs and labels, wanting to learn to print her own name, interested in pictures and adding to her speaking vocabulary faster than you can keep count of the words. Chapter 7 will tell you, in detail, about teaching her to read easily and happily yourself.

Second Language

The years between three and six, when your child's ability to absorb language with great facility is at its peak, are the ideal time to introduce him to a second language, if you are lucky enough to have the opportunity.

At this age, your youngster can learn a second language almost as readily as he learns English and without any sort of formal lessons, provided it is taught in the same way he learns English. He merely needs to hear it spoken frequently, naturally, and well by someone who can speak it like a native. A grandparent, a parent, a day-care teacher, a neighbor, or a household helper can be an effective teacher simply by speaking to your child only in the second language (or by speaking to him only in the second language in a special part of the house or during certain hours at the day-care center). Your youngster figures out for himself that to get what he wants and make himself understood, he must talk in one way to you and a different way to the person in his life who is using the second language or in the special area where the other language is spoken. He won't confuse the two languages, and he will use them with the appropriate person.

Your goal should not be to help your preschooler build up a large vocabulary but rather to establish the basic units of the second language in his growing brain, as described in Chapter 2. Then he can build on them later instead of having to learn the second language cold, using English sounds or speech units when he's a teenager or an adult.

It is important that whoever teaches your child the second language speaks it correctly. Bilingual children who come from disadvantaged homes where neither English nor their parents' native tongue is spoken well usually do poorly in school, research shows. And experiments in teaching a foreign language in elementary schools, using teachers who do not have a mastery of the language and who do not use a "direct" or "mother's" method, usually seem to be a waste of time.

If you aren't fluent in a second language yourself and don't know anyone who could teach your child by the "mother's method," you will probably not be able to give your child this opportunity. It just doesn't seem to work when parents try to teach a child a second language that they do not know via phonograph records or coloring workbooks or other techniques. Parents who try to learn a second language along with their youngster find that he learns more quickly and easily than they, as immigrant families for generations have discovered.

Math

Even if you never were a whiz in math yourself, you can help your preschooler discover and absorb many basic mathematical concepts long before she's ready for first grade. Whether she is eventually taught in school by traditional or new-math methods, she will profit greatly by these early-learning experiences.

In fact, your child will begin learning mathematical ideas in very simple form while she is still a toddler. Concepts such as "bigger and smaller," "light and heavy," "tall and short" are basically mathematical in nature. Grouping toys together, such as a pile of blocks and a handful of marbles, helps lay a foundation for set and subset theories. Simple matching games teach math concepts of "equal," "odd and even," and "more and less." Each concept helps lay a foundation in math on which your child can build later on.

The key to teaching a preschooler about math is to set the stage for her to make her own discoveries and to present ideas in the form of games that you both enjoy or practical uses for mathematical relationships she encounters normally in life. You gain almost nothing by trying to stuff her head with number facts learned by rote.

Because your preschooler will learn best by perceptual methods, mathematical ideas should be taught with interesting materials she will enjoy handling. For example, don't just teach her to count to 10 by rote, or by pointing to her fingers one at a time. Instead, encourage her to use anything she can move into groups—buttons, raisins, blocks, cookies, pennies—as she counts. Otherwise, she may get the idea that *four* means the fourth in a series, rather than all four in a set of objects.

Once your youngster has learned to count, you can invent dozens of delightful counting games to play with her. You can have her turn her back or cover her eyes and count how many times you rap on the table with your hand or bounce a ball or tap a glass with a spoon. You can ask her to count out the silverware and napkins to set the table for dinner or the number of small balls or peanuts or marbles she can drop into a clean, empty cardboard milk carton. You can go for "counting walks" together and look for items you've listed in advance: four white flowers, three rocks, two red cars, and one black dog. Or you can take a clipboard and help your youngster record her count of whatever objects interest her.

You can help your child learn about repeating patterns by giving him three or four kinds of macaroni and a sturdy string. Create a pattern by stringing one of each of the pasta shapes on the string, then challenge him to fill up the string and make a necklace by adding more macaroni in the same sequence you began.

You can teach your child the names of geometric shapes—circle, square, rectangle, oval, triangle, sphere, cube—and help him look for them wherever he goes. A tabletop can be a circle or a rectangle, for example. A circle can be seen in a button, a jar lid, a drop of water, or a slice of carrot.

You should also introduce your preschooler to the idea that zero is a number, too. The correct number of giraffes in the bedroom is zero. So is the number of bears in the bathtub. It is not "none." The difference may not seem important when your child is counting giraffes and bears that are not there. But it is crucial when he begins constructing written numerals. In writing the number 40, for example (meaning 4 tens and no ones), the second number is not "nothing," but "zero." The concept is even more obvious with larger numbers. There is a zero, not "nothing" between the 5 and the 7 in the number 507 (which means 5 hundreds, no tens, and 7 ones).

Once your child has learned to count from 0 to 9, the next step is to show him how to write the numerals he is counting. Most youngsters learn more quickly if you make large-size numerals for them to trace with their index and middle fingers. In Montessori schools, big sandpaper letters are used for this purpose. You can cut out a set of numerals from sandpaper yourself and mount them on squares of cardboard. Wooden jigsaw puzzles that match numerals with the proper number of dots or pegs or small animals are also available.

Several Montessori techniques can easily be adapted to teach mathematical concepts to your preschooler at home. For example, after your child has learned to count and to identify numerals, give her an egg carton with 10 compartments numbered from 0 to 9 and 2 compartments taped shut and 45 beads, beans, pennies, or buttons she is to distribute correctly into the compartments. The carton will give her some degree of self-correction and make it possible for her to practice and learn independently.

For another game, write a single digit on several slips of

paper and put them into a bag. Let your child draw them out one at a time and then get for you the corresponding number of items—blocks, leaves, buttons, or books.

Dice make an excellent device for helping preschoolers to learn about numbers in a games context and to reinforce learning already acquired. In one nursery school, for example, four- and five-year-olds play long, concentrated games in which one child shakes the dice and calls off the numbers to other children who chalk them on a blackboard and then add them up.

Any board game that involves dice or a spinner and counting can be useful in helping a child grasp number concepts. Four-year-olds can do quite well at Sorry and Parcheesi if one opponent is an adult or an older child who can help out, if necessary. A preschooler may shake a 3 and a 4 on the dice, for example, and count as he moves his marker, "one, two, three, one, two, three, four" to find the seventh space. But it isn't long before he announces "seven" after his shake, without the preliminary steps.

A deck of playing cards can also be turned into a learning game. You can explain that the ace card means one, then encourage your child to count the spots on the cards from ace to nine and match them with similar number cards from all four suits.

Playing bingo is a delightful, no-pressure way in which to help a child learn to identify and pronounce numbers between 10 and 75, especially if you call out the numbers like this: "Fifty-seven—that's five, seven." In a game situation, a child often wants to play and win so badly that he absorbs basic mathematical concepts without even realizing it.

Rummy-type games that give practice in number concepts are available in most toy stores, but they are generally intended for elementary school–age youngsters. Four- and five-year-olds with some experience in math can usually play the games but lack the ability to hold enough cards in one hand. This difficulty can easily be overcome by giving each youngster a large cardboard box, turned with its opening on the side facing the player, in which he can spread out his hand in secret.

Once your child has learned to read numerals, it's not difficult to teach her to tell time and to read a thermometer. Both of these skills are well worth the teaching effort. A preschooler finds it easier to accept the fact that it's bedtime or that it's too soon before dinner to have another cookie when the clock makes the ruling and not an arbitrary parent with whom the child can argue. Many a parent has sidestepped arguments about whether a child needs a heavy jacket or just a sweater by posting a code that goes approximately like this: above 70, no wraps; 65 to 70, sweater; 45 to 65, light jacket; below 45, heavy jacket and cap or scarf.

To teach your child about money, begin by helping her learn the names of a penny, nickel, dime, quarter, half-dollar, and dollar. Then, you can explain that we use money to trade for things we want and that we have different kinds of money so we can pay different prices for these things. Then play matching games with her to show that 1 nickel will buy as much as 5 pennies; that a quarter is equal to 2 dimes and 1 nickel or 5 nickels or 25 pennies or 1 dime and 15 pennies, and all the other combinations. After several short sessions of practice with these coin equivalents, your child should be quite knowledgeable about money and ready for a small allowance.

To teach your preschooler the concept of "odd and even," you can make a series of number cards, using index cards marked 0 to 9. Then let him place the corresponding number of buttons in pairs under each card so he can easily tell whether there is one left over.

Make a second set of cards and you can teach your child the concept of "same" or "equal" by putting out two identical numerals and corresponding numbers of buttons and by having him pair them off. Then, using two different numerals, with the correct number of buttons, help him discover the meaning of "more" and "fewer."

These cards and buttons are useful, too, in introducing your child to the idea of addition. First, lay out two numerals, with matching buttons, the sum of which is less than 10. Have him combine the buttons into one pile, count them, and find the matching numeral from your stockpile. Then you can show him how to write down what he has done, using the appropriate plus sign. Subtraction can be introduced in this same way.

Your child can also learn more complicated math ideas if you have the time and patience to work with him and he has the interest to play such games. For example, in Montessori schools, the concepts of "tens" and "hundreds" and "thousands" are taught by means of golden beads. These beads are available for the children to use as single units, in strings of 10, in squares in which 10 rows of 10 beads are securely fastened together, and in cubes that are painted to resemble 10 of the 100-bead squares.

The child learns to match the printed numeral 10 with a 10-bead string, the numeral 100 with the 100-bead square, and the numeral 1,000 with the cube. Then, for example, if he chooses a printed card that says 1,000, another marked 600, a 50, and a single-numeral card 3, he can stack them together to form for himself the numeral 1,653.

Parents who have used Montessori methods at home have devised several ingenious substitutes. For example, instead of beads, you can fasten sticky-backed tape that has a small, unitary design—flower, Santa Claus, circle, or bell—onto a cardboard and cut it in the required sizes. You'll need single units, rows of 10, and squares that contain 10 rows of 10 figures. For the 1,000-unit cubes, you can tie 10 100-figure squares together.

You'll also need some filing cards. On one set of cards, with a marking pen, write large-size numerals: 1,000, 2,000, 3,000,

4,000, 5,000, 6,000, 7,000, 8,000, and 9,000. Before marking the second set of cards, cut off about one quarter from one end, so that they can cover only the last three digits on the thousands cards. Then number them in ink: 100, 200, 300, 400, 500, 600, 700, 800, and 900.

The third set of cards is cut in half and numbered 10, 20, 30, 40, 50, 60, 70, 80, and 90. The fourth set is only one fourth as wide as the full-size cards and it is marked with single digits from 1 to 9. By stacking these cards in proper sequence, a child can construct any numeral from 1 to 9,999.

One game you can play with your child is to put the cards in piles on a table. Then say to your youngster, "Please get me four thousands." When he has succeeded, instruct him to find a certain number of hundreds, tens, and units and have him stack the cards properly to make the correct numeral. Then challenge him to lay out the same number of whatever equivalent you are using for the golden beads.

When your child can handle this game easily and happily, you can progress to more complicated forms of addition. First, have him construct two different numerals—1,433 and 6,354, for example—and lay out the "beads" that illustrate both numbers. First, he counts the number of unit beads in both piles, combines them into one pile, and finds the numeral card that corresponds. In this case, of course, it is a 7. In a similar way, he counts the tens, the hundreds, and the thousands, until he has 7 units, 8 tens, 7 hundreds, and 7 thousands. He forms the corresponding numeral and has the sum of the two original numbers.

At first, you'll want to use numbers that can be added without involving carrying. But when your youngster has become adept at adding, you can show him graphically how to carry. When he has 10 or more units, he can take 10 of them back to the original stockpile and exchange them for a strip of 10. Similarly, he can exchange ten 10-strips for one 100-square, or ten hundreds for one 1,000-cube. It's easier for him to understand if he performs the operation first with the "beads" and then sets up the numerals to match his answer.

If you wish, you can teach your child to subtract by much the same method. The easiest way is to have her set up a number with both beads and cards. The subtrahend should be formed only with the cards. Beginning with the units, have your child take away the number of beads called for in the subtrahend. When she has finished the operation, she can construct the correct answer with the cards. Your first numbers should not involve the concept of borrowing. But after the basic process has been mastered, you can introduce borrowing by having your child actually exchange a 10-strip for ten units or one 1,000-cube for ten 100-squares, so that she can perform her subtraction operation.

You can also show her how to check her results by adding the difference and the subtrahend to form the original number.

Short division can also be taught to a preschooler, using these Montessori-type materials. First, give your child a four-place number (with each digit an even number) to set up, using both beads and cards. To show him how to divide by 2, have your youngster take turns with you removing one 1,000-cube at a time from the pile set up to illustrate the dividend. If the dividend is 8,682, for example, each of you would have four 1,000-cubes. Do the same with the remaining digits, until each of you has four 1,000-cubes, three 100-squares, four 10-strips, and one unit. Then you can set up the number cards to indicate your quotient. In Montessori schools, the directress may vary the divisor by asking additional children to participate. For fun, she may suggest that the youngsters march once around the table each time they take a unit or a square or a cube.

When this step has been mastered, you can vary the dividends so that the digits cannot be divided equally by the number of individuals used as divisors. Then you can show your child how to change the leftover thousands or hundreds or tens into hundreds or tens or units that can be divided equally.

Science

A preschooler comes equipped with a probing, poking, questioning, exploring, insatiable interest in science of all kinds. Or at least she does until a parent or a teacher has discouraged or ignored or scolded her out of it.

Even if you can't tell a pipette from a test tube, you can do much to encourage the scientist innate in your child. Your aim shouldn't be to pressure her to memorize scientific facts but to absorb scientific attitudes—to question, to make sensitive observations, to look for cause and effect, to test conclusions, to wonder, and to marvel.

(Your encouragement of scientific interests and attitudes is important for your daughter as well as for your son. Research shows that most girls start out with the same type and degree of scientific interest as boys but are discouraged by lack of support and encouraging feedback from adults and are shunted away into other areas of interest long before junior high school.)

With practice, you'll discover many ways in which to encourage your preschooler's natural scientific bent. For example, find every way you can to help your child become more sensitive to her environment, to look beyond the obvious, to use all of her five senses to explore the world around him. In March, you can help her hunt for the first signs of spring in the tender shoots of green under snow-sodden leaves. You can encourage her to notice the differences in the shapes of leaves, the coloring of birds, the shapes of clouds, the sounds of a city or a suburb.

You don't have to live on a seacoast or on a farm or even in a wooded suburb to find natural phenomena to delight your child. You can make a special expedition to a park to watch a rising full moon on some crisp, clear October night. You can make the acquaintance of animal babies in a zoo or in a pet shop. You can collect leaves in a park. Find tiny fossils in crushed stone in a driveway. Watch a parade of ants scurry along a sidewalk. Grow small plants in jam jars on a windowsill. Marvel at floating castles and gray dust rolls of clouds. Take walks in the fog and in a warm rain. Learn the feel of the wind as it whips and whispers down apartment-house canyons.

One of the most fascinating ways in which to make nature intriguing to a city child—or any youngster—is to buy a good hand lens or magnifying glass. Even the tendrils of ivy clinging to a building, a spider on the wall, a stalk of geranium in a flower box, or a few grains of sand take on a magical aura when magnified.

One preschool science teacher suggests that simply giving a three-, four-, or five-year-old the cardboard center of a roll of toilet paper or paper towels to use as a viewer is useful when looking for interesting objects outdoors. Looking through the cardboard roll helps a child focus his eye and attention on a specific leaf or flower or other object and makes it easier for him to study it closely.

Another experiment you can conduct outdoors—either in a suburban backyard or a city sidewalk—is to encourage your child to stand perfectly still and try to identify all of the sounds that he can hear.

Your job isn't to try to teach your child precisely about what he observes. You don't have to know exact scientific names or explanations or make lessons out of what you do together. All you really need to do is to be interested yourself and invite your offspring to share your wonder.

Often, just following your child's lead is enough. Four-year-old Jeanne, taken by her mother on a routine shopping trip, became intrigued with smelling the flowers in the raised concrete boxes decorating the shopping center's walkways. She tugged on her mother's hand to share her discovery. Mother and daughter spent almost half an hour smelling the various types of flowers, comparing their scents, their shapes, and their coloring—happy and oblivious to other shoppers. This, too, can be called science.

"Now that Jeanne is ten and much too dignified to smell flowers in public, I remember that day with special delight," recalls her mother. "You need a small child for an excuse to take time to appreciate the small daily wonders of living."

Do try to answer your child's questions—even when they come when you're frantically busy trying to feed the baby, finish making dinner, and get the laundry started. If you must postpone his queries, take the initiative in reopening the subject. If you're on a crowded bus when your youngster asks you why that lady sticks out in front or what happened to the leg of the girl wearing a brace or why that man has no hair, you'll have to whisper you'll tell him later. Then do. You want him to understand that it's all right to question but that sometimes questions should be saved for a more appropriate time. After you've done this several times, you can probably avoid embarrassing questions in a childish treble by a look that says "Later" in recognition of an unspoken "Why?" in your offspring's eyes.

Sometimes, you'll discover that your youngster is satisfied with just a short, quick answer. "Why is that cloudy stuff coming out of the teakettle?" "Because it is hot."

But more often than most parents realize, a child is seriously questioning a physical phenomenon and would be fascinated by a more complex explanation of steam. And his interest could lead to a number of learning experiments with boiling and freezing water.

When asked a what-is-steam type of question, one mother replies to her child, "Do you want a long or a short answer?" Almost always the youngster answers, "Long!" and wiggles happily in anticipation of a fascinating learning session.

If you don't know an answer, tell your child, "I've wondered about that myself; let's find out together." Teaching your youngster how and where to find information to feed his boundless curiosity is one of the most valuable gifts you can give him during his early learning years. If you're stumped about finding adequate source material, ask the nearest librarian. Invest in an elementary science encyclopedia and look up answers with your child. Other possible sources of knowledge: a science museum (many exhibits are not too old for preschoolers), a natural-history museum, a TV science program, or a science-discovery kit from a toy store.

The Internet, of course, is an easy source to tap for information about almost everything. And parents should use it to gather information until children are old enough to use a computer themselves, which will be discussed in detail in Chapter 10. Sometimes when your child asks a what-would-happen-if kind of question, you can answer, "Let's experiment and see." What happens if you bring a snowball into the house? If you keep it in the refrigerator? The freezer? Is it really pure, clear water, if you let it melt? Is snow always the same? Do snowballs pack better in some snowfalls than in others? Can you make snow again if you refreeze the water? Can you make ice again after it has melted?

There are many excellent books describing experiments in the physical sciences that are written, usually, for elementary school youngsters but that are also suitable for preschoolers with the help of parents. The library nearest you should have several of these books. The experiments are not only stimulating learning activities but also delightful rainy-day fun for you and your offspring.

In trying these experiments, you can begin to encourage your child to have a scientific attitude about them. Before you begin, talk over these questions: "What are we trying to find out?" "How can we set up an experiment to discover the answer?" "What do you think will happen?" "What materials will we need?" Whenever possible, let your youngster perform the experiment himself. He'll learn far more that way than he will watching you.

When the experiment has been completed, urge your child to review precisely what did occur. Then ask him, "Do you think it would happen again this same way if we did it again?" "What did this experiment teach us?"

Your child will do a better job with these experiments if you've given him opportunities previously to pour water, to wash plastic dishes, and to measure dry materials and liquids with measuring cups and spoons.

No more than a brief sampling of science experiments for preschoolers can be included here, but they will give you an idea of materials you can find in your library.

For example, to help your youngster sense the reality of air, suggest that he crumple some newspaper at the bottom of a glass or a glass jar, turn the glass upside down and submerge it, straight down, in a pan of water for several seconds. When he removes it, he will find that the newspaper is not wet because the glass was already filled with air, which kept the water away from the paper.

To see the air itself, have your child repeat the experiment, this time turning the glass on its side after it is submerged in the pan of water and watching the air bubble up.

For a third experiment, suggest to your child that he submerge an empty glass in the water and turn it on its side so it fills with water. Then, show him how to tuck the end of a piece of rubber tubing into the top of the glass, turn it upside down again in the water, and force the water out of the glass by replacing it with air blown through the tubing.

Demonstrate to your child how he must empty the air out of a medicine dropper before he can fill it with water. Let him blow up a balloon and watch it jet around the room when he releases it. (On a visit to the nearest big airport, you can point out the jet planes that fly on this same principle.) Help him make a pinwheel on a pencil to demonstrate the force of moving air. Let him watch firsthand how you put air into a tire at the gas station and how beach balls and footballs are filled with air to make them more fun to play with.

Another experiment for a sunny day outdoors, or for a bathroom in wintery weather, is to give your child a chance to blow bubbles, using a straw and a small container of water mixed with liquid detergent. You can show her how to dip the end of the straw into the water, lift it out and blow gently to form a bubble. You can talk about how the air got inside the bubble and why the bubble soon pops, leaving a trace of water on the grass or on the bathroom floor.

You can even turn the pouring of fruit juice or a soft drink from a can into a science experiment. Punch one hole in one can and two holes in an identical can and encourage your small scientist to observe which empties faster. See if she can deduce why.

Experiments with water hold a special fascination for a small child, especially when she is permitted to perform them herself. For example, you can help her learn about evaporation by having her measure out a tablespoon of water in a shallow dish, set it in a warm place, and observe what happens to it. Add a drop of food coloring, if you wish, to make the experiment more interesting.

Next, suggest that she set out three shallow dishes, the first with one tablespoon of water, the second containing two tablespoons, and the third three, and watch to see whether the amount of liquid in the dishes affects the rate of evaporation.

Here's another experiment you can try when your preschooler comes indoors from play with a pair of wet mittens. Suggest that she put one in a warm place and another in a cold spot and observe which one dries more quickly. If it isn't mitten weather, try the experiment using dishcloths or washcloths dipped in water and wrung out. On a windy day, your youngster can experiment to see whether a wet dishcloth hung on a line in the breeze dries faster than one hung in a bathroom. On a hot, sunny day, you can give your child a squeeze bottle filled with water and let her make a design or a drawing on a sidewalk and keep track of how long it takes for the water to dry up.

To teach your child about another property of water, have her fill a small glass or a wide-mouth jar to the brim with water. Gently and slowly have her stir in about two table-spoons of sugar or salt, using a thin wire, such as a straightened paper clip. She should notice that the water does not run over, because the sugar and the salt will dissolve. Then have her repeat the experiment using sand and see what happens.

If your youngster has begun to understand about evaporation, ask him what he thinks will happen if he lets the salty or sugary water evaporate. Suggest that he experiment to check his conclusions by spooning out some of the salt or sugar solution into a shallow dish and check later to see what has happened.

When your youngster has grasped the idea that the air picks up water, ask him if he thinks the water can ever be taken out of the air again and suggest that you try to see if it is possible.

One of the easiest experiments is to take a glass of ice water and let it stand a few minutes on your kitchen counter on a hot, humid summer day or at a time when your kitchen is warm and steamy. Your child can observe the drops of water collecting on the outside of the glass.

Other ways to demonstrate condensation: Let your child squiggle or write letters on a steamy bathroom mirror after a warm shower. Show him how you can boil water in a pan on the stove and how the evaporated water will collect on the bottom of a second pan you have filled with ice and hold over the steam. Let him feel summer dew and autumn frost and make the connection between these phenomena and the idea of condensation. Let him run his finger over a car window that has fogged up in cold weather; talk about why it happens and how the car's defroster functions.

Your preschooler can have great fun experimenting—in the kitchen sink, bathtub, or plastic outdoor pool—to see what kind of objects will float and which will sink. Help her to keep a record of her experiments as she tests such everyday materials as blocks, bottle caps, paper clips, pennies, paper, pencils, crayons, cloth, capped empty bottles, capped bottles full of liquid, various types of soap, cork, empty milk cartons, and milk cartons full of water. Encourage her to form conclusions about why some objects float and others do not.

Some bright, sunshiny day, you can let your youngster—and her friends, if you wish—put on swimming suits and turn on the hose in the backyard so they can run in and out of the water. When they are ready to try something new, twist the nozzle of the hose so it produces a fine spray, angled so the sunshine catches the water drops just right and makes a rainbow for them to wonder about. You can talk about the colors they can see and how the drops of water act like prisms to break up the colors in the sunlight.

Experiments with sound usually delight preschoolers. For example, one of the simplest ways in which to demonstrate that vibrations produce sounds is to make a cigar-box guitar or a cereal-box banjo by stretching rubber bands of various thicknesses around the box. Your child can be helped to observe that the thinnest rubber band produces the highest notes when plucked and the thickest band the lowest. Tuck a thin block of wood or a strip of plywood under the rubber bands to act like a violin bridge. Have your child listen to the change in sound as you move the block to stretch the strings.

To help your child understand that the more vibrations per second, the higher the sound, tape a playing card to your child's upended tricycle so that the edge of the card is flipped by the spokes of a wheel as it revolves. Let your child spin the wheel by rotating the pedals and observe that the faster she turns, the higher the sound the card produces.

To demonstrate to your youngster that sound can travel

through other media than air, suggest that he take two wooden blocks or two flat stones or two small pot lids and bang them together, listening carefully to the sound. Then, in the bathtub or in a backyard pool, have him duck his head underwater and repeat the banging. He'll discover that it's much louder, because of the sound-conducting property of the water.

One child discovered an interesting variation of this principle. Lisa found that if she put one side of her face tightly against her brother's, she could hear him scratch his opposite temple much more clearly than if his face were only an inch or two away from hers when he was scratching. Her father explained to her that bone is also a good conductor of sound.

For other sound-conduction experiments, put a watch on a bare wooden table and have your child press his ear to the other end. He'll hear the ticking quite clearly. If you blow up a balloon and press it tightly between your child's ear and your ticking watch, he'll also be able to hear it distinctly.

You can make your child a can telephone this way: Find two empty metal cans with no sharp edges where the lids have been removed. In the center of the bottom of each one, punch a small hole with a nail. Through each hole, thread one end of a long, stout cotton string and tie it into a large knot or around a little stick to anchor it securely. Stretch the string tight and use as a telephone, with you speaking into one can while your child holds the other against his ear and listens.

For a variation in sound-conduction experiments, you can cut a piece of cotton cord about one yard long. Loop the center of the cord around a teaspoon and have your preschooler hold one end of the string in each of his ears, as he bends over slightly, balancing the spoon. If you strike the spoon with another spoon or a nail, your child will hear a sound like a church bell.

The world of growing things abounds with opportunities to help your young sprout gain a firm grounding in science, and you don't have to have a green thumb yourself to plant seeds of interest. Even if it isn't green-up time in the suburbs, there are dozens of experiments you and your budding botanist can try.

To demonstrate how a plant grows from a seed, buy a handful of large dried beans. Let your child try to break one of the beans open. When he finds it too hard to split, remind him that seeds usually need rain to start growing and suggest that he see what happens if he soaks several of the beans overnight in water.

The next day, your child will be able to peel off the coating of a bean seed and open it to discover the tiny shoot and root inside. Tell him that the surrounding sections of the bean, called seed leaves, are food for the baby plant.

To show your preschooler how the baby plants grow, try this: Line a glass with a wet paper towel. Keep water in the bottom during the experiment. Tuck one of the soaked beans between the towel and glass, where your child can watch it grow.

Cut off one of the seed leaves from a second soaked bean, carefully leaving the embryo plant, and add it to the glass. Do the same with a third, removing one entire seed leaf and half of the second. The difference in the growth of these three tiny plants demonstrates how much they need the food contained in the seed.

Radish seeds can be used to point up other essential needs of growing things. Fold two paper towels in the bottom of each of three glasses. Have your child put 10 radish seeds in each glass and cover each glass with a third folded paper towel.

In one glass, have your child sprinkle only a few drops of water. Soak the paper thoroughly in the second glass. Have your child fill the third glass almost full with water. Label each one and check the results in about five days. Help your youngster to understand that the seeds in the first glass did not get enough water; those in the third didn't get enough air.

Plants need proper temperature to grow, too, as you can

help your child to learn. In the bottom of each of two cups have your preschooler put a pad of wet, absorbent cotton. Sprinkle with birdseed. Cover the cups with saucers; place one cup in the refrigerator and keep the other at room temperature. Compare the results every day for a week.

Seeds can sprout in the dark, if they are wet, airy, and warm enough. But they also need light to grow into leafy plants after they have used up the food within the seed. Demonstrate this to your child like this: In each of two bowls, have your youngster place a wet sponge and sprinkle it with birdseed. Keep half an inch of water in the bowls during the experiment. Place one bowl on a sunny, warm windowsill; cover the other with a large pot or keep it in a very dark spot. Have your child check them every day for two weeks, but be careful not to let the second bowl stay in the light longer than a minute.

You can show your child other ways in which to make new plants besides starting them from seed. For example, put young pussy willow stems in water in your home and watch new roots grow from the bottom. After they are well rooted, the two of you can plant them outdoors.

Here's another way. Let your child cut a long leaf from a snake plant into two-inch pieces. Have him plant each piece about an inch deep in damp sand in a bowl. Keep the bowl covered with glass and in the light until new plants grow.

A favorite experiment to show how plants use water is this: Cut off the end of a white carnation stem underwater, place the carnation in a glass of water colored with bright ink, preferably red, and let it stand in the sunlight. Within a few hours, the petals will turn the color of the ink. You can even split the bottom half of the stem carefully and put each section in ink of a different color to obtain a two-tone bloom.

If you can't get a carnation, the experiment works, too, with a leafy stalk of celery you have freshened in water for half an hour.

On sunny days, you can help your child look for shadows

when you are outdoors together, noting that shadows aren't always the same size or in the same place. Then early one morning, you can suggest keeping track of your youngster's shadow for a day. Have him pick a spot to stand on the sidewalk and mark it with chalk. Then outline the shape of his shadow. Come back once or twice during the day—at noon and late in the afternoon—and have him stand in the same place and observe what has happened to his shadow. Then you can give him a flashlight and help him experiment to see that shadows are produced when light cannot go through a solid object, but that light can go right through a drinking glass or empty clear plastic bag without making a shadow.

Encourage your preschooler to make collections—insects, leaves, rocks, shells, pressed flowers—for the beauty of the objects and the pleasure of having them. When he runs out of shelf room to keep his collections, suggest that he begin to compare and classify his treasures, to keep his prizes, and to discard his duplicates. Then help him follow where these interests lead.

For example, suggest that your child start a collection of seeds and keep a count of how many seeds and what kind he finds in apples, grapes, peaches, cherries, watermelons, peanuts. Let him study closely dandelion seeds, milkweed seeds, an acorn, a coconut, and a maple seed. Ask him to guess how seeds can travel from one place to another. Then give him an opportunity to plant some of his seeds and watch them grow. (You'll have to do some background research first to guide this experiment to a fruitful conclusion.)

Today, there is only a thin line between scientific learning materials and some types of toys; both help your child learn more about physical phenomena. For example, magnets make fascinating playthings, especially if they are extra large and your child has a collection of nails, paper clips, and metal buttons with which to experiment. Help your preschooler to make a list of the household objects that can be moved about by a magnet and the ones that cannot. (Be sure to keep magnets away from TVs and computers.) And you can put paper clips on slips of paper that have the letters of the alphabet or the numerals he is learning and let him go fishing for them with a magnet that is on a string attached to a stick. He can "read" you the ones he hooks and throw back into the "pond" those he misses.

Other materials that can help children absorb scientific ideas in the guise of play include a large prism, field glasses, a see-through alarm clock that permits observation of gears in motion, and a stethoscope (a real one isn't expensive and permits a child to hear actual heartbeats and chest sounds).

Perception

Perception, as the word is usually used by educators, physicians, and psychologists, means the ability to transmit stimuli to the brain and interpret them accurately. It involves recognizing a voice as being Mommy's, a doll as being small enough to fit into a wagon, ice cream as being cold, a picture as representing reality.

Perception includes all of the senses—hearing, seeing, smelling, tasting, feeling. But because seeing is the key ability in learning, perception usually refers to the ability to see and to comprehend accurately in the mind.

To help your child sharpen his perceptual abilities, try playing some of these games with him:

- Arrange two to four blocks in various patterns and let your youngster copy the layout with identical blocks.

- Conceal a small toy in a paper bag. Let your youngster put his hand in, without peeking, and identify the object by touch alone. Vary the game by hiding several toys in the bag and by calling out which one he is to find and remove.

- Invent matching games of all types with lotto cards, color swatches from the paint store, numbers, letters, and magazine pictures pasted on cardboard.

- Try the Montessori activity of giving your youngster a box containing a dozen of each of four kinds of unshelled nuts that he is to sort by type into four small dishes. When he's adept at this, challenge him to try it blindfolded.

- Have your preschooler lie flat on the floor and ask him to identify different parts of his body as you point to them or call out their names. Vary the game by playing it while he is standing, sitting, and kneeling to help strengthen his perception of his body position in space.

- Set up an obstacle course for your child to follow through the house that will include crawling under a table, over the end of a sofa, around a chair, and jumping, hopping, rolling, and climbing. For fun, cut out foot, hand, and knee outlines and make a trail for your child to follow.

- Help your child learn about right and left. Identify his right sock and shoe and then his left sock and shoe as you dress him. Call out which arm he is to put into his sweater or coat first and which mitten he is to slip on first. Teach him that his knife and spoon go on the right, his fork on the left. When you are driving the car, point out when you are making a right or a left turn or ask him to tell you which direction you're going as you do it. And when you read to him, call his attention to the fact that words go from left to right along the lines of a page.

- With a small box and a block, have your youngster follow the directions you call out, putting the block into and out of the box, in front of and behind it, under it, to the left and to the right of it.

- Invest in two small pegboards. Set up a simple pattern

with colored pegs on one for him to copy on the other. Make the designs increasingly complicated as he progresses.

- Put several small objects on a table and let your youngster look closely at them for about one minute. Then ask him to close his eyes while you take one of the items away. Let him try to remember which object you've removed.

- Look at large pictures in a magazine with your child; encourage him to talk about what is going on in the foreground and what he can see in the background.

- Challenge your child to tell you, in order, all of the things he can see on a trip to the grocery store or on a walk to the playground or on some other familiar short trip.

- Plan walks with your child—to the park, through a shopping center, down a busy street, early in the morning, at dusk, in the winter, and when the weather's fine—to look for specific things. These could be colors, objects smaller than a breadbox, everything round, anything that is making a sound, people at work, or objects moving in the wind.

- Play a game with adverbs. Ask your child if he can demonstrate how to walk sadly, slowly, loudly, softly, proudly, fearfully, bravely.

- See how many different types of roofs you and your child can find in your neighborhood or on a car trip—hip, gable, flat, and single and double pitch. Or count how many different kinds of building materials you can see in the buildings you walk or ride past.

Concept Formation

Whether you help her or not, your preschooler will constantly be sorting out and combining and reorganizing and shifting the great mass of sensory impressions she is receiving and the perceptions she is acquiring, as she tries to understand the world around her. Often, she makes mistakes and she draws incorrect conclusions. But usually the fault is not in her way of thinking or in her reasoning abilities. She just doesn't have enough of the right information to begin with.

Four-year-old Carolyn hears her mother tell her father that Mr. Simpson, next door, has gone to the hospital. "What will they name the baby?" she asks, since her only knowledge about hospitals concerns mothers who have returned from hospital stays with new infants.

Donna, also four, is listening when her mother remarks to her older brother that she only has a dollar in her billfold. "Why don't we go to the toy store and get some more money," Donna suggests helpfully. Her brother hoots and calls her a dummy. She cries and through her tears says to her mother, "Well, every time you buy something in the toy store, you give the woman at the counter money and she gives you back more money." Donna's observations have been correct; she simply has not had the opportunity to learn that money can come in different denominations.

The exposure of small children to television has compounded this problem of concept formation. Television gives youngsters great masses of information and impressions for which they don't have enough background knowledge. Why does the Indian lady who comes to see the president wear a long sort of dress instead of moccasins and a feather? Why can't we use magic to make our kitchen floor shine like the man does on TV? Is that cowboy really dead like the robin we found in the backyard the other day?

Preschool children actually want to learn, can learn, do learn enormous amounts about history, geography, and economics without overt adult help, educators and psychologists are now acknowledging. They formulate surprisingly complicated explanations for facts they can't comprehend—not so much because they enjoy fantasy and magic, but because they crave understanding. And they are capable of dealing with important and significant ideas about the physical and social world.

Some educators who understand early-learning concepts are experimenting with ways to teach major concepts about social studies, economics, and the physical sciences to children in nursery schools and kindergartens. These programs generally take inspiration from the contention of Dr. Jerome Bruner, of the New School for Social Research, that "any subject can be taught effectively in some intellectually honest form to any child at any stage of development." They are backed by studies in which researchers and preschool teachers have recorded and studied the conversations of small children who strive to understand major concepts about life and death, God, outer space, the community in which they live, the world of work, cause and effect, and natural phenomena.

Designing new curricula for preschools and kindergartens to meet this new awareness of the intellectual needs of small children is under way in many day-care centers, nursery schools, and kindergartens. And research is being done in many academic fields to try to determine more precisely what key concepts small children should acquire as a basis for future learning. These key concepts are not to be taught by rote, researchers emphasize. But learning experiences should be designed to help small children discover and use these understandings for themselves.

It is rare to find a preschool where your youngster's needs to form significant concepts about the world are appreciated and directed. Even if you do, you as his parent still have the major role in guiding his development of accurate concepts.

What can you do to help your youngster? Several guidelines have emerged from the ongoing research: It's a help, first of all, just to appreciate your child's need to form concepts. Listen to what he says and try to understand the information or misinformation behind his remarks. Let this guide you into activities that provide him with facts he is apparently missing or has distorted in his thinking. Carolyn's mother and father, for example, just laughed indulgently at her. But her mother might have made it a point to read her a beginning book about where babies come from. She could have taken Carolyn to see the neighbor's new kittens and to the zoo to visit baby animals and talked casually about how they grew inside of their mothers. Some museums have exhibits depicting the development of unborn infants and displays in which baby chicks can be observed pecking their way out of their shells. Her mother could also have read her books about hospitals and what happens to people there and about the roles of doctors and nurses. None of this need be formal teaching. All of it can take place naturally and easily in the course of relaxed and normal interaction with a child.

For Donna, a complicated game of playing store might be useful. In some experiments with intellectual development in kindergartens, playing store has been successfully used to help youngsters understand not only the role of customers, food producers, manufacturers, and retailers but also about profit and pricing.

Donna's mother might have helped her daughter set up a grocery store in one corner and used it as a way to teach her about money, about making change, about the problem of getting produce and products to sell, and about how prices are determined.

In the course of such activities, a parent can guide a child into formulating questions he does not have answers for and can suggest that he take his queries to people who can supply him with missing information. A grocery store manager, for example, would probably be willing to explain to a small child the answer to a question he has thought through ahead of time with your help.

In addition to helping your child gain experiences that supply him with information to correct his misconceptions, you can also guide him into new ways of thinking about the information he has.

A bus trip, for example, can be much more meaningful to a preschooler if you help him fit it into an overall concept about transportation. Help him to think of all the kinds of transportation he can—boats, horses, cars, buses, trains, planes, trucks, in-line skates, rockets, bicycles, feet, helicopters—and talk about when he would use each one. Which methods would he use for hauling big packages? Which if he were in a hurry to go a long way? Which would probably cost the most money? This gives more meaning to short excursions on which you take your child and provides a foundation for future learning.

Children younger than first grade can absorb a surprising amount of learning about time, given some help, researchers have discovered. One good way to begin is to make a short, simple time line for your child. In a piece of string or rope, tie a knot about every foot to represent each of your child's birthdays to date. Then explain to him that the section of string in between the knots represents a year of his life. Talk with him about what events occurred during each of these periods—the time when he got his first tooth, when he first learned to walk, the summer you took that vacation trip to California.

Then make him a time line for yourself and point out some of the major events—perhaps when you started school yourself, when you were married, when you moved into your present home, when he was born.

Then you can tell him that a time line back to when Abraham Lincoln was president would stretch around your living room and kitchen twice. And one back to the era of George Washington, when our country got started, would go to the end of Jeff's driveway. A time line reaching to the year Columbus came to America would extend to the corner of your block and one showing the period of the first Christmas, when Jesus was born, would go all the way to his school. To make a time line that would represent the era when dinosaurs lived on this earth, you could need a time line that would stretch from your house to his grandmother's in the next state and back again 30 times, you can explain, for example.

It also helps your child gain some understanding about the changes that come with passing time if you can take him to a museum of history. Seeing the tools used by Indians or in ancient civilizations or even by pioneers in the United States gives him more observations upon which to base his developing concepts.

A preschool child won't be able to grasp completely the immeasurable periods of time that have swept over this earth or even to sort out all the events he has heard about according to chronology. But, Dr. Wann emphasized, "to assume that we should wait to encourage and help children to gain concepts of time and change until they can handle true chronology is to deprive children of one of the important learnings of early childhood. To defer help and encouragement in this area is to frustrate a basic intellectual need of today's young children."[1]

Maps make a good tool to help you orient your preschooler in your community, in your country, and in the world. Researchers who have worked with four- and five-year-olds, especially kindergarteners, find that they can grasp many major ideas associated with maps.

You might begin, for example, by helping your child draw a map of her room—locating chairs, bed, lamps, windows, door. She can learn that north is always at the top of the map and something about the concept of scale. Next, the two of you might construct a map of your block or your neighborhood, laying it out on the floor on a large sheet of white plastic or wrapping paper. You can crayon in streets and driveways, construct houses and buildings out of blocks, and use toy cars and trucks for traffic. From this point, it's relatively easy for your child to use and appreciate a map of your community and, eventually, a map of the United States. She'll be able to follow your route on a trip and to locate places talked about on television news programs with some assistance.

Because of frequent television programs about rocket launchings, most preschoolers have acquired many small pieces of knowledge about outer space. You can help your child form this smattering of facts into useful concepts by showing her a model of the solar system and explaining how it functions. (You can buy mobiles in the form of solar systems for her room or make one yourself with her help.) She's not too young to look for mountains on the moon with you or to grasp the basic principles governing eclipses, should one be visible in your area.

Adult occupations is another subject about which most preschool children have garbled knowledge and misconceptions. Where Daddy goes in the morning—and Mommy, if she holds a job—and why can be the basis for much learning, both by conversation and by actual experience. If possible, it's a valuable learning experience for a small child to go to work with his father or mother—perhaps on a Saturday or on a parent's day off—riding the train or bus, sitting at the parent's desk, and watching the kind of work that goes on for a few minutes. Both parents should make a point of talking to a child about what occurred in the course of their day and helping him understand not only what his parents do, but why.

You can also talk to your child about what other parents do—police officers, pilots, doctors, firefighters, salespeople, factory workers, construction workers, truck drivers, musicians, photographers, TV anchors, teachers—and the relationship of this work to the community's welfare. You can encourage him to make some beginning discoveries about the division of labor (perhaps by comparing the amount of time it takes you to check out of a supermarket when the checker does the bagging and when both a checker and a packer work on your purchases together). You can also note the tasks both mother and father do at home and help him discover why this kind of work is also important to the family.

You should also be helping your child learn that the old lines between male and female work are fading and that most jobs are now open to both men and women. A girl, in particular, needs to understand that police officers can be men or women, that girls can grow up to be doctors as well as nurses, that her sex should not be a limiting factor in what she will eventually choose to become.

A child's sense of sexual identity is established early in life and you don't want your daughter's ideas about being female to become limitations on the development of her ability. The changing role of women in society is something you should talk about with your child—boy or girl. You should discuss with your offspring how you and your spouse divide up family responsibilities and how you feel about what you both are doing. You can point out other families you know where parents have made different decisions about how to handle their responsibilities for home and job, and that some women combine jobs with homemaking while others do not. The point is to make your offspring—especially a daughter— aware that she does have choices about her life, that her sex need not be a limitation on the vocational or professional goals she may want to set for herself, and that there are many possible ways to combine home and career into a satisfying lifestyle.

If you are fortunate enough to have a two-parent family, you should make sure your child understands the special contributions both father and mother make. If you are a single parent, you should also talk to your youngster about how your family works and how you sometimes play both parental roles for his benefit.

A study of occupations can make a good, basic frame of reference for many of the short field trips you take with your child. For example, if he is getting bored with helping you buy groceries, suggest that he try to count the number of different types of workers in the supermarket on your next trip. Help him to observe which jobs take the least training and which require experience. And encourage him to speculate on other kinds of jobs that might be done behind the scenes or by other workers in other places.

Often you can take advantage of events in your neighborhood to help your youngster learn important concepts. For example, if there's a new house or apartment building being constructed in your neighborhood, you can use it to stimulate your child's formulation of concepts. Why do you think a bulldozer is used to dig the foundation, instead of people with shovels, you can ask your child. (His reasoning should lead him to observe other situations in which machines are employed to spare people hard physical labor.) Why does one group of workers only put in pipes whereas another crew does nothing but lay brick? Why is insulation placed between the inner and outer walls of the house? Why is a building inspector's permit tacked on that tree in front? What is the purpose of the blueprints the builder is reading?

You also should be aware that your child is constantly forming concepts in the area of social relationships. Often these concepts can be distorted, psychologists and doctors have discovered, by misinformation and incorrect assumptions garnered from television.

Melissa, age five, had been unusually weepy and upset, clinging to her father and unwilling to play with her friends, for the past two weeks. After much cuddling and questioning, she finally told her mother that she was afraid her parents were going to get a divorce. Melissa's mother could think of no reason why her daughter could have had such a mistaken idea, but finally the little girl whispered something about "that lady who had dinner with Daddy."

Then her mother remembered that she and her husband had invited a woman business associate of his to dinner about two weeks earlier. Melissa had connected the woman with a family-situation drama she'd seen on television in which a divorce had been precipitated by a dinner-table incident involving another woman.

Her mother assured Melissa that she and her husband intended to stay happily married and looked for experiences that would help the child understand more about family relationships. About this time, the entire family was invited to a wedding. Melissa's mother spent several days before the ceremony explaining to her daughter what would happen, what words would be said during the service, and how seriously she and her husband took the marriage vows they had made in the same way, long before Melissa's birth. Melissa listened spellbound to the marriage ceremony and for weeks afterward played "wedding" with her dolls.

One reason television has such a powerful effect on small children is that they usually can't separate reality from make-believe in the programs they watch. Often you can suggest play activities to your youngster that will aid him in making this distinction.

Lindsey's mother, for example, was concerned because her four-year-old seemed to believe everything she saw on television as being true and real. So she arranged for the child to visit an audience-participation show, see the cameras, and watch the program being produced. Then she encouraged Lindsey to play "television show" at home. Together they made a television "camera" by mounting a cardboard box on an old doll carriage base. Then they talked about whether they would put on a real-life program or a pretend story. For factual programs, Lindsey gave weather reports, neighborhood news, and helped her mother stage a cooking demonstration. For "made-up story" shows, she had her dolls act out policewoman plots and talking-animal dramas. And now she asks her parents to label programs she watches as being made-up or true whenever she isn't sure.

If you observe carefully how your child plays with other children and relates to them, you can also help her form intellectual concepts that will guide her social behavior in the future. Why should you share your toys with your guest? you can ask your child. How would you feel if you were Billy visiting at our house? Why do you suppose good manners are important? Why does Jamie act like such a bully and how can we help him to play in a nicer way with other children?

As your child begins to grasp new concepts based on her observations, you'll often notice that she plays them out, in variations, with her toys and with other small fry. If you listen to her conversations and watch her play, you'll usually discover how much she has actually grasped of the concepts you want to help her learn, and you'll have a good guide to the type of experiences to offer her next.

It will be years before your child can fully grasp and use most of the concepts you introduce her to as a preschooler. But they form a basic framework upon which she can build her future learning and make sense out of the great masses of information and detail her brain is recording.

Your child is going to be gathering information and forming concepts whether you help her or not. But with your assistance, she will form more useful concepts and fewer misconceptions and her future learning will be more efficient.

Toys

The years between three and six are the peak years for toys, the ages when your child most needs and most enjoys playthings. Many of the toys listed in Chapter 5 for toddlers are still appropriate for three- to six-year-olds. Some of the best playthings for preschoolers have already been mentioned in this chapter. But here is a quick summary of basic learning toys for this age group. Your child won't need them all, of course. Common objects around your house may be good substitutes for some of the items. But generally, he should have access to some playthings in each category:

- Blocks—well made and in as large an assortment as possible; simple, fit-together construction materials of wood or plastic, block cities, giant cardboard or hollow wooden blocks, if you can afford the money and the space.

- Toys to imitate grown-up activities—dolls, dollhouse, doll clothes, doll carriage, doll equipment, telephone, cash register, trains, trucks, planes, play money, an unstructured playhouse that can serve a multitude of purposes, doctor and nurse kits, farm and zoo animals, housekeeping equipment, gardening tools, carpenter tools. (Whenever possible, give your child the real thing instead of a toy. It works better, lasts longer, and gives a great sense of pride and accomplishment.)

- Materials to encourage creative arts—crayons, finger paints, colored pencils, chalk, blackboard, clay or the equivalent, poster paints, and paper of all kinds, from little colored notepads to large sheets of wrapping paper for murals. Invest in a stand-up easel if you have the space for it.

- Musical equipment—tape player, drum, tambourine, finger cymbals, triangle, bells, xylophone

- Props for dramatic play—costumes, costume box full of discarded clothing and large pieces of cloth, masks, hand puppets, hats, wigs, materials for playing store and school

- Games that teach numbers—dice, counting puzzles, dominoes, simple board games that involve counting, measuring tools, number rods, telling-time games

- Toys for loving—cuddly baby dolls, stuffed animals (which small boys need as much as little girls)
- Equipment for active, physical play—swing, wheelbarrow, wagon, scooter, tricycle, balls, trampoline-type bouncing pad, climbing apparatus, tree house, crawling tunnel, in-line skates, ice skates, merry-go-round, ride-'em trucks and trains, punching toy
- Toys to encourage sensory learning—inlaid puzzles, peg-boards, geometric insets, Montessori-type dressing frames, lotto games, color-matching games, kaleidoscope, flannel board with number and letter cutouts
- Science-discovery equipment—magnifying glass, magnets, prism, seeds, ant farm.

7

Should You Teach Your Preschooler to Read?

Teaching a preschool child to read is one of the happiest, most worthwhile, and most satisfying forms of early learning. It is also the subject of widespread research—with bright youngsters, disadvantaged children, three-year-olds, youngsters who are mentally retarded or emotionally disturbed or brain-injured, children of average IQ, four-year-olds, two-year-olds, and bilingual preschoolers.

Reading is being taught to preschoolers by parents at home, by psychologists in child-development laboratories, by educators in day-care centers, and by six-year-olds who like to play school in the family room. It's being taught phonetically, by sight-word techniques, by combination methods, and by no method at all. It's being taught with sandpaper alphabets, with newspaper comic strips, by first-grade primers, by television, by programmed readers, by cassette tapes, and by computer programs.

Regardless of method or motivation, most of those who try to teach preschoolers to read in any consistent way are generally successful. Those who have written about their experiences—in professional journals or in letters to the editors of newspapers—usually comment on the great joy, eagerness, and enthusiasm with which the preschoolers have learned.

The method with which I am most familiar is a 13-week series of daily cartoon strips which ran years ago in the *Chicago Tribune* and many other newspapers in the United States and England and showed parents how to teach small children to read by simple, phonetic lessons. It is described here in considerable detail because it shows how satisfying it can be for a parent and child to share the adventure of learning to read. And it illustrates how easily preschoolers can acquire basic reading skills if given some phonetic information in a relaxed and happy atmosphere with only a small investment of time by a parent. It also provides some insight into what parents should look for in a reading program. One parent who used the method wrote:

I doubt if you are fully aware of the door to a world of knowledge which the *Tribune* opened to children in the Chicagoland area. I do not see how you can begin to imagine the hesitant and curious way in which two of my little girls and I opened that door. Our doubt and curiosity soon gave way to an overwhelming enthusiasm and eagerness.

The older little girl started first grade this fall, reading as well as her second and third grade brothers. Our four-year-old spends many happy hours each week educating and entertaining herself. In our home there are no longer moans of "What can I do now, Mommy?"

My two little daughters and I have developed an understanding and a closeness that I never dreamed possible from our association in the field of education—an unexpected bonus from the reading strips. I am looking forward to the same delightful experience of opening the door to learning

for my other two babies and only wish, dear *Tribune*, that you had been around when the eight older ones were small.

Contemporary interest and research about teaching preschoolers to read began in the late 1950s. It was touched off, generally, by the discoveries about the functioning of the human brain itself and by concerns not only about providing learning stimulation for gifted youngsters but also about equipping disadvantaged children to succeed in first grade.

Now, it is commonplace to find youngsters entering first grade already able to read well. Popular TV programs like *Sesame Street* help youngsters learn to identify sounds and words. Many day-care centers and nursery schools make it a policy to offer reading readiness programs and beginning instruction in reading.

But the idea that children as young as three and four can learn to read if given a little of the right kind of loving, relaxed help is still not universally accepted. Many parents assume that teaching a young child to read would take more time than they can spare; if they cannot find a day-care center that offers a reading program, they see no problem in waiting for traditional instruction in first grade. School systems that have access to considerable data showing the benefits of providing preschoolers with early help in reading—either via programs for parents or in school-sponsored child–parent centers—often can't find the money to pay for such innovations. Others have been concentrating so much on diversity or special education classes that they have not been able to develop major new curriculum ideas.

Despite an enormous amount of accumulating evidence that preschoolers can learn to read easily and happily and with great immediate and long-term benefit, interested parents may still get some negative feedback from teachers they ask about the possibility. Some teachers still tell parents: Don't try to teach your child to read yourself. Reading is such an enormously complicated mental endeavor that even trained teachers sometimes fail to teach it successfully. So how can you possibly succeed? You'll use the wrong methods. You'll pressure your child. You are too emotionally involved to help your youngster. He'll ruin his eyes. Besides, he can't possibly learn until he has a mental age of six—maybe even seven or eight—so you're wasting your time and inviting emotional disaster.

Some well-known books on child care still echo these messages. Some learned educators still write scholarly papers for professional journals analyzing the reading process in ways that make it seem too impossibly difficult for anyone ever to learn, especially small children. Debates still persist about sight-word methods versus phonics versus combination techniques, about grouping and mainstreaming pupils, and about obscure technicalities involved in the reading process.

After the *Tribune*'s preschool reading series began to appear in print, dozens of parents wrote the paper with comments like this: "We're so glad to know it's all right to help our child with reading. He's learned so much on his own, from watching television and asking us questions about words. But we were afraid the school wouldn't approve."

One of the most curious facts in the history of American education is how long the mistaken idea persisted that children need a mental age of 6 or 6½ before they could learn to read. The notion was based on several studies that were made during the early 1920s and 1930s that showed that among first graders, those with a higher mental age learned to read better than their classmates.[1]

These findings were generally interpreted to mean that the older a child, the better she could be taught to read, and that youngsters with a mental age of less than six could not read. The occasional child who did come to first grade already reading was thought to be so highly intelligent that she learned to read almost spontaneously. Or her parents were suspected of pushing her to alleviate their own neurotic feelings of inadequacy.

More contemporary critics who have reviewed this evidence point out that all it really shows is that the higher a child's IQ, the easier she will learn to read. Furthermore, they point out, it isn't valid to draw conclusions about preschool reading from research that deals only with a small number of six-year-olds taught by a sight-word method in a formal classroom situation. As a result of this poorly done research, almost no attempts were made for decades to teach reading before the age of six and almost no children learned to read before they reached first grade. It was easy to assume that they couldn't.

But challenges to this smug assumption eventually developed—prompted in part by concerns about the worrisome percentage of youngsters failing to learn to read well in school and by new neurological findings about how the brain acquires and uses information.

Today, the teaching of reading to preschoolers is well under way in many different places in the United States. Today, there is no doubt that preschoolers can be taught to read—in several happy, satisfying, successful ways. For example:

In a Montessori school in Oak Park, Illinois, Bobby, four, spreads out a small, individual mat on the floor, then takes a collection of simple picture cards from a nearby drawer. One by one, he lines up the pictures in a row, down the side of his mat. He studies the first one, a dog. Slowly, Bobby sounds out the word under his breath. Still repeating the initial *d* sound, he goes to an open rack full of colored letters cut out of sandpaper-covered cardboard. He locates a *d,* takes it back to his mat, and places it beside the picture. Next, he finds an *o* and then a *g,* sounding out each letter as he walks back and forth.

Bobby successfully spells out *man* and *cat* and *hat.* Then he tries *bus.* But he can't remember what letter makes the initial *b* sound. So, for the first time, he asks for adult help.

"What says *b*?" Bobby asks the Montessori directress. She goes with him to a bin of large sandpaper letters that are glued on cardboard rectangles. Gently, she guides the fingers of Bobby's right hand so that his fingertips trace the sandpaper shape of *b* while she repeats the sound of the consonant. After learning the *b* sound through his eyes, his ears, and his fingers, Bobby is easily able to find it himself.

Without any more help or supervision, Bobby spells out the rest of the names on his picture cards. Then, he sits back on his heels, contemplates his work for a minute, and quietly returns all of the materials to their proper place.

No one has instructed Bobby to do the reading-spelling lesson. No one has supervised him or graded him or pressured him or even praised him for doing it. He could have chosen any of dozens of other activities. But he was sounding and making the words because he enjoys the learning and the sense of competence it gives him.

Dr. Montessori discovered that preschoolers could learn to read and write and enjoy the process enormously when she was developing her first slum-area school at the beginning of the century. Ever since, Montessori schools have taught preschoolers to read and to write. Dr. Montessori's textbooks—now published in several new editions in the United States—are full of descriptions of the eagerness and the enthusiasm with which her poverty-level youngsters learned to read. After studying their progress, degree of interest, and rate of learning, Dr. Montessori concluded that children learn to read most easily at ages four and five.

The widespread and enthusiastic revival of Montessori schools in the United States has been due in part to parents' interest in early reading. Today, the Montessori method of teaching reading and writing is one of the best and most complete available to preschoolers. Much of the entire Montessori program aims at educating a youngster's five senses and is designed to culminate in the joyous and exciting discovery by preschoolers that they can communicate by reading and writing.

A child in a Montessori school learns to write before she learns to read. And she learns with such ease and pleasure that most elementary school teachers find it difficult to believe. She begins by learning how to control the muscles in her hand—by manipulating equipment designed for this purpose, by working with geometric form boards and inlaid puzzles and by tracing and filling in geometric shapes with a pencil. Then she practices tracing sandpaper letters with her fingers as she learns the sounds these letters make. In this way, she learns all of the physical motions necessary to write before she ever risks making a mistake by actually trying to write with pencil on paper. When she is ready to try, she usually succeeds immediately and joyfully.

Dr. Montessori's classic book, *The Montessori Method,* describes the tremendous excitement and delight with which her small preschoolers discovered that they could indeed write real words, as a result of previous training of the senses and having learned the sounds of the letters. "The first word spoken by a baby causes the mother ineffable joy," she wrote. "The first word written by my little ones aroused within themselves an indescribable emotion of joy."[2]

Only after a child has learned to write well does he learn to read, Dr. Montessori believed. He should be taught reading by sounding out the words phonetically, then repeating them rapidly until he understands them. Often reading, too, comes with the same burst of excited joy with which a child discovers that he can write.

Four-year-olds, on the average, take only a month or six weeks from the first preparatory exercise to achieve their first written words, said Dr. Montessori. Five-year-olds need only about one month. "Children of four years, after they have been in school for two months and a half, can write any word from dictation and can pass to writing with ink in a notebook," wrote Dr. Montessori. "Our little ones are generally experts after three months' time, and those who have written for six months can be compared to the children in the third elementary. Indeed, writing is one of the easiest and most delightful of all the conquests made by the child." Moving from writing to reading takes about two weeks, reported Dr. Montessori.

The same easy progression from writing to reading has also been noted by Dr. Durkin in her studies of youngsters who learned to read at home before they entered first grade. More than half of these children were intrigued with printing words before or at the same time they became interested in reading. Such a child would draw or scribble with an ordinary pencil, or write on a blackboard at home. Then he would start to copy letters of the alphabet. Soon, he would begin to ask questions about words ("Show me my name!") and about spelling. And from this interest, he would advance naturally into reading.[3]

Educators who teach young children to read usually take great precautions against pressuring a child into reading. The youngsters' only reward, in their programs, is the joy of discovery, the feeling of accomplishment and mastery, the fun of knowing. Yet even skeptics who aren't convinced of the value of preschool reading acknowledge with surprise the intensive interest, concentration, and delight with which children use the reading materials. The same kind of fascination and enthusiastic concentration marks much newer computer programs that are designed to help young children learn to read. In preschools, kindergartens, and first grades where they are available, children are generally so eager to use them that careful schedules of taking turns must be worked out.

The warmth, praise, and enthusiasm of human teachers play a greater role in some of the other ways in which preschoolers are being taught to read today. It is almost impossible for parents to play the detached, neutral role of a Montessori directress or to refrain from reacting with excitement and enthusiasm to a child's happy successes in decoding written words.

A few of the reading materials available to parents who want to teach a child to read at home are built around what is essentially a sight-word or look-say method of reading in which the youngster is encouraged to identify words by their shape as a whole instead of decoding them phonetically. Some preschoolers can—and do—learn to read in this way. But phonetic reading methods, which teach a child from the very beginning that printed words are just written-down sounds that he can easily learn to decode, do a better job of teaching reading than do sight-word techniques.

Debate does still persist on using phonics versus the sight-word method, or its modern counterpart, the "whole language" approach, in which children are encouraged to guess at what a word means on the basis of its context. But almost all of the best-conducted and most complete research studies on the subject show a clear-cut and continued advantage for youngsters who learn by techniques that introduce phonics at the very beginning of instruction. After several years of trying "whole language," many school districts have returned to teaching phonics again. Concerned about declining test scores, several states have mandated that schools include explicit instruction in phonics.[4]

Using magnetic resonance imaging, researchers at Yale University's Center for Learning and Attention have even identified differences in the way the human brain reads using phonetic or sight-word methods. Phonetic readers experience increased blood flow in the language centers of the brain as their brains literally processed the sounds, uniting them into words. Magnetic resonance images (MRIs) of sight-readers showed no such increase in blood flow.[5]

When the *Chicago Tribune* decided to develop a comic-strip feature to help teach preschoolers to read at home, a phonetic plan was chosen. This one was developed by a nursery school teacher, Mrs. Dorothy Taft Watson, and included several games and learning activities.[6]

"This is a game to teach you what the letters say," a parent begins by telling a preschooler. Showing the child the large letter *h* in the comic-strip panel, the parent points out, "This looks a little like a chair."

The next panel shows a little boy running. The parent reads, "Harry ran home so fast, he was out of breath." With the next panel, "He fell into the chair and all he could say was 'h - h - h - h - h.' "

Then the parent encourages the youngster to run across the room, pretend he's out of breath, and collapse into a straight-backed chair as he makes the out-of-breath *h* sound.

Finally, the parent suggests that the child listen for the *h* sound in words like *hat, helicopter, heart,* and *hammer*. If the child is still interested, the parent asks him to think of words he knows that begin with an out-of-breath sound and writes them down for him, calling his attention to the initial *h*.

"A very young child usually does better if he doesn't even know the names of the letters at first, except for the vowels, which sometimes make the sound of their own name," explained Mrs. Watson. "Later on, you can easily teach your youngster the alphabet by means of the familiar alphabet song," she suggested. The sounds that the letters make are what's important in decoding printed words—not the names of the letters.

The second comic strip teaches *m*, linking the sound with *Mary, moon, mouse, milk,* and *monkey* and the shape with a pair of child's mittens held together and upside down, thumbs outside. Next comes *p*, associated with the noise a papa makes pretending to puff on a pipe. This time the parent writes down a series of words starting with *p* and asks the child to draw a circle around each *p* as she sounds out the words. (Lowercase letters are used throughout the initial parts of this program and most others for preschoolers; capitals are taught later on.)

Parents should play the game of letter sounds with a child for only a few minutes at a time, according to Mrs. Watson. She suggested that each session be no longer in minutes than the youngster's age in years—three minutes for a three-year-old, five minutes for a kindergartener. But the game can be played several times a day, provided the child is interested and enjoys it.

As a child learns the sound of a letter, she is encouraged to look for it in places other than the comic strip—on cereal packages, highway signs, labels, headlines. Many mothers wrote the *Tribune* that they had invented games to be played in the car or while doing housework that involved the child's listening for initial consonant sounds in strings of words or sentences concocted by the parent.

"Remember that for preschoolers, phonics is still very much a game—just as learning to walk and to talk were games," advised Mrs. Watson. "Keep it light, happy, and relaxed. Your child has no deadlines to meet, no tests to pass, no possibility of failure."

"Your child will often forget the sound of the letters, particularly at first," explained Mrs. Watson. "Just tell him the right answer at once. Don't make him guess or wallow. Do praise him delightedly for each sound he learns and each word he sounds out. Your child will learn far faster when he's motivated by praise. And most important, do share his excitement at his own cleverness and the new world that is opening to him."

Next *s* is taught, linked with snake. Then comes *w* with its windy sound, emphasized by having the child hold his hand in front of his mouth as he says *witch, wild, wagon, wolf.*

The letter *t* is learned in association with the *t-t-t-t-t-t*-tick of a clock and *r* becomes the *r-r-r-r-r-r-r-r* sound of a big, cross dog, which a child can have ferocious fun imitating.

When a preschooler has learned the sounds and shapes of these six consonants, all of which make a consistent sound, he's ready for his first vowel. Parents can tell preschoolers that vowels are "fairy letters" because they can do magic tricks with other letters and that every word must have one, Mrs. Watson suggested. The first one to teach is the short sound of *a* as in *apple*.

Then comes the exciting minute when a preschooler is ready to roll consonants and a vowel together to make his first word, *hat*. To emphasize the smoothness of this procedure, the *Tribune*'s comic strip shows a snowsuited child rolling the *h* and *a* and *t* into a snowball.

Starting with the eighth comic-strip lesson, a preschooler is able to read a very simple comic written for her, using only the sounds she has learned to identify and blend together. For the rest of the 13-week newspaper series, she gets a new comic every day to read by herself, as well as instructions in a new sound or reading technique.

"When your child begins putting consonants and vowels together to make words, it's important that he learn to do it smoothly and quickly, so he will recognize the word he is sounding out," Mrs. Watson stressed. "You may have to work with him several days before this comes easily and naturally. Tell him he need not sound a word he already knows. He should just read it right off."

As the lessons proceed, a preschooler learns the sound of *j, l, z, b*, and *d*, reading easy comics and playing simple games based on letter shapes or sounds. For example, a child can act out *d* by marching about, making the *d-d-d-d-d* sound on a pretend drum.

The fairy letter *e*, as in *egg*, comes next. The letters *ck* together are taught as a *k* sound. With *g*, a preschooler learns the hard sound, as in *gag*. But he is also told that sometimes *g* sounds like a *j*, and if he can't make sense out of the word using the hard *g*, he should simply try the alternative.

Parents are encouraged to make up simple games to play with their children, using these basic sounds. For example, a 16- or 20-square bingo-type card can be drawn, using letters instead of numbers and raisins or small jelly beans as markers. A parent can be cooking or washing dishes as she calls out the sounds for the youngster, who shouts out his own name when he has succeeded in marking a row up or across. Then he gets to eat the markers.

After a youngster has learned the consonants and short vowel sounds, the *Tribune*'s reading program begins to teach him shortcuts. First, he learns a few common digraphs—two letters that join together to make a special sound of their own, such as *ch, sh, qu, ph,* and *th.*

Linguists point out that *th* actually makes two different sounds, as in *then* and *thin.* But this is a subtlety that doesn't trouble preschoolers. Almost always, without being told, they will choose the correct pronunciation without realizing the difference.

After the common digraphs come phonograms, groups of letters that almost always sound the same, such as *ook, ank, ink, all, ight, atch, or, er, aw,* and *oy.* These word patterns make it easy for small children to learn some of the most irregular vowel sounds and consonant combinations. And by blending these parts of words with initial consonant sounds, a preschooler can increase his reading vocabulary rapidly and easily.

At this point, a parent should teach a child the names of the five vowels, according to Mrs. Watson. A youngster is taught one simple rule about when a vowel says its own name: When two vowels come together in a word or have only one other letter in between in a short word, the first one usually says its own name and the second one keeps quiet. For example, if a youngster already knows how to pronounce *at,* this rule makes it easy for him to learn *ate* and *eat.* And it gives most children a wonderful sense of mastery and competence to be able to apply this rule to read *rob* and *robe, kit* and *kite, hat* and *hate,* and *bat* and *boat* and *bait.*

Critics of phonetic reading methods always point out the

inconsistencies in the English language, such as the different sounds of *ough* in *cough, rough, bough, dough,* and *through* (the worst single example of sound-spelling inconsistency in English) and subtle shades of differences in the pronunciation of vowels. But advocates emphasize that 85 percent of all English words are completely phonetic and almost all of the rest are at least partially so. And it's far easier to learn the spelling of the 44 basic English sounds and a few rules about when to use which than it is to memorize every word by its total shape, as some reading methods teach.

When a child does discover such an inconsistency, a parent should merely tell him that it is a "naughty letter" that doesn't follow the rules, Mrs. Watson suggested. Most preschoolers are delighted at this idea and have no further difficulty.

As he begins to read easy books (many of which are still being written from word lists used with look-say methods, rather than according to phonetic principles), a child will encounter a few common words that don't follow the phonetic rules he's learned so far. It's easiest just to tell him what each word says when he comes across it and have him learn it as a sight word, according to Mrs. Watson. Such words include *could, father, friend, once, one, pretty, said, says, shoes, sure, there, to, too, very, where, would,* and *you.*

Once a preschool child has learned the sounds of the consonants, the sounds of the long and short vowels and rules about when to use which, and a dozen common sight words, he can proceed independently in reading. Eventually, he should be taught the names of the consonants. And he should learn the alphabet. (It's easiest with the familiar song that follows the "Twinkle, Twinkle, Little Star" tune.) But from this point on, he'll absorb almost everything else he needs to know from practice.

"Julie was four when your first lessons started," one mother wrote to the *Tribune.* "She whizzed through about sixty of the lessons, but then lost some interest. She just wants to read books instead. Now she has very little trouble reading her sister's third grade reader. And she's trying to teach her little three-year-old brother to read. Thank you for making reading such a wonderful experience for our little girl."

"Parents should not be afraid of helping their children with reading," emphasized Mrs. Watson. "The subject has too frequently been surrounded by a maze of technical terms and suggestions. Too many people think of reading as being far more complex and difficult than it really is and tend to find deep and complicated reasons for any simple mistake a child may make.

"Teaching a child to read is actually quite easy," she said. "You can hardly go wrong. Anyone can easily learn the simple, basic letter sounds suitable for a preschool child. And it is surprising to see how easily and enthusiastically an extremely young child will often learn them. Phonics can be started—as a game, of course—when the child is just learning to talk.

"My own children began as babies, running in and out of my kindergarten and picking up their letter sounds along with nursery rhymes. If they saw a picture of a cow, they knew the cow said 'moo,' and if they saw a printed 'm' they knew it said 'm-m-m.'

"It is easy to teach a child the rudiments of reading," commented Mrs. Watson. "It is also a privilege and such an enjoyable experience that it would be a pity to miss it. Moreover, these early years are usually periods of high intellectual curiosity in the child. His interest is keen. He wants to learn. And he will do so more easily than he may later on. A four- or five-year-old who discovers the magic of letters will often spend endless hours experimenting with every bit of printed matter he can lay his hands on. Presently, he will discover that he can read—and then the world is his."

Giving parents a preschool reading program for their children via a newspaper comic strip was such a revolutionary concept in education that it might stir up a controversy, *Trib-*

une editors thought. First-grade teachers, especially, would disapprove of the suggestion that part of their primary job could be done at home by a parent.

So the great burst of enthusiasm that greeted the preschool reading series caught the paper by surprise. What was intended as a public-service feature suddenly became one of the hottest circulation ideas in years. More than 60,000 parents asked the *Tribune* for reprints of parts of the series they had missed or mislaid. Almost twice that many bought paper-covered reprints of the reading strips since the series ended. The entire 13-week reading program has been published in many other newspapers and repeated twice since in the *Tribune*. Thousands of delighted parents have written the *Tribune* about their experiences using the material with their youngsters. The *Tribune* now even gets an occasional letter from a college student thanking the reading program for setting him on a successful academic career that has led to admission to a prestigious university.

"My three-, four-, and five-year-old children are learning so much about reading from your comic strips," wrote one mother. "Our two-year-old listens and our nine-month-old baby eats whatever she can reach—the reason why we are missing two of the lessons. Can you replace them, please?"

"We need the last four comic strips," wrote another parent. "We were out of town for the weekend. The neighbors were saving the papers for us but decided to keep the reading strips for themselves."

The mother of a 4-year-old boy and a 30-month-old girl described her experiences with the reading lessons this way:

Jimmy, my oldest son, will be five in December. He was very enthusiastic about learning to read. Last summer, he was more interested in going over his comic strips than playing outside with his friends. "Reading" his new sound was the high point of each day.

The time spent daily in learning each new sound and

going over the old ones varied from two or three minutes to fifteen. I found it very important for the child, as well as myself, to find a time when there were few distractions, such as a favorite TV program for him or demands of caring for the two youngest children for me. When either of us was tired, rushed, or had our mind on something else, nothing was accomplished.

I had some difficulty in convincing him that the sounds could be put together to form words. Jimmy has now reached the point where he can recognize on sight most of the common short words and is not afraid to tackle the long words.

After the first eight weeks, I purchased a beginner's dictionary, which I found was very helpful in building up Jimmy's self-confidence. Now he is reading books in the easy-read series. He reads to anyone who will listen to him—his father, sister, friends; even delivery men cannot escape without listening to a sentence or two. Another side effect of learning to read is that his speech has improved; each word is said clearly, and mistakes in pronunciations can be corrected easily.

Linda was only two and one-half when the reading strips started and, like most younger children, she tries to imitate every word and action of her older brother. I intended to use the series with her next year when Jimmy starts kindergarten, but I have already shown her several of the comic strips to teach her sounds that she was unable to say. I now believe that she will complete the entire series and be able to read long before next September.

I have recommended the series to three mothers whose children are having difficulties with reading in the first grade. One of them even offered to buy the scrapbook I made of the comic strips. But I wouldn't part with it for the world. It will always have an honored place in my home. My son is a walking, reading testimonial to its effectiveness.

* * *

Kindergarten and first-grade teachers did indeed make up the largest group of individuals writing the *Tribune* about the preschool reading program. But contrary to expectations, almost all of them had high praise for the idea. This was particularly true of former teachers who retired temporarily to care for small children of their own.

"I am a first grade teacher in an Indiana school," wrote one. "I think you'll be interested in knowing that my best student is also one of yours. Would you kindly send me the entire series so I can use it with all my pupils?"

In some schools, kindergarten and first-grade teachers sent notes home to parents, suggesting the use of the reading strips. Explained one, "This kind of idea certainly helps the teacher of the first grade. The children entering the class then have some idea of phonics and reading and they aren't so lost."

"We have a kindergartener in our house and I am also a first grade teacher," wrote an Iowa mother. "I was overjoyed to find your excellent series. Now my five-year-old girl is delighted that she can read as well as her third grade sister. I only wish my own pupils had this same opportunity. This is certainly not pushing a child—but helping him develop his own potential. These children in my first grade class have good minds, but no one has encouraged them to use their minds. It is like having an arm in a sling; if it's never exercised, it will eventually become unusable."

As interest in early learning has soared in recent years, the number of easy-read books; workbooks; and audio, video, and computer programs billed as teaching reading to young children has multiplied. Unless parents are careful, they could spend a lot of money on materials that merely confuse a child and retard his learning. Here are some guidelines:

- The method of teaching should be phonetic and begin by showing a child how written symbols are merely sounds written down. It's surprising how much material fails by this standard. Most easy-read books for beginning readers are still based on the old look-say sight-word lists that a child cannot easily decode but must guess at by their shape and defeat the idea that reading is a logical activity that youngsters can master. Alphabet books, for example, typically begin with "A is for apple," although the name of the letter *A* does not make the vowel sound in *apple*. Many workbooks and computer games simply expand on these problems.

- Young children don't need a lot of expensive software to learn to read. Parents can make simple matching lotto-type cards to help a child learn to recognize the letters and easy words. You can make bingo cards using sounds and then short words. You can put signs and labels on items around the house. And you can call attention to words—on cereal boxes, in the grocery store, on the TV schedule, on traffic signs—whenever you are with your child. A computer program may be fun for a child to operate, but some of them are unnecessarily cutesy and distracting. And reading and a reading lesson on a parent's lap is more effective and welcome than a computer game.

- Like many toys for young children, much early-reading material is full of gimmicks that distract attention from the learning. One widely marketed learning-to-read video even counseled children not to look at letters at all but to outline the shapes of words and memorize them. Imagine trying to memorize hundreds of thousands of abstract shapes without learning any means to decode them!

The debate about whether children younger than six *can* learn to read has generally been resolved. It's obvious that preschoolers can read and read fluently and with great enjoyment. But some influential critics still contend that even though it's possible, it's not a good idea to help a youngster learn to read before he starts first grade.

The opposition to preschool reading uses several arguments. First, the critics charge, too much pressure is bad for preschoolers, and it must take pressure to get children younger than six to accomplish first-grade-level work. For example, commenting on the program developed by the Denver public schools to give parents television instruction on how to introduce reading to four-year-olds at home, one professor of education wrote in a professional journal, "We shudder at what can happen when thousands of eager parents launch an attack on their young children."

Pressure *is* bad for small children. Furthermore, it's usually ineffective. Even greenhorn parents who might be inclined to pressure a youngster discover long before their firstborn is two years old that pressure doesn't work—in getting a child to nap or to use the toilet or to eat peas or to wave bye-bye or to say thank you to the nice lady for the cookie.

The Denver program reported no evidence of pressuring from parents. This 16-week experiment that gave parents instruction on how to teach their small fry about beginning consonant sounds, letter forms and names, and letter–sound associations for some consonants brought much enthusiastic response. Of parents participating, more than 80 percent said that the instruction was helpful to them and important for their children. About 75 percent said they would appreciate having more help with early reading and that they intended to continue beginning-reading activities with their offspring.[7]

Observers who have studied other early-reading programs have not discovered any evidence of pressures or negative emotional reactions. Even in the cases of four preschoolers, now reported in professional literature, who failed to learn to read in research programs—all twins with low IQ, emotional difficulties to start with, and a family background of poverty—researchers found that the youngsters enjoyed the program and scored better on psychological tests afterward than they had previously.

Actually, an earlier start in reading reduces the pressures of learning by introducing a youngster to reading at the age when her brain is most able to acquire language and her fascination with words is at its peak. When reading is taught individually and informally by a parent at home, a child isn't pressured by first-grade competition. She doesn't have to try to make the top reading group or feel humiliated in the lowest section. She doesn't need to be concerned about grades or tests or keeping up with anyone else. She is free of the fear of making mistakes in public.

Every first-grade reading method requires much repetition of words and sounds. The writers of primers often boast about how many times they can use the same word on a page or in a story. The total vocabulary introduced in a first-grade sight-word reading program ranges from about 110 to 300 words. It's no wonder it takes rules and discipline to keep a six-year-old's eager, active, space-age, television-conditioned mind on "Oh, look. See the girl. See the boy."

But two-, three-, and four-year-olds enjoy repetition. What is boring at six can well be fascinating at three. What a first grader does only at a teacher's insistence, a three-year-old may easily do by his own choice and initiative.

The critics who still think no one but a trained teacher can help a child learn to read ignore not only the new research on the subject but also a youngster's ability to learn spoken languages. They also ignore the skill with which a majority of parents learn to adjust their child-rearing methods and teaching techniques to the individual personality and progress of their child.

In studying the backgrounds of 49 youngsters who read before entering first grade to find out how they learned, Dr. Durkin of the University of Illinois found a surprising factor. Sixteen of the youngsters said in interviews that they had been taught to read by an older brother or sister. Checking out these statements with parents, Dr. Durkin learned that the older child had been solely responsible for the teaching of reading in only 4 cases. For 24 other youngsters, however, an older brother or sister did contribute to the reading instruction. Having a sister about two years older who likes to play school has a great deal to do with early-reading ability in a preschooler, suggested Dr. Durkin.

So easy can it be for some preschool children to learn to read that they almost seem to teach themselves. For example, William H. Teale, of La Trobe University, Bundoora, Victoria, Australia, compiled considerable research on children who learned to read before starting first grade. He found there were usually four factors present in their home environment:

1. A wide range of easy reading material was readily accessible, including not only books but signs, names, TV captions, and other material. TV program guides were favorite early reading matter for these youngsters, who also picked out words in newspapers, cookbooks, and labels on food products.[8]

2. Someone in the home helped the child learn what the printed material says, both by volunteering information ("That sign says 'stop'") and by answering a child's questions about words, and made it clear to the youngsters that printed words convey important and interesting information. Parents in these homes did considerable reading to their preschoolers and one or both of them were avid readers themselves. "In many ways reading became an integral part of daily living," Dr. Teale noted. "The early readers saw people reading and responding to print. They themselves were read to and came to understand that reading is yet another mode of communicating."

3. Children who learned to read early in these studies almost always had access to pencil and paper and enjoyed drawing and scribbling.

4. People in the home environment who were important to the child—not only parents but brothers, sisters, aunts, or grandparents, for example—responded to what the youngsters were trying to do.

"In short," said Dr. Teale, "the children got feedback about reading in response to their felt needs and in a manner which preserved the general language arts concept of reading."

A study of how 37 youngsters in a class for gifted children in Palm Beach, Florida, learned to read, either before they entered first grade or almost immediately after, showed that generally the same factors were involved, with some individual differences. Several parents said they helped their youngsters learn to read, some by means of phonics, a few with a combination of phonics and sight words. Six children learned to read incidentally, largely by asking questions persistently about letters and words and names on TV. Two preschoolers started reading in Montessori schools, three in nursery school. The parents of almost all of these youngsters had read to them throughout the earliest years of their lives, beginning by the time they were first able to sit up.

Parents who are teaching reading at home are routinely cautioned to stop the instruction the second the youngster seems bored or frustrated or inattentive or uninterested. Most parents do this quite naturally and successfully, as letters to the *Tribune* indicate. One mother wrote:

You should have seen how interested and excited my three-year-old boy was to learn the sounds of the letters. I believe now that if a child can tell a knife from a fork, he can tell an "a" from a "b." It's that simple.

I never pushed my children. Rather, they kept after me to teach them another sound. I only gave them one at a time and added another only when they could identify the last one on cereal boxes, newspaper headlines, and the like. I

think we mothers don't always realize that we are really the child's first and most important teacher.

The wife of a missionary temporarily stationed in Portugal taught her four-year-old to read, using the reading strips from the *Tribune* mailed to her by the boy's grandmother. She wrote:

Jon just turned four in October. We began in September. Every day, five days a week, he wants a new letter. And we review from the beginning each time. His enthusiasm overwhelms me. My mother has been sending me a week's comic strips at a time, and if Jon happens to see them, he is quite insulted that he cannot learn the new ones right away. Tonight, as he went to bed, he asked, "Tomorrow, will I learn a new letter?" Outside, he calls our attention to signs, and many times a day he can be heard muttering letters and words, "h-a-m—ham!" and "f-a-s-t—fast!"

I am thoroughly enjoying teaching him, despite the fact that I have never had any training. In fact, I've never had any college work.

Twenty years after the *Tribune* series ran, an Iowa father wrote to the newspaper, reminiscing about the experience he shared with his now college-age sons:

Every day we cut out the page printed in the *Tribune* and pasted it in a scrapbook, until we had the entire workbook. Our oldest son was ready to read and our effort became "a dad thing." He would perch on my lap and we would go through some portion of the workbook, usually stopping when he began to squirm. Needless to say, he could read when he entered kindergarten, first reading the sign on the classroom door, much to the amazement of his teacher.

About a year later, I approached our youngest boy, but he was not ready to read and we put the workbook aside. When

206

he was nearly five years old, we tried again and he took to reading just as his brother had done. And just like his brother, we had fun doing my "dad thing." Upon entering kindergarten he could read, probably on a second- to third-grade level. His esteem went through the roof early in the school year when the teacher came down with laryngitis and let him read the "book of the week" to his fellow classmates.

Many parents are troubled about what happens when a youngster enters first grade able to read competently and independently. They fear that such a child will be a problem for the teacher and out of lockstep with the educational processes.

But most kindergarten and first-grade teachers are elated to find a pupil who is already able to read. Primary teachers are continually urged to try to meet the individual needs of their pupils—and it is easier to help the first grader who can read than the one who cannot.

Almost all first grades are divided into first, second, and third reading groups, with two groups working independently while the teacher gives reading instruction to the third. Or they are organized about individual learning programs so that each youngster works at his own speed. As enthusiasm for preschool reading continues to grow, chances are that most first grades now contain more than one child who could read fairly well before the beginning of the school year. These youngsters can form their own reading group. Or if one child is far advanced beyond the top reading group, it is quite easy for the teacher to keep him occupied and interested—if only by giving him a library book to read. Ungraded primaries and those with individual learning programs also make it easier for early readers to continue working at their own pace.

But what if an early reader draws a poor teacher, one who resents his accomplishments and lets him know it? It's difficult to conceive of an adult worthy of the name of *teacher* who would penalize a six-year-old for already knowing how to do something he is supposed to be learning. But it has happened and it can happen again.

If a first-grade teacher is so insensitive to the feelings of a child and so unenthusiastic about achievement in learning, the whole class is probably in for a difficult and unhappy year. A first grader who draws such a poor teacher—and there are a few among the hundreds of thousands of elementary teachers in this country—will probably have unusual difficulty in learning to read in that class. Parents can count it a blessing that their youngster already knows how to read, if he's trapped in such an unfortunate situation.

Since a majority of youngsters do learn to read in first and second grade, why encourage a child to read at age three, four, or five? It isn't worth the effort, even assuming it succeeds, critics also contend.

On the contrary, a preschool reader gets a head start in first grade and maintains his advantage all through elementary school, according to increasing and well-documented evidence. His IQ is likely to be increased permanently.

An earlier start in reading is an advantage for children throughout elementary school, according to studies made in California and New York public schools by Dr. Durkin.[9]

In her first study, in California, 49 youngsters entered first grade able to read at grade levels ranging from 1.5 (first grade, fifth month) to 4.5 (fourth grade, fifth month). The median grade level was 1.9. Their IQs ranged from 91 to 161. Five years later, 15 of the children had been double-promoted. Of these, 12 were still attending school in the same community and were available for further testing. Their mental age ranged from 10.9 to 17.2, with a median of 14.0.

The earlier the youngsters started reading, the greater the advantage they gained, Dr. Durkin's research shows. For example, 12 of the youngsters began to read at age three; their reading level at the time of the last follow-up averaged 9.2. Fourteen children were five years old when they started to read. Although the average IQ of this group differed from that of the three-year-old readers by just one point, they were reading at only 7.6-grade level.

The lower the child's IQ, the greater he profits from having a head start in reading, Dr. Durkin's research also suggested.

Preschool help with reading does not lead to problems of learning in school, Dr. Durkin stressed, in summing up the findings of her five-year study. None of the children involved in her research had an academic problem. And a majority of the bright preschool readers did better in reading after only five years of school instruction than nonearly readers of the same IQ level did after six years of schooling.

No learning problems resulting from an earlier start in reading were detected, either, in a major long-term study of the teaching of reading in kindergarten conducted in the Denver public schools between 1960 and 1966. The study involved about 4,000 youngsters who were followed closely from kindergarten through fifth grade.[10]

Organized reading instruction in kindergarten for youngsters in all ability ranges and from all types of background did not produce any harmful social or psychological results, the extensive Denver research showed. It did not trigger problems of school adjustment or create dislike for reading. No more of the early readers developed visual defects or reading disabilities than did the control-group youngsters who followed a traditional timetable for learning to read in school.

The kindergarten readers who got an accelerated reading program later on had significantly higher reading rates at the end of fifth grade than did the youngsters who followed the traditional program or who got a stepped-up reading program without the kindergarten head start. The kindergarten readers had a larger vocabulary. They did better on reading comprehension tests. And they also scored higher in word-study skills, in arithmetic concepts, language, social studies, and, to some extent, in science.

Reading can be "quite effectively" taught to large numbers of typical kindergarten pupils in a big-city public school system, the Denver study concluded. Pupils in all ability groups benefit proportionately. And the earlier start in reading has a measurable, lasting effect at least through fifth grade, provided the school program is adjusted to take advantage of the early start.

However, the benefits of the early start tend to be lost after first or second grade if the traditional school program doesn't give the early readers a chance to build on their skills at a faster-than-usual rate, the Denver researchers found.

A preschooler can't see letters well enough to read, and she will ruin her eyes if she's pressured to try, some critics have also charged. This has been a common and persistent assumption, but researchers who have studied early readers have not been able to find any evidence of eyestrain or damage. Parents who know how fast very young children can discover tiny objects—pins, beads, buttons—on the floor usually discredit the theory that preschoolers can't see well enough to read. New studies about visual abilities of newborns have led doctors to revise their old concepts about vision in young children. Early reading, particularly if the letters are large and clear, may actually be good training in visual perception, some advocates of early reading explain.

The eyes of most children are physiologically ready for reading at the age of 12 months or before, according to ophthalmologists. Normal children can focus and accommodate at least by the time they are a year old. (Actually, by 3½ months, a baby's vision is almost as accurate as an adult's and probably better than that of most people over age 40.) So learning to read at an early age is not an eye problem.

Teaching a child to read will rob her of her childhood and prevent her from achieving the social and emotional growth that is the chief developmental task of the preschool years is another argument critics hurl at advocates of early reading.

But how many children have a life so full of fascinating toys and happy play that they can't spare even 10 minutes for reading? (The Denver reading program found that youngsters made significant gains in reading ability if parents spent as little as 30 minutes per week working with them.) A four-year-old whining, "Mommy, what can I do now?" or parked in front of the TV is a more typical picture of early childhood.

There are other arguments that are often used against early reading: Preschoolers won't read for meaning; they'll only call words or recite them like a robot. Young children don't hear well enough yet to discriminate between words and sounds. And they may not know the precise meaning or range of meanings of words.

All of these sound just like arguments against permitting a child to learn to talk. Yet no one worries about "talking for meaning." No one claims that a child is too young to handle the abstractions of spoken language or that he may use a few words he doesn't completely comprehend. No one even frets very much when a baby who has just learned to say "Daddy" applies her precious new word one bright morning to the man who lives next door. Even the critics who contend that a preschooler can't understand a book if she reads it herself still urge parents to read to their children, yet they express no concern that the youngsters may not understand precise word meanings.

Some questions about preschool reading do, however, remain to be answered by extensive research in the future. For example, if 6½ is not the minimum mental age at which a child can learn to read, is there in fact a minimum age at all? When Dr. William Fowler was director of the University of Chicago Laboratory Nursery School, reading was taught to three- and four-year-olds using a method he developed that stresses sound–letter relationships, word patterns, play orientation, and careful programming. He found that bright three-year-olds often do as well and in some ways better than bright four-year-olds.

The Denver public school research suggests that the average child should be about 4½ to profit from instruction in reading, although youngsters with special aptitude and interest could begin earlier. Some advocates of sight-word programs urge that a start be made at age two. Montessori schools begin pre-reading sensory stimulation at about three.

Dr. Durkin suggested a simple way in which to tell when a child is ready to read: Give him interesting opportunities to learn and see what happens.

Can the advantages of preschool reading instruction be made available to all children, even those whose parents are not willing or able to help them at home? The experiences of the Montessori schools and those in a few other nursery schools and day-care centers do show that reading can be taught in a carefully prepared environment, without the one-adult-to-one-child relationship that is ideal for informal teaching at home. Television programs like *Sesame Street* also help give millions of children some exposure to reading fundamentals.

An increasing number of public school kindergartens now provide five-year-olds with some reading instructions, but it is rarely as much as an interested parent can give an eager child at home. More day-care centers and nursery schools are offering some very preliminary reading experiences. But most are laboratory schools in university settings to which most parents do not have easy access. A few educators have proposed moving the starting age for public schooling up to four, the better to capitalize on children's early learning abilities and to offer a start in reading. But such a school system reorganization is enormously difficult and most administrators are too hampered by budget shortfalls and other problems to tackle it.

If you have a preschooler now, you can't wait for reading instruction to become available at the nearest nursery school. What should you do?

You should teach your preschooler to read—because research to date shows she has much to gain and nothing to lose. Everything you teach her will help her, even if you begin teaching her and don't follow through to the point where she can read independently. Even if she learns only a few words or a few sounds, she will benefit. No matter which method you choose, she will not become confused later on in first grade if the teacher uses a different technique.

But don't try to teach your preschooler to read unless you really want to, unless both of you will enjoy the process. Don't pressure her to learn so much every day. Don't drag her away from any other fascinating occupation to read. And don't attach any penalties to her not learning if she isn't in the mood. Stop the minute she acts the least bit bored or restless—or before, if you can manage it. Most people who have taught small children emphasize that you're more likely to bore a child by going too slowly than by proceeding too fast.

If you were not taught to read by a phonetic method when you were in first grade, you'll probably be surprised at how logical and simple a modern phonetic or linguistic reading program is. Investigate a program of this kind before you begin helping your child. You should use reading materials with large type, preschool educators say.

Your child may be one who enjoys making reading a formal game of "school," especially if she's itching to go to school with an older brother or sister. Unless this is so, don't attempt to make reading instruction anything formal. Just cuddle your youngster up close, as you do when you read to her. Show her a new sound or a new word. Review a few of the ones she already knows. Be enthusiastic about what she remembers. Tell her matter-of-factly what she has forgotten. Then give her a happy, loving hug before she goes back to other activities. You probably won't spend more than 10 minutes a session. After your child has learned a few sounds or words, you'll find reading games are a delightful way in which to keep her happy.

The more you expose your child to printed words, the

quicker and easier she will learn to read. Some parents have used the technique of hanging labels on a table, a toy box, a bed, a doll. Buy your child all the books you can afford. Make your local library a regular stop, and let her choose her own reading materials.

Do read to your child, happily, lovingly, frequently. The children who did best in preschool reading research were those whose parents read to them at least 60 minutes every week. A love of reading is one of the best legacies you can give your child—and one of the best assurances that she will be able to keep up with the future.

8

How You Can Encourage Your Child to Be Creative

Kim, four, spends a busy November morning digging up black dirt in the backyard and filling little cardboard boxes with it. When her mother asks her why, Kim explains that these are to be her Christmas gifts for her brother and the other boys she knows.

"What boys like best is to get dirty and play in the mud," Kim tells her mother. "When the snow covers all the ground, they can't find any mud. So I am going to give them some for Christmas."

Gregg, five, is a tinkerer. In the last month alone, he has tried to take apart the toaster, pull out and rewind a cassette tape that belongs to his brother, find out what makes the hands on the clock move, and discover how fast he has to slide back and forth in the bathtub before the water swooshes out.

Randy, three, asks questions almost nonstop every minute he's awake. "Where does the night go in the morning?" "Why is the sky always up?" "Where was I before you had

215

me?" "Why amn't I Johnny?" "Why doesn't it rain up sometimes?"

All of these preschoolers show evidence of possessing creative intelligence to a high degree—as do most young children. Yet, according to recent research, it's likely that this gift will be blunted or ignored or misdirected or discouraged or punished out of the youngsters long before they reach high school, and their promise will be only partially realized.

"Creativity" is a name now given to a particular component—probably several components—of intelligence. Researchers have identified dozens of separate intellectual talents comprising overall mental ability and estimate there may be almost as many more factors not yet recognized. The usual type of IQ test measures only six to eight of these elements. Educators and psychologists have become especially concerned with creativity in children in recent years because it seems to be the essence of genius—and an essential characteristic of those individuals who make original contributions to the world.

Creativity means far more than talent in art or music. It includes the whole range of creative and adventurous thinking in every field: scientific discovery, imagination, curiosity, experimentation, exploration, invention. It is the ability to originate ideas, to see new and unexpected relationships, to formulate concepts rather than to learn by rote, to find new answers to problems and new questions for which to seek answers.

A creative child has intelligence of the highest order. In fact, many researchers and educators now group children as "gifted/talented" or as "gifted/creative/talented." But he may or may not score well on an IQ test, which measures chiefly academic areas of mental ability. Research on creativity in children is far from complete, and most of what is known has been learned in studies of school-age children. Valid tests of creativity are difficult to develop because by definition they are concerned with producing many fresh ideas and unorthodox solutions, rather than one "right" answer. So the tests are hard to score and evaluate.

But most researchers agree on these points: (1) Almost all small children possess a considerable amount of creativity. (2) Creativity can be increased by deliberate encouragement, opportunity, and training. (3) It can also be dulled almost out of existence by some child-rearing and educational practices.

It is important that parents understand how to identify and cultivate creativity in very young children, for the tender sprout of creativity needs to be encouraged and guided almost from birth, according to Dr. E. Paul Torrance, a well-known expert on creativity in children. (In some cultures—and, to a lesser extent, in some cultural groups in the United States—certain kinds of stifling early environments produce individuals who are not open to new ideas and whose production of good innovations is very limited.)

"If we observe how infants handle and shake things and twist and manipulate them in many ways, we find some of the earliest manifestations of creative thinking," said Dr. Torrance. "Since the infant does not have a vocabulary, he can learn little by authority. Thus, by necessity, much of his learning must be creative; that is, it must evolve from his own activity of sensing problems, making guesses, testing and modifying them, and communicating them in his limited way."[1]

Beginning about age 3, a child's creativity usually begins to increase, according to Dr. Torrance and other researchers. It seems to reach a peak between 4 and 4½. Then it drops suddenly about age 5, when the youngster enters kindergarten (probably because of pressures from teacher and classmates to be more conforming). Creativity then rises slowly in the first, second, and third grades, said Dr. Torrance, until there is a sharp drop in the fourth grade.

What are the signs of creativity that you can watch for in

your small child? Several researchers have compiled descriptions of creative children you'll find useful. For example, an enormous bump of curiosity is typical of a creative youngster. She loves to experiment, to test the limits of situations. She questions constantly and usually in a penetrating way or on an offbeat tack that can annoy a busy parent or a preoccupied kindergarten teacher who doesn't understand this special type of intelligence.

A creative child isn't often put off by an overly simple answer, or at least not until her basic creative instincts have been blunted. She is particularly sensitive to answers that don't make sense in relation to other facts she knows. Often she invents long, complicated explanations for phenomena she doesn't understand.

A creative youngster is particularly sensitive to what she sees, hears, touches, and experiences. You'll notice this sensitivity not only in the pictures she draws or finger-paints but also in her surprising understanding of other people and other people's problems. She delights in learning precisely the right word for an object or a feeling or a color. And she enjoys sharing these special observations with an adult who is also aware of them.

A creative child generates new ideas like sparks; many of them are offbeat or silly, but a few are surprisingly original and good in relation to his age. He often gives uncommon answers to questions and suggests unusual solutions to problems. He finds unexpected uses for common objects, like the five-year-old who constructed a "nutcracker" for her father's birthday present out of an empty paper tube, a heavy bolt, and a string.

In one test of creativeness designed for school-age children, youngsters are told to list all the uses they can for a brick, other than building. An extremely creative boy or girl may think of 35 or 40.

The imagination of a creative youngster is unusually active, delightful, and full of humor. Many preschoolers can turn this vivid imagination on deliberately and do so with great delight. Researchers who study creative children often comment about their playfulness and note that many highly achieving, creative adults talk about playing with ideas or inventions.

It is characteristic of a creative youngster to attempt tasks far too difficult for him. But instead of considering his failures frustrating, he accepts them as challenges—at least some of the time. His attention span is longer than usual for his age. And he may become so preoccupied with his own thoughts or projects that he may not pay attention to what his parents are saying to him.

Unusual flexibility is another mark of a creative youngster. He is open to suggestions, new ideas, to almost any activity an adult describes as "a new experience." Research shows that in comparison with others, a creative youngster tends to be more self-sufficient, resourceful, stubborn, industrious, introverted, complex, and stable.

Because creativity implies independent thinking, a creative child often seems to be in conflict with her teachers in preschool or kindergarten or with her parents. She may ignore or be ignored by many of her classmates. Teachers may consider her disruptive and impertinent. Deciding to what degree she will give in to social pressures toward conformity may cause her emotional upset, even before she reaches first grade. It helps if a parent is able to talk with her tactfully about these differences, encouraging her to develop her own ideas while still enjoying common activities with playmates.

Even parents who feel quite liberated and nonsexist about appropriate male and female activities may be surprised at how many sexist attitudes their offspring seem to absorb from television, playmates, and other sources. You may have to make a point of telling your youngster that toys and games and future plans aren't limited to one sex or the other.

Because he enjoys being independent, a creative child often objects strenuously to what he considers unnecessary rules and controls. He usually prefers to work by himself on his own projects rather than to participate all of the time in the group work that dominates so many day-care centers, nursery schools, and kindergartens.

How can you encourage and increase your child's creative abilities? Although research in this field is still incomplete, many positive recommendations can now be garnered from numerous studies. Many of the suggestions for increasing creativity in small children are virtually identical with recommendations already made in previous chapters in regard to overall intelligence. By stimulating a small child to see, to hear, to touch, to manipulate, to explore, and to try for himself, you can foster creativity. A parent who talks happily with a small child—and listens seriously in return—is helping creativity to grow. So is the parent who is enthusiastic about his child's achievements and projects and who encourages his innate curiosity.

In addition, experts on creativity make these recommendations:

- Help your youngster to feel and value his uniqueness, to find satisfaction in expressing his feelings, to experience the joy of creation. Too often, a child feels that he could not possibly think up a worthwhile idea, and so he doesn't follow through on the ideas he does have.

  A child needs what Dr. Carl R. Rogers, of the Center for Studies of the Person in La Jolla, California, called "psychological safety" to express his ideas in new and spontaneous ways. A parent who laughs at a youngster's ideas, even in an indulgent way, or who pushes off suggestions with a what-could-you-know-you're-only-a-kid attitude usually convinces his child quite easily that his thoughts couldn't possibly be valuable or worth developing. Of all the image makers in our society, none is more powerful or more damaging than the adult who casually derogates his own child.

- When you can, let your youngster plan some of her own and your family's activities and use her ideas when it's possible. Even a two-year-old can sometimes decide whether she'd rather have a picnic in the backyard or eat indoors as usual. A four-year-old should be permitted to select which of two or three play outfits to buy (after you have restricted the choice to those suitable in price, size, fabric, and style). Preschoolers should have occasional opportunity to plan family menus ("Which meat shall we have? What vegetables? What for salad?"), weekend fun, and treats.

  Permitting a child to make such decisions not only makes him feel that his ideas are worth consideration, but it also helps him realize that decisions have consequences. If you recognize and respect your child as an individual, you'll find that his urgent drive for independence will not be so likely to erupt in undesirable ways.

- Encourage your child to become more sensitive to her environment, to ask questions, to experiment. Many of the suggestions already listed in the section on science in Chapter 6 are useful in this context, too.

- Science activities provide good opportunities to help your child understand that not all experiments succeed and that an experiment that doesn't succeed isn't necessarily a failure.

  "Most parents find it extremely difficult to permit their children to learn on their own—even to do their schoolwork on their own," commented Dr. Torrance. "Parents want to protect their children from the hurt of failing."

It is important to teach children how to avoid failure when possible, of course. It is urgently necessary when their physical safety is involved. "But overemphasis may deter children from coping imaginatively and realistically with frustration and failure, which cannot be prevented," said Dr. Torrance. "It may rob the child of his initiative and resourcefulness. All children learn by trial and error. They must try, fail, try another method and, if necessary, even try again. Of course, they need guidance, but they also need to find success by their own efforts."[2]

If this sounds like too rigorous a concept to impose on your child, remember the process by which she learned to walk. How many times did she fail and fall? How long did she try without giving up? How much of the process did she do by herself, without active help or motivation from an adult?

As you study your own child and his reactions to experiences, you'll come to know about how much adult help he needs to function creatively and when he is apt to get discouraged and quit.

• Don't be deterred by traditional concepts of "readiness." New research shows that they are often inaccurate. If you constantly wait to introduce your child to new experiences and new materials until you detect signs of "readiness," you will keep him from being creatively challenged and stimulated.

"Readiness" too often becomes what Dr. Torrance called a "holding-back operation." He said that this reluctance to let children try for fear of failure is one of the most powerful inhibitors of creativity operating in the early childhood years.

"The usual defense of holding-back operations is the fear that the child will become frustrated by failure," said Dr. Torrance. "The ability to cope with frustration and failure, however, is a characteristic shared by almost all outstanding individuals. Certainly, almost all highly creative scientists, inventors, artists, and writers attempt tasks that are too difficult for them. If they did not attempt these overly difficult tasks, their great ideas might never be born."[3]

- Invite your child to try what one educator calls "creative calisthenics" with you. These aren't formal lessons but are games you can play while riding in the car or doing dishes or waiting in the dentist's office.

  For example, you can play "How many ways could you use a pencil?" with your youngster. Take turns thinking up as many different, nonwriting uses as you can; for example, a mast for a toy boat or a perch for a birdhouse. Then substitute other common objects for the pencil, such as an empty milk carton, a paper cup, a spool, or an old tire. Be encouraging and happy about his responses—not critical.

- Apply the old necessity-is-the-mother-of-invention gambit. Give your child the need to think creatively by handing him an occasional mind-stretching problem or tough question to ponder: "What would you do if you were lost in the shopping center?" "How could you make a birthday party more fun?" "What can we make with the leftover lumber in the garage?" "How can we find out which is the shortest way to the park?" "What could we use to make trees around the dollhouse?" "What would help George stop being such a bully?" "What would you do if you had to be the teacher in kindergarten tomorrow?" "Can you invent a good game to play in the car?" "If you had a television station, what kind of programs would you put on?"

  You can invite your child to hypothesize by asking him "What if . . ." questions and, if possible, letting him test out his answers: "What if you put a block into a glass that's full of water?" "What if we let a glass of milk sit outside of the refrigerator for a day or two?" "What if you mix red and yellow finger paint?" "And what if you then add blue and green?"

It's also fun to push a what-if game into the realm of fantasy. "What if it never got dark?" "What if everything you touched turned into gold?" "What if adults kept on growing as fast as children?"

- Encourage your youngster to appreciate new experiences—from watching a carrot top sprout in a dish on a windowsill to solving new problems; from observing the subtle shadings in a sunset to learning a new scientific concept (ice cream melts at room temperature, chocolate melts if left in the sun).

- See that your child has a quiet place and time to work on her own, without having to participate in a group, even a family group, all of the time. Most day-care centers and kindergartens, as well as elementary schools in general, place heavy emphasis on sharing and on group activities. Without your active efforts, your youngster may have almost no private time for individual, creative activity. Yet all good ideas begin in a single, individual, human brain.

  Richie, a four-year-old attending a university lab school, was working with great concentration on discovering the relationships between number rods. He placed a four-unit rod next to a six-unit one, thought for a minute, and was reaching for a two-unit rod when Mike snatched the materials away. Richie shouted in protest and tried to wrestle the rods back. At this point, the teacher intervened. She divided the rods between Richie and Mike and lectured Richie on sharing. But Richie's moment of discovery was lost.

"Don't interrupt a child who is working even to praise him" is a principle emphasized in Montessori schools to protect this irreplaceable instant of creative discovery.

One thing that makes it particularly difficult to provide young children with time to be creative on their own is television. If the TV set is turned on, it becomes such an easy magnet that youngsters simply relax and watch whatever is on without feeling a need to start a project of their own. The most effective way to prevent television from preempting too much of your child's irreplaceable early years is to turn it on only for a limited number of specific, carefully chosen programs and not permit indiscriminate viewing.

- Motivate your child to follow through on his ideas. Too often, brilliant innovations are lost because their inventor did not have the self-confidence or self-control to complete their development. During the preschool years, you can often encourage follow-up by questions like, "How are you going to finish your picture?" or "When you're done with your drawing, let's make a frame for it." Sometimes you can offer additional raw materials. Or you can suggest some positive actions: "I like your idea about rearranging your room. If you'll help, we can fix it your way right now."

- Don't worry if your preschooler enjoys making up stories or weaving fantasies or playing highly imaginative or imitative games. It's a normal part of preschool development. You'll probably be more comfortable about your youngster's use of his creative imagination in these ways if you help him label his stories "made-up" or "pretend" when they are. Set an example yourself by telling him whether the books you read to him are fact or fiction and the TV programs you watch are real events or playacting.

- Often you can spur creative activity in a youngster by giving her a good reason for trying to be creative. Plan a backyard art fair, for example, with children's masterpieces clothespinned to a clothesline for relatives and neighbors to view, and you may stimulate a minor renaissance on your block. Start a young marching band, and interest in rhythm instruments among preschoolers will double. Introduce word games on long car trips, and your offspring's awareness of words and their usage will sharpen. Write down some of your youngster's imaginative stories to paste in a scrapbook, and the quantity and quality of the stories will increase.

- Don't teach your child how to do everything step by step, but leave room for his imagination to flourish and for his brain to function. This doesn't mean, of course, that you let your youngster flounder with no preliminary guidance or instruction at all, or that you let him try to work out his own method for such basic physical maneuvers as tying shoelaces. Your youngster does need to learn, for example, the rudiments of using paint and brush, how to hold a pencil, how to manipulate scissors. But his creative feelings will be stifled if you insist on holding his hand to show him how to draw a horse or if you correct his drawing yourself when he has finished.

   Marcie, almost five, was invited to a birthday party at a Manhattan store where children could select from a variety of plaster objects they could paint in colors of their choice. She picked a mermaid. After she had finished, as cake and ice cream were being served, she happened to notice that one of the shop's staffers was unobtrusively touching up the mermaid and adding some new colors. She had a tantrum and was still upset when she got home and told her mother. Her mom called the plaster shop and explained what had happened. The store owner invited Marcie back to choose another model and gathered her workers to hear the little girl tell them, "You don't change an artist's work unless you ask her first."

- You can make positive suggestions when your youngster seems to need them. Often these can be in the form of questions that stimulate her own thinking. If she crayons a horse, you might ask, "Where is the horse going?" "Is someone coming along to ride him?" "Is he standing in a field or beside a barn?" If your young artist is unhappy about the looks of her horse and asks for help, you can suggest that the two of you find some pictures of horses to give her more ideas, rather than tell her specifically what to do.

  If your child is making up a story, you can say, "I'd like to know more about that doctor; what did he look like?" Or "Where do you suppose that spaceship came from?" Or "How did that boy feel inside when the giant grabbed him?" Sometimes you can suggest, "What other kind of an ending could you think of for your story?"

  One good way in which to encourage creative storytelling is to play round-robin story with your offspring. He begins a story, starts to develop a plot, and then stops, often in midsentence, for you to pick it up. You carry the story line a little further, then toss it back to him.

  You can set a pail of water in the corner of the sandbox to make sand-castling more successful. You can locate a big empty cardboard packing box for your backyard cowboys and Indians to turn into a fort or a jail or for your miniature Martians to use as a spaceship. You can suggest costumes and props when your youngsters need new ideas for imaginative play—paper bags, empty cartons, and canned goods for playing store; stamp pad and index cards for playing library.

- Recognize that creative efforts are often messy. Paints spill. Bug collections add clutter. Experiments with seedlings take space and time. Cherished leaf collections gather dust and crumble. A preschooler who is constantly pricked by fear of being scolded or spanked for making a mess isn't going to feel much of the adventurous excitement of being creative. It's much safer and easier just to watch television.

  You will need rules about cleaning up afterward and limits about where in your house finger paints may be used and rock collections displayed. But it may help to remind yourself that no one wins prizes or scholarships or fame for being neat. One mother commented, "I used to fret about how messy my children's rooms are most of the time. Now I just call them 'creative' instead of 'messy,' and I shut the doors when we have guests. I feel much better and my children are happier."

- Do reward your youngster for his creative efforts—by praise, encouragement, and interest; by sharing with him the inner joys of creation; by valuing his creative results, even if they don't come close to adult standards. Your surprise and pleasure at what your youngster has discovered or thought or made or said will encourage him to keep trying; your indifference will dampen his innate creative sparks.

- Enjoy being creative yourself and share your feelings with your child. Talk about the color scheme you are trying to create for the living room; the effect you want to achieve in your garden; the solution to a problem you've just worked out; the new recipe you're experimenting with. Let her know when your efforts to be creative aren't spectacularly successful. If the new dessert sinks out of shape or the new casserole seems too dry, you can be casual about it and comment that at least you've learned something and the next one will probably be better. This will help your child to feel that she need not be assured of success before she undertakes a project, and it makes it easier for her to experiment.

Provide your child with plenty of good, simple art materials. Encourage her to use these experimentally and without constant supervision, discouraging criticism, or fear that she will make a mess for which you will scold her.

All forms of creativity, even in scientific and engineering fields, are related, many researchers believe. Stimulating your child to be creative with art materials helps him develop sensitivity, originality, flexibility, and imagination—talents necessary for creative thinking in other areas.

Knowing just how much to supervise and suggest is a creative art itself. But if you study your child's individual reactions to your suggestions and comments, you'll soon discover just how best to encourage his efforts and his originality. This is one major reason for being aware of your offspring's need for creative stimulation: You are in a position to know him better than any teacher can and to work with him individually.

You should, of course, show your child the basic ways to use these art materials. But you shouldn't insist that he make his sky blue just because the real sky is or form his clay dog into better shape yourself. It helps to spur your child on if you comment favorably on what he has produced. But your remarks should be sincere, specific, and enthusiastic, in proportion to the effort your youngster has expended.

"You always say what I have drawn is 'interesting,' and half the time you don't even look at it," complained one perceptive five-year-old. "I hate that word *interesting*."

You don't need to spend a lot of money on commercial products labeled as stimulating creativity; most of them aren't as effective as the simple materials listed below. Before you buy such a toy or game, be sure to think through how your child will use it and whether you can supply the same thing yourself.

Raw materials for preschool art range far beyond crayons and paper, although these will probably be the first craft materials your child uses. Creative art can also be inspired by

- A package of white paper plates, to decorate with crayons, to turn into picture frames, to make into clocks by adding numbers and hands, or to edge with bells for a tambourine

- Peanut shells, to paint or ink with faces and to use as fingertip puppets

- Paper lace doilies, to color for place mats or to trim with ribbon for hats or to use as clothes for clothespin dolls

- Large sheets of white, dull-finish oilcloth, to map out the streets of your neighborhood. Encourage your youngster to crayon in the houses he knows or to build them with blocks. Add toy trucks, cars, and tiny dolls for a working community.

- Assortment of small, multicolored pads of paper, to mark for parking tickets, plane tickets, paper money, or just to stimulate drawing

- Old sheeting, to cut up and crayon for place mats or dollhouse bedspreads or costumes. Colors will last longer if you place the sheeting color-side down on newspaper, cover with a damp cloth, and press with a hot iron.

- Finger paint in the three primary colors, to stimulate freewheeling art and experiments with color. You can buy it ready-made or mix your own, using liquid laundry starch and food coloring or powdered poster paints. Apply to white shelf paper dampened with a sponge or use it directly on a laminated plastic tabletop, which you and your pint-size Picasso can sponge clean quickly afterward.

For new varieties of paint, combine food coloring with a squeeze of toothpaste or a daub of hand lotion. Both make a delightful finger paint.

As an alternative to fingers in finger painting, try a comb, a small rag, a notched piece of cardboard, or an old hair roller. To add a new dimension to a finger painting, let it dry, then add more color with a paintbrush, or make a second finger painting on top, using a different color. Or try adding a few small dabs of finger paint to a piece of paper, smear slightly, fold in two, and open to discover an unpredictable double design. Or finger-paint over squiggles of crayon.

One mother plopped her rambunctious Rembrandt into the bathtub, made "finger paint" by adding two or three drops of food coloring to several squirts of father's foamy shaving cream, and afterward cleaned up both art and artist easily with a soapy bath.

- Long lengths of brown wrapping paper, to make magnificent murals or life-size paper dolls by tracing around real children and crayoning in their features and clothes

- Chalk, to use on bright or black construction paper, as well as on sidewalks and slate. Or soak sticks of colored chalk in cold water and rub on a sheet of paper that has also been soaked or sponged wet. You can draw with the sides or ends of the chalk, or even rub the chalk about with your fingers. Lay the finished design on a fold of newspaper to dry—and preserve it by spraying it with a fixative. (Hair spray does nicely.) On a sunny day, you can let your child chalk a design on the sidewalk, then decide how she wants to erase it: by letting the rain wash it away, by spraying it away with water in a squirt-type bottle, or scrubbing it away with a brush and a pail of water.

- Collage collection, for young pop art. In a box, assemble a big assortment of bright paper, bits of ribbon, interesting fabric swatches, trimmings, headlines, old Christmas cards, string, seals, stickers, buttons, old postcards, magazine pictures. Your young Michelangelo glues or rubber-cements his choices to construction paper or cardboard or posterboard to make original designs or unique birthday cards.

- Potatoes, to slice in half and use with paint or ink to stamp out patterns and designs. To make other unusual prints, walk fingers across the paper in paint patterns. Or try fork tines, bottle caps, half an orange, a celery stick, corks, carrot halves, clothespin heads, a spoon, checkers, or small blocks dipped into paint.

- Poster paints, for paintings. For unusual variations, instead of a brush, try a feather, a small sponge, a toothbrush, or a wad of paper towel. Or put poster paint and a little liquid laundry starch into an empty plastic squeeze bottle and use it to apply paint to paper, varying the amount of squeezing, the distance from the paper, and the speed of hand movements. Combine with other colors, in other old bottles.

- Clay or its equivalent, for sculpting. A five-pound bag of ceramic clay from an art store is most fun. But children also enjoy the homemade kind (equal parts of salt and flour, with water added gradually to get the right consistency and powdered paint or food coloring mixed in, too, if you wish). Using cookie cutters, tongue depressors, pipe cleaners, and a rolling pin with clay may stimulate fresh ideas.

- Crayons, basically for drawings. Or your youngster can make crayon rubbings by laying an object with an interesting texture—penny, wood, leaf, corrugated paper, string design, sandpaper, or checker—flat on a firm surface. Cover with paper and rub over it, using the flat side of the crayon.

  Or he can shave (with a dull knife or grater) flakes of old crayons into a sheet of shelf paper. You can cover this with another paper and press with a warm iron to melt the crayon. Then, your child can add more to the picture, if he wishes, with black crayon or he can scratch lines into the colors.

- Waxed paper, to make translucent pictures. Spread out a sheet of waxed paper, and on it arrange colored shapes and bits of bright tissue paper in overlapping designs. Add crayon shavings and wiggles of colored thread. Top with a second sheet of waxed paper, cover the whole creation with a piece of plain paper and press it into semipermanence for your child with a warm iron.

- Enrich your preschooler's life with music in every way you can. Your preschooler will enjoy and profit from having an opportunity to use simple musical instruments, such as an octave of bells, xylophone, rhythm sticks, finger cymbals, a triangle, drums, a tambourine. Or she may also enjoy simple experiments with an autoharp, a piano, or an electric organ if you have one.

  A tape recorder or CD player she can operate herself, plus her own CDs or tapes, gives a preschooler great delight and a good introduction to music. She will also enjoy and appreciate some classical music that has a definite melody, especially if you tell her something about the composition. CDs or tapes that introduce the instruments of the orchestra are also helpful.

  You've probably been singing lullabies to your baby

since you brought her home from the hospital. Gradually, you can add other songs, folk tunes, ballads, musical comedy tunes. She'll enjoy learning a song in a foreign language and singing games and songs with accompanying finger plays.

You can help your preschooler discover more about music by talking about how music makes you feel or want to move about. Good examples: *Peter and the Wolf;* almost any Sousa march; *Swan Lake;* "The William Tell Overture," with its storm and quiet aftermath; "The Skater's Waltz"; "The Flight of the Bumblebee"; Dvořák's "Largo."

- Encourage your child to let stimuli from one artistic field suggest creative activities in another related area. For example, suggest that he make up a dance to go with ballet music, paint an illustration for a favorite poem, make a dust-jacket design for a book you've just read to him, dictate a story for you to write down about a painting he's just made, or finger-paint to music.

- You can also suggest to your child that he try to express some of his strong feelings—sadness, fear, worry, joy—in creative activities such as artwork, poetry, or acting.

Nurturing your child's creativity is one of the most delightful privileges of parenthood. Many of your happiest hours with your child will be the times when you share his adventurous thinking and work together on creative projects.

It is urgently important that your child's creative abilities be firmly established before she starts first grade and encounters the stifling, stunting effects of groupism or a teacher who makes it clear to her that she'll get along better if she just obeys orders and doesn't ask questions. Perhaps your youngster will be fortunate enough to have a teacher who knows how to stimulate and value creativity; but even so, he must deal with 25 or 30 other pupils and cannot give your child what you can. The conforming pressures of classmates will also begin to inhibit and blunt your child's creativity. Unless she has already been sold on the delights of thinking and creating for herself, she will find it easy to fall prey to demands for conformity and mediocrity and the desire not to be different in any way.

9

Montessori Ideas You Can Use at Home

What do little children like to do most of all?

To learn.

What should schools for preschool children teach?

To read, write, and understand mathematical concepts; to be self-disciplined, self-reliant, courteous, and orderly; and to love learning.

Why?

Because the years between two and six are the time when such learning can be absorbed most easily and happily by a child's developing mind.

These tenets, basic to much of the recent research about early learning, were also held by Dr. Maria Montessori, an Italian physician, who put them into practice in the early 1900s with great success. In eclipse for decades in the United States, although not in Europe and India, Dr. Montessori's ideas, techniques, and equipment were rediscovered in the 1960s by American educators and parents who see in them a practical and successful way in which to put into operation what the early-learning theorists are talking about. Not only did Dr. Montessori formulate many of these theories herself almost a century ago but she also worked out the best and most complete educational methods to date for implementing these concepts.

"Today, many educators go to great lengths not to admit they are plagiarizing and mining Montessori for ideas in the field of preschool education," commented a school superintendent. (Dr. Montessori, for example, developed child-size furniture, educational toys, inlaid wooden puzzles, programmed instruction, and much of the other equipment now used in modern preschools.)

Since the rediscovery of Montessori ideas by American parents and educators, enthusiasm for Montessori education has grown enormously. There are now thousands of Montessori schools in the United States and on five continents. Many of them were started and are supported by groups of well-educated parents who realize that their three- and four-year-olds are ready for something more mentally stimulating than bead stringing and finger painting and who appreciate the respectful care with which a Montessori program treats youngsters and protects them from pushing as well as from boredom.

Although most Montessori schools concentrate on three- to six-year-olds, some are now expanding to offer infant and toddler programs. Parents who were enthusiastic about their children's progress in Montessori preschools have also pushed the development of elementary and junior high schools with a curriculum based on Montessori principles. An increasing number of public school districts in many states have set up Montessori elementary schools as magnet programs to give parents a choice in the kind of education their children receive.

Even today, Dr. Montessori remains one of the best sources for practical ways in which to stimulate the mental development of preschool children. There is much in her books and concepts and in the Montessori schools that you can adapt for use at home with your child, whether or not you wish to consider sending her to a Montessori school.

After Maria Montessori was graduated from a medical school in Italy, her first job was working with children in Rome who were classified as mentally retarded. So successful were the methods she developed to stimulate their learning abilities that many of these youngsters equaled or surpassed the records of normal children in school examinations.

So Dr. Montessori asked herself the logical question: What are we doing wrong with normal children that they can be outperformed by the mentally retarded?

Eagerly, she accepted the offer of a job to start a nursery school in one of the early Italian housing projects in an extremely poor area. The sponsors of the school had only one goal—to provide supervision for preschool youngsters while their parents worked and to keep them from damaging the buildings. But Dr. Montessori saw in the school an opportunity to test out her theories about how the minds of very young children learn.

So poor were the youngsters that Dr. Montessori told their mothers that if they had only bread and water to eat, they should make hot bread-and-water soup, so it would seem more filling. The curriculum also had to include such basic instructions as how to take a bath.

In this "Casa dei Bambini," teaching children from the most appalling slums, Dr. Montessori developed the educational philosophy and techniques that were to prove so successful with youngsters from every kind of socioeconomic background. Among the principles she worked out are these:

1. A child, unlike an adult, is in a constant state of growth and change, and the ways in which he changes can be modified greatly by his environment.

2. A young child wants to learn. The task of the adult who loves him is to encourage, to provide opportunities for learning, to permit him to learn by himself.

   "Who doesn't know that to teach a child to feed himself, to wash and dress himself is a much more tedious and difficult work, calling for infinitely greater patience than feeding, washing, and dressing the child one's self," Dr. Montessori wrote. "But the former is the work of an educator, the latter is the easy and inferior work of a servant. Not only is it easier for the mother, but it is very dangerous for the child, since it closes the way and puts obstacles in the path of the life which is developing."[1]

3. The mind of even a very young child has great capacity for absorbing a tremendous variety of experience, even though he can't express it verbally. "The most important period of life isn't the age of university studies, but the first one, the period from birth to the age of six," said Dr. Montessori. "For that is the time when man's intelligence itself, his greatest implement, is being formed."

4. A young child absorbs almost all of his early learning from his environment. To foster learning, his environment should be "prepared" so that he can choose freely from it the learning activities for which he has developed a readiness.

5. The very young child learns much through movement, and his movements should not be restricted any more than is necessary for his physical safety and to avoid interference with the rights of others. He needs great opportunity to move about, to explore, to learn through every sense organ of his body.

6. A youngster goes through specific stages in develop-

ment when it is easier to acquire certain types of learning than it ever will be again. This is obvious in the development of speech, for example.

"Children pass through definite periods in which they reveal psychic aptitudes and possibilities which afterward disappear," said Dr. Montessori. "That is why, at particular epochs in their lives, they reveal an intense and extraordinary interest in certain aspects of their environment to the exclusion of others."

7. Sensorimotor activities play a great role in a child's learning. The more opportunities a youngster has to feed sensory stimuli into his growing brain, the more his intelligence will develop.

8. Children learn best in an atmosphere of freedom combined with self-discipline and in an environment prepared to help them learn. The child, said Dr. Montessori, must be free within the classroom to follow his own interests, to move about, to work freely at activities of his choice. But freedom cannot exist without self-discipline and without the development of skills that make a child relatively independent of help from an adult. Limits also must be imposed to protect the rights of others.

9. The teacher must not impose learning upon a young child and must not intrude upon what the child is learning by himself. She should not substitute her will for the child's or rob him of the satisfaction of working on his own tasks.

10. A youngster should be able to learn at his own rate, at his own level of readiness, without being forced to keep up with or wait for a group.

11. A child develops a sense of his own worth by doing any simple task well—whether it is scrubbing a table, pouring water from a pitcher without spilling it, or

multiplying 15 times 8. He needs great opportunity for such successes.

12. When a child is given a chance to learn when he is ready to learn, not only does he increase his intelligence but he also gains contentment, satisfaction, feelings of self-confidence, and a desire for further learning.

The great success Dr. Montessori had with her slum-area children drew distinguished educators and visitors from many parts of the world to the "Casa dei Bambini" during the early 1910s. Montessori schools were started and flourished in many parts of Europe and later in India. A few were opened in the United States. But teacher training in this country was generally inadequate. The movement ran headlong into the educational concepts of John Dewey; it was often misinterpreted and misunderstood and it quickly withered.

Dr. Montessori continued to teach, lecture, and write in Italy, throughout Europe, and in India until her death in 1952. It was not until the early 1960s that interest in the Montessori method began to revive in the United States, sparked by new research into the importance of early-childhood learning and by the urgent need to find better ways of educating youngsters from poor and disadvantaged families.

The swift spread and obvious success of Montessori schools in recent years have been major factors forcing hard new looks at this country's traditional concepts of preschool education. Some early childhood educators, however, are critical of what they see as a lack of emphasis on social and emotional development in the Montessori curriculum and consider it too rigid and ritualistic for middle-class American youngsters. Others argue that all of the valid Montessori ideas were long ago incorporated into nursery school programs here.

It is true that some of the Montessori equipment, such as inlaid puzzles and child-size furniture, have become part of standard early childhood education. But many critics have taken the tools of Montessori while missing the blueprint for what the tools are expected to accomplish. They have not grasped the Montessori concepts about the absorbent mind, sensitive periods, freedom to work individually at learning tasks of a child's own choice, and the importance of intellectual work at an age when youngsters are so eager to learn.

Except for the size of the children and the furniture, almost everything in a Montessori school differs from what is found in the usual day-care center or nursery school. And everything in a Montessori school—from the colors of the learning materials to the tone of the directress's voice—is precisely planned to stimulate a young child to learn.

For example, when Erica, four, bounces into her Montessori classroom, she begins the morning by hanging up her own coat. First, she spreads it out on a low table. Then she inserts a hanger into the shoulders, fastens the buttons, and hooks the hanger over a low rod. She learned this technique through the programmed instruction that breaks down activities into small steps that she can master. The purpose is to capitalize on a preschooler's fierce desire to "do it all by myself" and to help her gain as much independence as possible from adults in her personal care.

Then Erica changes her shoes for bedroom slippers to help her feel comfortable and to keep down the level of noise that might distract the youngsters from their learning projects.

After a quick "Good morning" to the directress, Erica is free to choose any of the learning activities she wishes. She can use the material as long as she desires. And she is never urged to share it with any other child who happens to want it at the same time. Her activity is respected seriously as "work" and no other youngster is permitted to interfere, in contrast to other types of day-care centers where sharing is emphasized regardless of what a child is attempting to accomplish by herself.

In a Montessori school, learning is an independent—not a group—activity. Each child works at his own speed, in his own way, with materials he chooses because of his own ability level and interests. He doesn't compete with any other child. He is neither held back nor pushed for the sake of keeping pace with the group.

The adult in charge of a Montessori classroom is called "directress" instead of "teacher" to emphasize the different kind of relationship she has with the children. Her function is to prepare the environment in which a child can learn, to guide his self-teaching, to answer his questions. She is a "catalytic agent," explained the director of a Montessori teacher training center. She does not impose learning upon a youngster but stimulates him to learn for himself. She seldom praises his accomplishments, so that he learns to look for satisfaction in his work and to learn to please himself, not someone else.

Erica walks quietly around her classroom for a few minutes. Then she pulls out a small piece of rug from a cubbyhole, spreads it on the floor, and picks up a set of number rods, marked off in alternating red and white units. With them she begins to set up a problem in subtraction. When she has arranged the rods to her satisfaction, she gets sandpaper numerals and a minus sign to illustrate her mathematical operation.

Jane, 3½, has chosen one of the "practical life" activities. Using a plastic pitcher, she dips water from a big plastic container marked "nice clean water" and with a sponge and cloth cleans the tabletops. When she's finished, she pours the water into a second container labeled "dirty old water" and puts her equipment away.

Over by the long row of windows, Jack, four, is arranging a "1,000-bead chain," hooking together strips that each contain 10 beads until they number 1,000. At each 100-bead interval, he lays out identifying numerals. Jack's project takes him almost an hour, but he doesn't tire of it. When he encounters large numbers later on in elementary school, he'll have a concrete idea of what these symbols mean.

Toby is taking apart and reassembling an inlaid wooden puzzle that is a map of the world, saying the names of the continents under his breath as he handles them. Julie is matching an assortment of bells with eight other bells arranged to make an octave, learning to appreciate subtle differences in sounds and in the patterns they make. Two five-year-olds are reading quietly to themselves. Another is writing words in his notebook.

Three-year-old Marcia is carrying a pile of pink blocks in precisely graduated sizes over to her small rug to build a tower. Like most of the Montessori equipment, the blocks are self-teaching and self-correcting. The child using them can tell for herself when she is right and when she needs to correct an error. Like almost all Montessori equipment, the pink blocks are beautifully designed and free of gimmicks that would distract from their purpose and their subtle sense of good design.

When each child has finished a project, he usually smiles in satisfaction, pauses for a minute or two, then puts his equipment carefully away in its special location. After that, he chooses another activity. Occasionally, the directress stops by his rug to see what he's accomplishing. But usually, the inner feeling of achievement is the child's only motivation and reward.

When young children are engaged in such learning, "there is both an earnestness and a peace about their activities," explained Paula Polk Lillard, a founder and director of a Montessori school in suburban Chicago. "The pleasure that the children are experiencing is evident; but its outer manifestations are muted. Sometimes a young child will exclaim, 'I did it!' in a triumphant tone. More often the reaction is a light in the eyes or a quiet smile and perhaps the soft-spoken words, 'I did it again.' This calmer reaction of the young child in discovery is sometimes misunderstood by adults when they visit

Montessori classrooms. We are accustomed to seeing children in settings that do not foster this deeper reaction to the environment. It is important to understand that the joy that comes to children in this all-inclusive exploration is intense, although the children's outward appearance is one of seriousness and concentrated effort."[2]

After the youngsters have been working with great concentration and interest for about 90 minutes, the directress quietly begins to walk along an oval stripe painted on the floor of the classroom. Soon, most of the children are following her, except a few who are still too intent on their own projects. Gently, the directress leads the youngsters in activity games designed to strengthen their muscles and give them more mastery over their bodies. They sing two songs in French and play a counting game in French.

Then comes the silence game. Seated around the oval, the children squeeze their eyes shut and sit as motionless as they can. The silence game has two purposes: to show a youngster his progress in self-mastery and to increase his auditory sensitivity.

When all is still, the directress calls each youngster softly by name. One by one, each tiptoes silently to his own little table, painstakingly pulls out his chair, and sits down.

"We teach the children to be silent not because an adult says so but in order that they can hear better," explains the directress. "We teach them how to pull out a chair quietly because it gives a child great pleasure to be able to control the chair and himself well."

Juice break comes next at a Montessori school—but it differs from juice time in other nursery schools. Here, the children take turns pouring the juice themselves, carefully, with great control and no spilling. With great concentration and a tiny smile of pride on her face, a three-year-old carries a tray of little glasses to the other children and distributes them. The pitcher and glasses aren't plastic or paper but glass; Montessori children take pride in knowing they can handle real things correctly, even if they are breakable.

The Montessori emphasis on self-discipline has raised doubts and opposition from some critics who may be confusing self-control and inner discipline with the rigid control imposed by adults. But Montessorians explain that only through inner discipline can an individual become truly free to learn. Only when he has mastered learning techniques and materials is he free to be creative. Only when he understands reality can he be truly imaginative.

The Montessori program for toddlers offers even younger boys and girls the same kind of orderly, calm environment full of a rich variety of attractive learning materials. Busy toddlers practice pouring dry materials such as rice and small nuts until they are adept at pouring water and fruit juice without spilling. They concentrate with obvious satisfaction on scrubbing tabletops, bathing and dressing dolls, putting together puzzles and stacking blocks, mastering self-help skills, walking along low balance boards, and testing their powers of observation with matching games.

The directresses in the toddler program use the same quiet tone of voice and respectful manner toward their charges as those in the preschool classes. And the youngsters learn to respond in the same courteous manner.

When a two-year-old boy suddenly begins to push a little girl off a rocking horse, yelling, "You go away—now," the directress doesn't scold him or insist that the girl share the toy. Instead, she quietly reminds the girl to tell the boy firmly that she is using the horse now and that he can use it only when she is finished. It's a Montessori principle that a child's learning activities should be protected from interruptions, even for sharing.

Preparation for learning to read begins even in the toddler classes, as teachers play games that help the children listen and identify initial sounds of words and names. Even these lessons are designed to have a sense of ritual, to teach mastery of materials. For example, for a language game, a toddler gets an attractive woven mat from a low shelf and spreads it out carefully on the floor. Then she brings a small basket full of fruit and sets it precisely on the mat. As she takes each piece of fruit from the basket and puts it carefully on the mat, she calls out its name, emphasizing the initial sounds as the directress repeats the words as well: "orange, apple, pear, banana, grape." She then calls out the children's names in turn, again stressing the initial sound: "Alyce, Bobby, Michael, Peter, Betsy." When the game is done, the first child carefully puts the fruit back in the basket and returns it to its place on the shelf, then rolls up the mat and stows it properly. Again, she is learning not only self-control but that activities have a beginning and an end and that orderliness makes learning easier.

Not all Montessori schools are alike. Many, especially those affiliated with the American Montessori Society, have added more creative activities, more music and art, and new kinds of learning materials to the traditional Montessori program. But some schools still try to stick faithfully to the original Montessori methods. And others are simply day-care centers and preschools that have incorporated a few Montessori ideas and a little Montessori equipment without offering a genuine Montessori experience. Even the name *Montessori* is now in the public domain, so it can be used anywhere by anyone for any purpose. As in choosing any day-care center or preschool, you should check into the qualifications and philosophy of the staff, observe the activities, and make sure it is what you want for your youngster and what he needs.

Whether or not you want to consider enrolling your child in a Montessori school, you may be interested in reading some of the books by or about Dr. Montessori that are listed in the bibliography. Parts of most of these books are obviously out of date and do not apply to contemporary children.

But they still contain a wealth of ideas and insights into the gentle ways that can foster the learning development of small children.

Not all Montessori activities are applicable to homes and parents. Some depend upon the establishment of a large "prepared environment" in which a child is free to choose her own learning tasks. And a parent can't maintain the same type of low-key, rather impersonal relationship that a Montessori directress has with a child.

But many Montessori ideas and techniques do work splendidly at home. Accurate, well-made copies of some Montessori equipment can be found in good toy stores and in school supply catalogs. Other materials have been adapted into games and equipment quite similar to the Montessori originals. Parents who understand Montessori purposes can often make or find inexpensive substitutes that accomplish the same learning purposes.

In adapting Montessori ideas for your child, it helps to keep in mind these guidelines, which have been worked out for parents by Montessori directresses:

- Teach your child with real things. If you take time to show her how to handle materials and equipment carefully, she will be capable of far more than you realize.

- When you want to teach your youngster a new activity or skill, plan it out first as a programmed teaching exercise. Break it down into small, precise steps. What points of interest does the activity hold for your child? How can possible error be controlled by the activity itself, not by your verbal instructions? (In helping a child learn how to polish shoes, for example, a Montessori directress slips a piece of white paper under the shoe. The youngster can tell immediately when the polish is not going on the shoe because of the marks on the paper.) Can you isolate a single learning element you want your youngster to absorb?

- When teaching a small child, slow down your movements. Use as few words as possible. Let your movements guide your youngster's eyes to what she is to learn. (For example, in teaching a child how to use scissors, show her how to pick them up safely, to hand them to someone else, and to cut a straight line. Then let her practice, progressively, on thick straight lines, thinner lines, curves and angles, and finally on pictures.)

  The purpose of this type of teaching is not to direct every move your child makes or to force your methods on her. It is simply to give her a successful way of doing something she wants to do urgently at this stage in her life. She can do it other ways if she wishes. But at least she will know one sure way that she can count on.

- Cultivate the art of not helping your child whenever he can do a task for himself. "Any unnecessary aid is a hindrance to learning," commented Dr. Montessori decades ago.

- Whenever you can, arrange your home and equipment so that your child can manage for himself. Make his table and chair low enough, his toy-storage shelves accessible, his clothing equipped with fasteners he can work, his closet rod the right height. Then don't do anything for him that he can do for himself.

- Give your child enough time to do a task without hurrying. He usually works at a slower, more deliberate speed than an adult and needs to repeat activities often, even after he appears to have mastered them.

- See that your preschooler has as much choice as possible over her own activities and learning. She can't live up to her potential unless she has the opportunity for independent work.

- Don't insist that your youngster try a new activity if she isn't interested. Don't make her stick at a learning task when she doesn't want to.

One reason for the great success of the Montessori method is this freedom of choice offered to the child, for a youngster's responses and interests are the best guide adults have to his level of readiness for learning. And this technique is a parent's best protection against undesirable pressuring and pushing.

- Make discipline in an activity interesting whenever you can. Say, "See how quietly you can close the door." Or "See if you can spread the peanut butter all the way to the edge of the bread."

- Don't ever rob a child of the feeling of satisfaction of having done a job all by himself. Don't do over any activity that he has done while he is watching. If he is not succeeding and is becoming frustrated instead of continuing his efforts, suggest a more simple but related game or project that will help him acquire the necessary skills. For example, if he is having trouble controlling a pitcher when he wants to pour a glass of water, encourage him to try pouring easier substances, such as sugar or rice, from one container to another, until his muscular control has improved.

- Whenever you can, protect your child from interruptions while she is concentrating on any activity, even if it seems pointless and repetitious to you. Her learning is work of the highest importance, and if you have respect for her and what she is trying to do, it will be much easier for you to teach her respect for others and their work.

- A useful Montessori way of helping a child learn the exact name of an object is called the three steps of Seguin (based on a teaching technique of Dr. Edouard Seguin, a nineteenth-century philosopher and educator who had great influence on Dr. Montessori). First, put three objects—for example, a paint chip of red, one of blue, and one of yellow—in a row in front of the child. First, point to the red and say, "This is red." Then, pointing, say, "This is blue" and "This is yellow." Then tell the child, "Point to blue. Point to red. Point to yellow." In the third step, the teacher or parent changes the order of the objects and pointing to each one asks the child, "What is this?"

Some learning activities based on Montessori techniques and ideas have already been described in this book. But here are others that you and your child will enjoy and that will help educate his senses and aid in his mental development:

- For a happy game that develops motor skills, draw a wide circle or an oval on the floor with chalk. First, let your child walk it, placing one foot directly in front of the other and precisely on the mark, until he can balance well. Then, encourage him to try it carrying a glass of water without spilling it as he walks, or a bell without letting it ring, or a beanbag on his head without letting it slip.

- To stimulate your child's tactile sensitivity, cut out matching pieces of cloth of several different textures—velvet, silk, seersucker, corduroy, chiffon. When your child can match them easily by sight and touch, blindfold her and let her try it by touch alone.

- Put a dozen simple objects in a paper bag, with the top tied just tightly enough to let your youngster slip her hand in. Ask her to identify each object by touch before taking it out.

- For a game to foster visual perception, you can get two sets of paint chips from a hardware store and mount each one on cardboard to make a color-matching activity. (Some parents use two sets of spools of thread in a range of hues.)

  A two-year-old can begin by matching just the three primary colors. Later, various shades of each color can be added to make the game more challenging. As he becomes more skilled, a child can learn to arrange the shades in order from lightest to darkest. (Children in Montessori schools learn to match and arrange 64 different shades.) Finally, in a color-memory game, you can show your youngster one shade, then send him into another room to choose the matching hue from a pile of all the colors.

- Obtain four small medicine-type bottles of opaque glass with droppers. Into one, put lemon juice and into another, vinegar. Into the third, put sugar and water, and into the fourth, a diluted syrup. Drop a little from one bottle at a time onto your child's tongue and ask her to identify whether it is sweet or sour. Most preschoolers delight in making appropriate faces for the sour substances.

- To sharpen your child's auditory abilities, take small, empty salt shakers or little cardboard boxes and fill pairs of them with different substances—sand, gravel, rice, pebbles, for example—that make a noise when your child shakes them. First, he should learn to match the pairs of sounds. Later, he can arrange them in order of loudness.

- You can play the same kind of game by obtaining half a dozen small glass or plastic bottles that you can cover with paper, three with one color and three with another. Then fill one of each color with a fragrant spice from your kitchen and repeat, using two more spices. Uncap the bottles and let your child smell them, then match them by their scent. You can add more pairs of spices as he becomes adept at recognizing them.

- This basic technique can be adapted to help your child learn many different types of things. For example, you can buy or collect two identical, inexpensive sets of mineral specimens. First, have your child learn to match the minerals. Then teach him their names. Later, he can learn to arrange them according to hardness or group them into other classifications.

- Lotto cards of different kinds can be used to help your child learn about animals—first by matching them, then by learning their names, and finally by classifying them according to families or habitats. Other subjects you can use in this way include leaves, trees, dinosaurs, flowers, insects, birds, and geometric shapes.

- To help your child learn more about herself, have her lie down on a large sheet of wrapping paper and trace around her with a thick pencil. She can then color in her features and her clothing and cut out her outline.

- To stimulate her ability to observe accurately and record her observations skillfully, let your youngster use a windowpane instead of paper for drawing. She can trace the shapes that she sees through the glass on the window with crayon and learn easy lessons in perspective, shapes, comparative sizes, and structures by herself. She'll even enjoy polishing the window clean again with a commercial cleaning solution.

- For a game that combines finger dexterity with size discrimination, you can put screws and matching nuts of several different sizes in a small bowl. Your child can unscrew the nuts and put them on one side of the table and the screws on the other. Then she can rematch and reassemble them.

- Young children in Montessori schools voluntarily choose and enjoy a variety of "practical life" activities. You can arrange most of these experiences easily for your youngster at home. For example, you can provide him with two plastic bowls or basins, a small pitcher, a sponge, a small towel, and an apron. Then you can show him step by small step how to put on the apron, fill the pitcher with water in the sink, carry it over to a low table, and fill one of the basins carefully with water. Then, after your demonstration, he can dampen the sponge with water, squeeze it, and use it to wash tabletops or the floor, squeezing out the dirty water into the second bowl and freshening the sponge again in the first bowl. When he is done, he should empty the bowls in the sink, dry them with the towel, and put them and his apron away. For variations, your child can use similar equipment and procedures to bathe a doll or, with an added scrub brush, wash and dry dishes or clean other washable objects. Most young children in Montessori schools enjoy such activities and repeat them often.

10

Computers
and Preschoolers

How much can a preschooler do with a home computer? Push a few buttons to call up some flashy graphics that hold his attention about as long as most new toys? Practice programmed drills with number facts? Begin to write before she learns to read? Discover some basic elements of computer programming that will ease her way into the technology of the twenty-first century? Nudge his brain into logical, orderly thinking? Stretch her mind with an open-ended opportunity to think in new ways?

Three-, four-, and five-year-olds are doing all of the above—with a concentrated enthusiasm that surprises traditional educators but not computer buffs or adults keyed into early-learning concepts.

Computers are now standard equipment in most pre-schools, kindergartens, elementary schools—even some day-care centers. There is a booming market for software programs created just for preschoolers, and new sites for children open almost daily on the World Wide Web. An estimated 60 percent of U.S. families with school-age children have computers at home.

Few extensive studies about the effects of computer use by preschoolers are yet available. But education experts, nursery school teachers, parents, and youngsters themselves bubble with enthusiasm as they see how computers not only help with traditional kinds of learning but offer the possibility of entirely new dimensions in thought and logic.

The few early-childhood educators who raise doubts about the benefits of giving a preschooler computer access to do because they consider a computer rather like another television screen—a mesmerizing medium that tends to deprive a youngster of time to socialize and interact with the real world. Or they see it turning a home or school into a video arcade hypnotizing children with moving stick figures, flashing lights, and sometimes violent scenes. Some parents worry about the possibility of exposing their young children to predatory strangers, pornography, or misinformation on the Internet.

Even Seymour Papert, the Massachusetts Institute of Technology professor who has spent his career helping children learn to work with computers, said he worries "about the psychological and spiritual consequences of children being more independent of their parents in their exploration of the world. But for better or worse, this will happen, and it will be far more likely to happen for the worse if parents act like cyberostriches, putting their heads in the sand in denial of the looming changes in the learning environment."[1]

Computers are revolutionizing learning—and changing old ideas about what young children are capable of doing. Beyond guiding animated creatures through fanciful mazes and designing new outfits for digital Barbies, children are using computers to explore increasingly sophisticated concepts. "They can understand coordinates at ages three and four, and do plotting of computer graphics," said Dr. Ann McCormick Piestrup, a founder of the Learning Company, now one of the nation's leading makers of software for children. "They can visualize things in three-dimensional space with positive and negative numbers at the age of seven—which is the youngest I've tried it; perhaps younger children could do it—and then perform transformations on these objects similar to what is taught in college and graduate school."[2]

Children as young as three can begin using a computer advantageously, and although they need some close supervision and adult help at first, preschoolers can become quite independent. Three- and four-year-olds can learn to log on, maneuver a mouse, take care of diskettes and CDs, and find letters on a keyboard. They can follow simple on-screen instructions like "okay," "next," and "quit," and that may jumpstart reading and a desire to read more.

In fact, the sense of control and competence young children seem to feel about using a computer suggests that it may be a good way to help them develop feelings of autonomy. Youngsters who learn to use computers in nursery school or kindergarten may well be more comfortable with the technology than their parents are, which provides an enormous boost for a young ego. "For the first time in history, kids are in a position to leapfrog ahead of their parents," observed technology critic and author Steve Bennett. "Kids understand computers intuitively and can acquire knowledge easily, which creates a wonderful opportunity for them to become essential guides for parents who are unfamiliar with computers and have, in effect, entered a foreign territory with a strange new language. With this new mentoring role for children comes unprecedented power."[3]

But just because a child is comfortable and happy at a computer, she is not necessarily having a valuable learning experience. "It's so easy to buy the gear and go about our business, proud that our kids are using a computer, rather than watching TV or getting into trouble on the streets," Bennett warned. "It's also so easy to simply assume that if our kids are doing something on the computer, they must be learning. That may or may not be true. A young child aimlessly clicking a mouse and listening to cartoon animals go 'bleep' isn't having a learning experience. Neither is an older child playing five hours of a 'slice 'em and dice 'em' game each day."

How can you help your child use a computer for learning? "Educational" software programs are being introduced so rapidly by such a variety of computer companies and educational publishers that it is impossible to critique individual examples here. But most fit into the following kinds of learning categories.

Electronic Flashcard Machine

Some of the software touted for preschoolers does little more than show them a series of flashcard images that can be matched or moved around by punching keys or moving a joystick. Some are really drill-and-practice exercises and they usually reward correct answers with smiling faces or dancing cartoon figures or electronic sound effects.

These programs do give young children a chance to begin using a computer—with all of its powerful fascination and mystique. They can make youngsters feel important, successful, and competent and give them the learning satisfaction of being the cause of an electronic effect. Preschoolers can learn about shapes by manipulating them on the screen. Children can match, compare, and contrast colors and sizes; drill on number facts; and learn letter shapes.

But except for the fun and learning experience of working the computer itself, most of this kind of learning can be done as well, or better, by manipulating real things directly. Preschoolers can understand concepts like "bigger and smaller" and "under and over" much better by lifting and shifting concrete objects rather than electronic symbols. Some of the software programs suffer from being cutesy and so gimmicky that they distract from what they intend to teach.

Electronic Teacher

Most programs used in schools provide what is known as computer-assisted instruction. These programs are designed to take a learner step by step toward a specific educational objective, providing drill and practice in the process.

A good computer teaching program offers a child several happy advantages. It can help him learn at his own speed. It can give him encouraging praise as happy feedback and reinforcement when he's right. It can let him move ahead to fresh challenges as soon as he's ready, so that he isn't bored.

A computer can correct a child's mistakes gently and in private so that she need not fear being embarrassed or ridiculed by trying and failing in public. And if she is making a pattern of errors that suggest she has missed an element in a learning sequence, it can back up and try another way to teach the same point.

But these programs give youngsters what are essentially electronic workbooks. They aim to move children more efficiently and happily toward traditional educational goals imposed on the learner by a teacher-programmer. And, said one critic, they have no more influence on student achievement than changing the truck that delivers the groceries improves children's nutrition.

Electronic Simulator

Some software programs offer to transport a child's imagination to other times and other places. Books and movies do that, too, but a computer program can go further and ask the child to participate and even save the day in a make-believe adventure.

Programs that put a youngster in the middle of the Amazon jungle or on the Oregon Trail and ask her to balance resources and ration supplies all the while battling disease and rattlesnakes can be more than entertaining. They give her a chance to feel responsible for others, to test strategies, reevaluate, and try again. Along the way, she may also learn some geography and history and some new perspective about the kinds of hardships real people faced long before the computer age.

Similarly, games that let youngsters build robots, manage railroads, construct office towers, plan cities, and land aircraft help them learn a variety of interesting concepts—not the least of which is a feeling of mastery over a small world of their own creation. These programs also may spark a child's curiosity in how real office towers run and how real cities are laid out. A youngster who has "managed" an office tower may find urban elevator rides more interesting for years afterward.

Many of these kinds of programs are better suited for somewhat older children. Preschoolers may need a sibling or a grown-up to help, but they can be eager participants when a family plays together. And some of the simulated-activity programs come in scaled-back versions for children who aren't yet reading.

As valuable as these experiences can be, some computer enthusiasts and educators think that computer technology holds even more promise as a tool for a youngster's own imagination, in such roles as the following.

Electronic Canvas

Some of the first things young children discover about computers is how to create bright visual effects with programs that let them wash color over the screen, create rainbows, fill a garden with flowers, and direct shapes and patterns to dance across the screen. What a youngster is learning is not only another way to create art but also how to manipulate a marvelously responsive medium.

Yet critics point out that producing art by pushing keys is a pale imitation of the richer creative experiences children get when they use even such simple art materials as crayons or finger paint. And with basic art materials, children can be much freer in mixing colors and using their imagination than when they are limited by a machine.

Electronic Pencil

Four- and five-year-olds have been taught to write and read by computer programs ever since the mid-1960s. Today, several programs are available that teach preschoolers simple reading and writing skills—some of them building on Dr. Montessori's theory that writing comes first and easiest to a young child, who then discovers he can read not only his own words but other written words as well.

Writing with a simple word-processing program is ideal for young children for several reasons. Punching a keyboard is easier mechanically than printing out letters or using script, and freed from this painstaking labor, children can more easily turn out sentences and little stories that have substance and hold their interest.

A computer makes it easy to correct and erase mistakes and to polish their creations, so that children can take great pride in the results. Experimental programs with five-year-olds in kindergartens show they can turn out logical, coherent stories of three and four paragraphs, with a little help with spelling.

Electronic Mud Pie

The "mud pie" metaphor is Dr. Papert's. An associate of Jean Piaget at the University of Geneva in Switzerland for six years, Dr. Papert believes that the best kind of computer programs for a child are those that enable him to design his own programs—in short, a digital mud pie that he can shape into anything he can imagine.

In Dr. Papert's view, most educational software is either "instructionist"—that is, school-style learning in the guise of a game—or "constructionist"—in which children learn by writing their own games. With instructionist software, he explained, "The machine asks the question. The kid responds. The machine creates a threat in the game. The kid responds. By some sleight of language, this is called interactive—as if the two sides, human and machine, were in a relationship of equality. To my mind the position of the child here is, in the most essential respects, basically passive."[4]

When a child builds her own game, however, she is mastering the material and the medium and mixing them with her own unique and creative approach. As Dr. Papert put it, "The question is: Will the child program the computer or will the computer program the child?"

Even a young child can learn the basics of programming. In the 1960s, Dr. Papert invented a programming language called LOGO specifically for use by children, who learn the fundamental concepts by directing a little "turtle" symbol in geometric patterns on the screen. More recently, Dr. Papert extended the idea to a far more advanced program called MicroWorlds, which enables children to design their own multimedia presentations. Children can create books, newspapers, video games, interactive reports, and other projects, using text, recorded dialogue, sound effects, their own drawings, or pictures downloaded from the Internet. They can experiment with color and speed changes—whatever they can imagine and their equipment can supply.

Many elementary schools have adopted MicroWorlds as an exciting teaching tool for older children. But preschoolers who are not yet reading can experience the same thrill of creating their own programs with iconic and animated versions such as Make My Own Castle and Make My Own Treasure Island.

The advantage to such child-controlled programs is not just that they facilitate creativity. They also help to build a child's computer confidence and let him master a technology that will play an ever more important role in his life. "I do not want to see another generation of children grow up to be people for whom anything technological is an unintelligible black box," declared Dr. Papert. "If you can use a computer game, you should know how to make one."

It's hard to believe that as recently as 1990, the Internet was a little-known network linking military computers with computers in a few high-tech universities. In the twenty-first century, the World Wide Web will be as vital a part of your growing child's life as the telephone and the television were in the twentieth century. The Internet already offers a wide variety of learning experiences that you and your child can share together. Though its vastness can be daunting even for an adult, it helps to think of the Internet as playing the following kinds of roles.

Electronic Library

Imagine having instant access to almost any newspaper, magazine, museum, university, television network, nonprofit organization, and company headquarters in the world, 24 hours a day, usually with no admission fee. With an on-line service and a few search engines, you have that access—and you can take your child along to almost any place in the world.

Although your preschooler won't fully appreciate this extraordinary resource until she is older and doing homework assignments, you can give her a taste of the vast stores of information available on the Web and show her how to bring some of it home. Pick a topic she enjoys—dinosaurs, hamsters, figure skaters, anything. Use it as a key word, cast an electronic net, and see what kind of information comes back. Spend as much time as you can clicking through the Web sites and pages your search yields, showing your child the wide variety of material she can find. If you are overwhelmed with general sites about dinosaurs, show her how to refine the search to specific types. Let her print out pictures and make her own scrapbooks or collages.

Your youngster will need an adult or older sibling to help in searching, at least at first. But even if she isn't reading yet, she can appreciate pictures and enjoy the search. Recognizing even a few words will allow her to navigate a Web site; you can show her how to maneuver the mouse until she finds a link. You will probably find that the more she uses the computer, the more words she will pick up automatically, and the more she will want to learn.

As opportunities arise, teach your child to be a savvy Web consumer. Try researching the topic with different search engines and see what different information they turn up. Get across the notion that not everything she reads there may be true or useful. Does this information about sea turtles come from a big, famous museum, or is it some children writing about their pet? How can you tell the difference? Set up a site about your own family, and update it frequently. Show her how to save the addresses of favorite sites so she can find them quickly again.

Most on-line services offer content-filtering programs that will automatically screen out sites with language or pictures that are inappropriate for children. Some are far more restrictive than others, so you may want to experiment. Do you want a program that blocks every single site that mentions the word *sex*—even in a basic reference to gender? Remember that exploring the Internet *with* your child is the most effective filter of all.

Take your child on virtual field trips. Some national parks and historic places—even the White House—have Web sites that offer click-through "tours." Research other cities or vacation spots before you go there. Some art museums let you browse through their collections. It's not too early to show your preschooler the difference between a Picasso and a Renoir. You can zoom in on favorite paintings, print out copies, and even save them as "wallpaper" on your computer desktop.

Like so much else with computers, learning to read will vastly increase what your child is able to do on the Internet. For example, once he can navigate by himself, give him simple assignments just for fun: Find an interesting fact about an animal or pick a place you'd like to go or the top news story of the day.

By age five, Hillary was so at ease with her Internet searching skills that she peppered her spoken language with computer lingo. ("Mom, when are we going to have lunch? I'm hungry. Key word: *Hungry!*")

Electronic Post Office

Giving your child his own e-mail address—or better still, letting him select one himself—can be a thrilling introduction to cyberspace. And the words *You've got mail!* may be the single most powerful incentive your child ever has to learn to read and write. Encourage older relatives and friends to send your child messages frequently. Help him find friends his age with e-mail addresses of their own. Teach him to respond promptly; "reply" buttons make it easy.

Sending and receiving e-mail can let your child develop a very special relationship with grandparents or cousins. Even before he can write, your child can send photos or drawings via e-mail with the aid of a digital camera or scanner. Most on-line services have instant messaging capabilities so your child and a grandparent or friend can "chat" just as they could on the telephone. Your child can dictate messages for you to write until he can manage on his own.

E-mail is also a splendid way to write "chain stories." Have your child write or dictate the first line of a story, then send it to a friend or relative and ask him to supply the second line. Continue passing it back and forth, or include other friends and relatives, asking each to add a new sentence to the growing saga.

If you have access to e-mail where you work, have your child send you messages there, and message him back. Or arrange a time each day for a private e-mail chat.

Electronic Playground

As your youngster will soon discover, cyberspace is filled with Web sites designed just for children. Most on-line services feature entire sections devoted to them. If you let him, your child can spend literally hours going from link to link.

Like everything else on the Web, such sites run the gamut from intriguing information that can pique your child's curiosity to thinly disguised advertising for brand-name products. There are sites with stories, games, puzzles, on-line magazines—even music and videos to download. There are sites devoted to popular TV shows, movies, bands, and cartoon characters. Many invite your child to leave messages on bulletin boards or to enter chat rooms to talk with other kids.

Explore these options together and help your child evaluate which sites are fun and which are boring. Show him how to mark favorite sites so he can find them easily again. Even when he is young, you can teach him the difference between advertising and other information. Ask him, "Is this telling you something you really want to know, or are they just trying to get you to buy something?"

Just as you wouldn't let your young child go to the playground or the shopping mall all by herself, don't let her wander through cyberspace without some supervision and guidance. Teach her that "chatting" to people she doesn't know can be dangerous. Some forms of content-filtering software block all forms of "chat"—even among relatives and friends.

If you don't want to restrict your child's access that rigidly, you should give her some basic safety rules for the Internet—just as you would for the playground. Explain that people can pretend to be anyone they want in cyberspace and that she should never agree to meet someone in person that she has met only on the Web. Tell her never to answer questions about her body or give out her name, her address or phone number. If she ever finds herself in such a situation, she should immediately tell you or another grown-up.

Also tell your child to be wary of Web sites that ask for similar types of information. Some insist that visitors register before they are admitted, and providing a screen name and e-mail address is generally safe. But some sites that cater to children offer to send them samples or free gifts in exchange for information like their street address, phone number, school name, and answers to questions about their buying habits. Although the worst that may happen is that your family ends up on another mailing list, such practices are the electronic equivalent of luring your child with a promise of candy. Teach her to always ask you first before providing any information over the Web. That also applies to on-line shopping sites, especially those that let you leave your address and credit card number on file for easy ordering.

The very best way to ensure your child's safety on the Web, and to help him appreciate all its wonders, is to explore it with him. Set aside a special time each day or each week to go on Internet excursions together. That applies to trying new software products as well. In some families that value learning, the computer is fast taking the place of the television as an activity everyone can share—and it helps establish what Dr. Papert calls the "family's learning culture." Youngsters who see their parents continually exploring new ideas and learning about things—be it baseball, Jupiter, or volcanoes—will grow up thinking that learning is an ongoing adventure, not a chore relegated to children.

Will you handicap your child's future if you don't get him a computer and an assortment of software for his third birthday? No. But if you can possibly afford it—and prices are dropping steadily—one computer that your whole family can share would pay dividends in learning for years. And for a child growing up with otherwise limited resources, access to the Web in particular can be a great equalizer. There are growing concerns that in the future, there will be an ever-widening gap between those who have had the opportunity to use a computer and those who have not.

If buying your own computer is not possible, try to help your child find at least some access to one at school or at a local library or learning center. Some photocopy stores let customers rent computers by the hour, and some children's software retailers let youngsters try out programs for free or a small hourly fee.

Dr. Papert thinks that because of their early experience with computers, the rising generation of children could be a revolutionary force for technology in the future. "Those who at home had these richer learning experiences with the computer are beginning to appear in school as a kind of nuisance because they are demanding 'Why aren't we doing here what we know how to do at home?' " he said. "The cohort of young people who grew up with a computer from the beginning has not yet hit school with its full force. It will very soon and when that happens, I predict that we will see an irresistible pressure to change the structure and the content and the nature of schooling."[5]

11

How to Safeguard
Your Child's Brain

Kevin was four on the wintry day that his father bundled him up and took him for a ride on the new sled he'd gotten for Christmas. The afternoon was brisk and bright and a fresh fall of snow covered the nearby beach where Kevin had enjoyed playing the previous summer. But the temperature was falling. And a chilly wind was rising off the lake.

Suddenly the sled hit a hidden bump and flipped on its side. Kevin spilled out and, before his horrified father could catch him, tumbled into the water. His bulky snowsuit quickly filled with water and the boy rapidly sank out of sight into the dark, icy lake.

Kevin's father screamed for help and ran into the water, searching desperately for the child he could no longer see. A passerby dashed to help. Another flagged down a police car that radioed for paramedics and an ambulance. Frantic minutes went by—perhaps 20 in all—before Kevin's body was found and pulled to the surface. Even though they assumed he was dead, the police officers began cardiopulmonary resuscitation.

Just a minute or two later, the paramedics arrived. They began pouring oxygen into the boy's lungs while continuing to pump on his chest in an effort to restart his heart. They, too, detected no sign of possible life, no pulse, no heartbeat, no movement of the eyes, no response. Still, they worked on in the chilling cold, hating to give up, hating to lose a child. Frantically, they rushed Kevin into the ambulance and continued their efforts on the way to a children's hospital nearby.

At the hospital, a team of dedicated physicians took up the seemingly lost battle to save Kevin. They were hoping that two factors might tip the deadly odds against the child: The bitter cold might have quickly lowered the demands of Kevin's body for oxygen so that his brain might have survived. And the "diving reflex" might have channeled whatever oxygen the body had to the brain in a desperate strategy to survive.

Then the impossible happened. Kevin's pulse began to flutter. His heart started to beat on its own. And his breathing resumed, first in gasps and then with more regularity. For days, physicians kept the little boy sedated, using every medical means to minimize damage to his brain and to make his recovery as complete as possible.

But when Kevin at last regained consciousness, it was apparent that some brain damage had occurred. He had forgotten most of his four-year-old's explosive vocabulary. He had difficulty walking. And he had to relearn most of the skills he had acquired in the last two or three years of his short life.

With months of extensive therapy—at the hospital, at a rehabilitation center, and at home—Kevin has been improving steadily. His motor skills have returned. So has his speech. He started school in a class for children with learning disabilities, but eventually, physicians hope, most of the traces of his tragic accident will disappear.

Just how much intellectual ability a child has at any given

time is the result of three interacting factors, according to Dr. Richard Masland, former director of the National Institute of Neurological Diseases and Blindness.[1] These factors are:

- The basic genetic quality of the youngster's brain and the rest of his central nervous system, which he inherits
- Changes in or damage to this central nervous system by injury or disease, either before or after birth
- The impact upon the child's brain of his environment and his experiences

You can't change the first factor—the quality of the brain that your youngster possesses. That is determined by the complex of genes carried within the egg and sperm that joined at his conception. These in turn reflect his biological heritage from both his father's and his mother's families for innumerable preceding generations. The third factor has already been discussed at length in this book.

This chapter is concerned with the second of Dr. Masland's factors—what you can do to protect from injury and disease the brain your child has inherited, so that it will develop optimally and function effectively.

In the United States today there are at least 5 million individuals who have been diagnosed at some time in their lives as being mentally retarded. Probably an even larger number of people function inadequately throughout their lives because of a lesser degree of mental retardation or slight, unidentified brain damage or dysfunction.

In recent years, medical researchers have discovered that a substantial percentage of boys and girls who have behavior problems; who have trouble learning in school; who are overactive, hard to discipline, poorly coordinated, easily distracted; and who have specific learning disabilities may suffer from minor brain damage or dysfunction. Often this damage is so subtle that it can't be detected by the limited diagnostic techniques doctors now have. But it can sometimes be assumed because the child's symptoms match those of youngsters with proven brain injury and because the case history indicates when the damage probably occurred.

Children with minor brain damage are usually average, or above, in overall intelligence. But because of their difficulties and distortions in perception and because of other problems, they usually have a struggle learning to read and aren't able to make full use of their intelligence. Often these learning disabilities trigger secondary emotional problems, too.

At least 50 percent of all mental retardation can be prevented, even with the limited knowledge now available, the American Medical Association has estimated. So can much of the learning disability caused by brain injury. Many of the known ways to prevent brain damage lie chiefly within the control of parents—either before a child's birth or after. That's why it's important for you to learn about possible dangers to your child's brain and the ways in which you can protect him from learning disabilities and mental retardation—just as you guard his physical health from injury and disease as much as possible.

Odds are excellent that your child will be born with a normal, healthy brain, which will continue to grow and develop throughout childhood without injury. But a youngster's mental abilities are not something to leave to chance. You owe it to your offspring to learn all you can about the preventable causes of mental retardation and learning disabilities and to give him all the protection you can.

Below are some of the most important ways.

Consistent Medical Care

Arrange to have your child in the care of a skilled and up-to-date physician who will give him regular medical checkups and all recommended immunizations.

It's become tempting, in recent years, for parents to be casual about immunizing their children to what used to be common diseases of childhood, like measles, whooping cough, and mumps. Widespread immunization programs have drastically reduced the incidence of these illnesses so that parents can easily assume that their youngsters simply will not be exposed to them. Some mothers and fathers also worry about the possibility their child could have an adverse reaction to the vaccine.

But measles (the regular, "red," two-week variety that doctors call rubeola), in particular, has not yet been eradicated by the vaccine that became available in 1963, despite widespread hopes that it could be. Although more than 96 percent of American schoolchildren have received at least one dose of the vaccine, localized epidemics continue to occur—particularly among older children in high schools, on college campuses, and even in hospitals.[2]

Measles used to be considered a childhood nuisance, a necessary but rather minor evil. But measles can kill and is also the most serious cause of mental retardation of all the common childhood diseases. About 1 in every 1,000 measles victims suffers a serious complication, such as pneumonia or encephalitis, and one third of these are left with severe, permanent brain damage. Researchers also report that measles, even in a mild form, may be a cause of less severe degrees of mental retardation, learning difficulties, and personality or behavior changes. Measles "can knock the edge off children's IQs," warned Dr. James L. Goddard, when he was commissioner of the U.S. Food and Drug Administration. And the danger of brain damage from measles is greatest among preschoolers, researchers point out.

Today there is no need to risk even the most remote chance that measles could take the edge off your child's intellectual abilities. The American Academy of Pediatrics has concluded that some children didn't respond to the vaccine because they were given it at too young an age, because of technical problems, or because they received it at the same time as im-munoglobulin, which may have interfered with its effectiveness. The AAP now recommends that all children have a second dose of the vaccine between ages four and six to prevent school-based outbreaks.

Health experts still hope that with the cooperation of parents—and the United Nations and governments worldwide—measles can eventually be eliminated, as has smallpox. But it won't happen if the level of immunization falls. And until it is eliminated, you owe your child protection against what can turn into a tragic or deadly disease.

Besides measles, there are other infectious diseases and disorders that can damage the brain of a child who was born healthy and normal and thereby limit his intelligence. Most of these, fortunately, are rare. Others are uncommon complications of diseases as ordinary as mumps and chicken pox. Some of these afflictions, like cretinism, can be corrected rather easily if diagnosed and treated early in life. Some can be prevented completely by routine shots on standard schedules. Some come on insidiously, slowly; others start with convulsions and fever and fear in the night.

No layperson can hope to know enough about all of these brain-damaging hazards to children. You don't need to. But it is important that your child be under the regular, routine care of a good physician who keeps informed of new research and who is as close as your telephone.

It is safer today to raise a child in the United States than ever before in history. Good routine care and preventive medicine are two major reasons why. But it is still up to parents to take the initiative to make sure these are available to their children. For example, be certain that your child's hearing and vision are checked as early as possible—so that her fast-growing brain doesn't become wired without that critical sensory input. Vision screening isn't usually done until a child is three years old, but even newborns can and should be examined for eye problems. If you suspect that your baby is not focusing or tracking or responding to changes in her field of vision, be sure to alert your physician. Similarly, pediatricians are now urged to check all infants for possible hearing loss before they are three months old and to correct any problem, if possible, before it interferes with language and speech development. If you notice that your baby isn't responding to noises around her, let your doctor know.

Accident Prevention

Take reasonable precautions to prevent accidents that can injure your child's brain.

Sometimes you feel as if only a wrestler could keep your seven-month-old squirmer from wiggling off the table while he's being diapered. Or only a professional athlete could supervise a two-year-old explorer closely enough to stop him from tumbling down the stairs or off the top of the bookcase. Or only a Marine sergeant could bellow emphatically enough to make a four-year-old sit safely still in the car while you're driving.

But you must protect your child against accidents. Injuries involving the head can cause brain damage, which is reflected in loss of intellectual ability.

"If parents could see what happens to a child's electroencephalogram [EEG] when he's hit on the head or falls down stairs and is knocked out for a minute or two, they wouldn't take accidents so casually," commented Dr. Frederic Gibbs, a neurologist and pioneer in the use of the EEG for brain research.

Accidental injuries cause about half of all deaths among children between the ages of 1 and 14. At least a hundred times that many youngsters suffer nonfatal injuries.[3]

Almost all head injuries can be prevented. In fact, many

safety experts are urging that the word *accident* be replaced by *injury*, to avoid even suggesting that what happened was a chance event that could not have been prevented.

Two cardinal principles to remember in protecting your baby or toddler from falls are these: She's stronger and quicker than you think. And every day, she can do more than she did yesterday.

Starting the day you bring your infant home from the hospital, you should make it a habit not to leave her alone on a table or counter or in a bathinette, even for the second it takes to turn around for a fresh diaper. Even before she learns to roll over, a baby can dig her heels into a tabletop and shove herself off.

Never leave your baby alone in a high chair, either, even for the minute it takes to answer the phone. The day your baby crawls the first inch—or even before—put up gates at the top and bottom of every staircase. Police other members of your family to make sure that everyone locks the gate behind him. And be ready to get new locks or safety catches the minute your baby learns to pick the old ones. As soon as she can learn, teach her to go up and down stairs safely, holding on or sliding down on her padded bottom.

Train yourself to put up the sides of your baby's crib without fail. And when your toddler is old enough to begin climbing out by herself, keep an old mattress beside the crib to cushion tumbles. Or promote her to a youth bed. She may get up and inconvenience you sometimes when she's supposed to be sleeping. But she will be safer from falls. Be sure, too, that your windows are safely screened, especially above the first floor.

Be extremely wary of infant walkers. Many parents buy them in the mistaken belief that they will keep their baby safe while she is learning to walk, but often the opposite is true. In one recent year, 25,000 children, most of them between the ages of 5 and 15 months, were treated in hospital emergency departments for walker-related injuries. Parents themselves have reported that between 12 percent and 40 percent of infants who use walkers suffer some kind of accident. Many of the most serious come from falling down stairs, which can result in severe head injuries. One study found that more than a third of falls with walkers occurred even though stair gates were in place.[4]

Concerns about safety have prompted manufacturers to make some modifications and issue warning labels, but the AAP has recommended that infant walkers be banned completely, and that existing ones be destroyed.

The dangers of head injuries are greatest, of course, in cars. Auto accidents are the leading cause of death and serious, permanent physical and mental disability among children. Children who are not wearing safety restraints when an accident occurs continue moving in the original direction of the car like flying missiles until they strike something solid or are thrown out of the car. Consumer Product Safety Commission data shows that 85 percent of children younger than age five who are hurt in car accidents have head injuries that can cause permanent neurologic disability.

Crash tests carried out by traffic experts show that it is not possible for an adult—even wearing a lap and shoulder restraint—to prevent a small child on her lap from smashing into the dashboard and windshield if an accident occurs, even at low or moderate speed. If the adult isn't wearing a seat belt, the force of her body also crushes against the youngster from behind.

Child safety seats and seat belts are the most effective way to reduce the number and severity of car-accident injuries, and almost all states require them. As a result of such laws and education campaigns, use of seat belts has increased dramatically in recent decades—from about 15 percent nationwide in the 1950s to an estimated 68 percent in 1998. Still, riding unrestrained remains a major source of traffic deaths and injuries. Roughly half of children under age five who die in crashes every year were not buckled in, and half of the rest wore adult seat belts that didn't provide adequate protection.[5]

Parents are often careless about strapping their children in for every trip, especially when they're tired and rushed and only going a short distance. Yet the sad fact is that most young children who are killed or badly injured in cars are in vehicles driven by a parent, during the day and within a few miles of their home. Parents also become less conscientious about buckling in their children as the children get older. One government study found that while 96 percent of parents always used a child seat for their newborn babies, only 17 percent did so for their five-year-olds.

So many youngsters continue to die or suffer tragic brain damage in auto accidents that the AAP conducts a major, ongoing campaign to educate parents how best to protect their offspring.

The AAP recommends that

- Infants ride in rear-facing child safety seats, buckled into the backseat, until they have reached both 20 pounds and one year of age. Until a baby is that big, her neck muscles are not strong enough to protect her head from snapping forward in a crash, which could cause serious neck and spinal cord injuries. The seat should be snug and at a 45-degree angle to support the baby's head and keep an airway open.

- Bigger children should ride in front-facing child safety seats, also in the backseat, as long as they can fit in them comfortably—that is, with their ears coming below the top of the seat, and their shoulders below the strap slots. A child will be too big when she weighs about 40 pounds and measures 40 inches.

- Children who have outgrown safety seats should ride in booster seats until they can wear an adult seat belt properly, with the lap belt low and tight across their hips and the shoulder belt across their shoulders, not their face or neck. Numerous youngsters suffered fatal injuries—even in the backseat—because a shoulder harness hit their bodies at the wrong level.

Even well-meaning, safety-conscious parents may think that their baby is safer in the front seat where the driver can see her and help in case of choking or other problems—especially if there's no one else in the car. But experts say that the risk of a child's suffering a serious injury in a crash is far greater than the risk of experiencing a life-threatening problem during a ride. Some parents also argue that a car ride is a great opportunity to discuss the scenery or have a heart-to-heart talk with a child, which is more difficult when the child is riding behind. Nevertheless, the AAP recommends that all children under age 12 ride in the backseat, buckled, even if it requires chauffeuring fewer children than you had planned.

Keeping children out of the front seat has become even more critical given the threat that air bags pose to them. Starting in model year 1998, all passenger cars are required to have dual air bags—for the driver and front-seat passenger—and many cars built before that have them as well. Federal statistics credit air bags with saving several thousand lives since the 1980s, but they have also caused the deaths of several hundred people—including approximately 1 child for every 10 adults they saved. Sadly, many of these fatalities occurred in car crashes that were otherwise survivable. The air bag killed the children, not the collision.[6]

The force of an air bag inflating at speeds up to 200 miles

per hour is particularly dangerous to children and short adults because their heads are at the same level as the onrushing bag. With a larger adult, an air bag is generally at chest level, and it usually expands fully before making contact. An unbelted or improperly belted child is especially at risk, since he may be thrown forward or off the seat by the collision. The air bag may strike him on the head or neck while it is still inflating, causing a serious or fatal injury. An inflating air bag can even seriously harm a child strapped into a safety seat in the front, and it can force the back of a rear-facing infant seat violently into a baby's head.

Many parents and consumer advocates have protested that air bags do more harm than good where children are concerned, but so far, to no avail. Federal law even prohibits car dealers and repair shops from disarming them. Exemptions to the law are granted only in rare cases such as cars that have no backseat or infants who require constant monitoring for medical problems. Installing a manual cutoff switch requires a similar waiver.

Unless and until such laws are changed, the best way to protect your child is to keep him buckled into the back, as far away from the air bag as possible.

Bicycling, skateboarding, and in-line skating also pose considerable safety hazards for children. Epidemics of injuries rise and fall as these activities wax and wane in popularity, with head injuries among the most common and most serious. Lightweight, low-cost helmets are now widely available, and in some areas, they are required by law to be worn. One study showed that wearing a helmet can reduce the risk of head injury by 85 percent and brain injury by 88 percent. Yet many children refuse to wear them, and many parents don't insist.

The AAP recommends that even if they do wear a helmet, children younger than five should not go skateboarding because their center of gravity is higher than that of older children and they have less muscular control, so they are at even higher risk for head injuries.[7]

The AAP also strenuously opposes boxing for children (as well as adolescents and young adults) because of the possibility of brain and eye damage. Even though the overall risk of injury is higher in other "collision sports" such as football, rugby, and ice hockey, the academy notes that boxing is "the only sport where direct blows to the head are rewarded and the ultimate victory may be to render the opponent senseless." Numerous studies of professional boxers have documented that multiple blows to the head can cause dementia pugilistica, a chronic swelling of the brain. Even amateur boxers are at risk for brain and eye abnormalities.[8]

Protection Against Poisoning

Of all the substances that can accidentally poison a small child, the one most likely to leave permanent brain damage is lead.

Two thousand years of human history—and a batch of worrisome studies—all confirm that lead hurts the human brain and erodes the intelligence. It accumulates in the body, especially in young children, causing irreversible brain damage, harming other organs, leading sometimes to death. We know enough now to avoid poisoning from the lead water pipes and wine containers that did so much damage to the ancient Romans that historians say it may have contributed to the fall of the Roman Empire. But lead remains a common, preventable threat to the mental and physical health of many young children.

Airborne lead from industry and from car and truck emissions settles on crops, soil, water, and urban streets and playgrounds. Studies show our diets today have a hundred times as much lead as those of our prehistoric ancestors and that our bodies have accumulated a thousand times as much lead as theirs.

For most of us, the level of lead piling up in our bodies isn't known to be dangerous. But hundreds of thousands of young children, especially those living in what are called "urban lead belts" in large cities, are suffering from what worried physicians describe as a silent epidemic of lead poisoning. As a result, they are growing up with impaired intelligence and health. And the adverse consequences will last a lifetime.

Lead poisoning usually develops slowly, over several weeks or months, as the damaging substance accumulates in the body, especially in the brain. First symptoms are unusual irritability, followed by digestive upsets and tiredness and often by convulsions and death. Even when a child recovers, the chances of permanent brain damage are high—inevitable, according to some doctors.

Until recently, most concern about lead poisoning in young children focused on old housing, where some toddlers and preschoolers habitually nibble on peeling, sweet-tasting, lead-based paint. Tacitly, the problem was blamed on greedy, neglectful landlords and parents who didn't supervise their toddlers well.

But more recent studies suggest that much of the burden of lead accumulated in the bodies of young children really comes from environmental pollution, particularly from car and truck emissions.

Rising awareness of the dangers of lead poisoning prompted the federal government to require steep cuts in the amount of lead in the nation's gasoline in the 1970s and 1980s—and the reported incidence of lead poisoning in young children did drop sharply, by as much as 37 percent between 1976 and 1980. But gasoline is just one source of lead contamination. It's estimated that it would cost more than $28 billion to get rid of all the lead-based paint in buildings in the United States. And health officials fear that many children with elevated blood levels of lead still aren't being identified because of inadequate screening.

The Centers for Disease Control and Prevention recommends that all children be tested in areas of the country where more than 27 percent of the housing was built before 1950 and where more than 12 percent of one- and two-year-olds have had elevated lead levels. By law, all young children enrolled in Medicaid and other federal health programs must be screened regularly, since lead poisoning is five times more common for such youngsters than others. But a recent federal report found that only about 18 percent of such children actually do undergo lead tests.[9]

What's more, health officials aren't sure what level of lead in the blood is safe. The old level used to diagnose lead poisoning—80 micrograms per 100 milliliters of blood—was too high, researchers now say. Evidence suggests that with levels as low as 20 micrograms, children can experience a drop in IQ along with behavioral disorders.

What can parents do to reduce the hazards of lead poisoning—and its insidious brain damage—for their children? Those who live in an older home, regardless of its cost, should make sure there is no peeling paint, especially around windowsills, that a child could chew or lick unobtrusively. Paints designed for indoor use now contain only a minimal amount of lead; but parents should check the labels on any paint they buy for use inside their home and in repainting toys and not let a teething toddler chew on anything that has been coated with paint intended for exterior use.

Dirt and dust in some urban areas where truck and auto traffic is high may be contaminated with dangerous amounts of lead, studies show. This airborne lead pollution may be a major reason why so many children in these areas show indications of lead poisoning and why the incidence of learning disabilities among them is so unusually high.

Researchers who have made studies of the levels of lead-contaminated dust in homes where small children live recommend extra effort be made to keep the dust cleaned up, especially around windowsills and floors near windows. They also emphasize the importance of keeping children's hands clean, to lessen the risk that they will get lead-contaminated dirt in their mouths.

12

The Joys of Having
a Bright Child

If you surround your youngster with the sort of mentally stimulating, encouraging home environment described in this book, will he become a "bright" child? Will she be classed as highly intelligent when she goes to school and will she be placed in top reading groups and in fast-track programs?

That's too sweeping a promise to make about a specific child at this point in the research about the development of intelligence in children and the effects of early learning. But it's a likelihood that many behavioral scientists and educators are studying seriously.

You can raise the intelligence level of almost any youngster a substantial degree by a stimulating, warm early home environment. That much seems certain. Whether your child was born with a poor, average, or superior mental potential, an enriched environment will raise his eventual level of intellectual functioning, regardless of the genes he has inherited. If your youngster has been lucky enough to inherit an average or above-average brain to start with, chances are great that a warm, loving, mentally stimulating environment from infancy will help her develop into a bright or gifted youngster.

Bright and *gifted* are terms often used interchangeably to describe the kind of boys and girls who have superior ability and who consistently do better, develop sooner, or learn more and faster than children generally in any area of significance. Dr. Paul Witty, who spent most of his career at Northwestern University studying bright youngsters, defined giftedness as "consistently remarkable performance in any worthwhile line of endeavor."

Others who have studied highly talented youngsters define giftedness as the "ability to think, generalize, and to see connections and to use alternatives" and as "ability to think in the abstract, to perceive cause and effect relationships, and to project ideas into the future."

The Gifted and Talented Children's Education Act of 1978 defined "gifted and talented" children as those "possessing demonstrated or potential abilities that give evidence of high performance capabilities, in areas such as intellectual, creative, specific academic or leadership ability, or in the performing and visual arts." (Many state education departments also use this definition. With cutbacks in federal involvement in education, states now have much of the responsibility for developing programs for the gifted.)

Sometimes schools identify bright and gifted children by IQ test alone. Most prefer to add teacher evaluation, grades, and other criteria. Most programs use a broad definition that includes children who are highly capable not only in academic work but also in the creative arts and who show unusual leadership abilities.

A stimulating home environment in early childhood has played a part in the lives of an impressive number of highly intelligent and highly gifted individuals of great achievement. And when researchers probe into the background of school-age children rated as gifted or mentally superior by IQ tests, they typically find a stimulating home life and often deliberate planning by parents to help their children learn to use their brain.

Dr. Robert J. Havighurst, of the University of Chicago, put it this way: "Boys and girls who are mentally superior have become so because of (1) a home and school environment which stimulated them to learn and to enjoy learning; (2) parents and other significant persons who set examples of interest and attainment in education which the children unconsciously imitated; and (3) early family training which produced a desire for achievement in the child. When these influences act upon a child with average or better biological equipment for learning, the child will become mentally superior."[1]

On the other hand, if a youngster who is born with superior biological endowment does not receive adequate early stimulation, she will not develop into a bright or gifted individual, researchers point out. It has been estimated that much of the potential of at least half of our gifted children is wasted for lack of early opportunity to learn at a sufficiently fast and enriched rate.

But even if it is possible that you can help your youngster become mentally superior, is it desirable? Do you want a bright child in your family?

"I couldn't care less about a high IQ. I just hope my kids turn out to be nice, average, normal youngsters," you occasionally hear a parent say. Some fathers and mothers—and even a few teachers—still picture a highly intelligent child as being a pale, puny prig who wears glasses and is just as inferior socially, emotionally, and physically as he is superior mentally. But they're just as mistaken as those who used to argue that genius is only a thin line away from insanity.

Another widely held—and mistaken—idea about gifted children is that they are pouring energy and effort into intellectual activities to cover up a painful inadequacy in another area of their life. No such evidence exists in dozens of excellent

Contrary to some fears that gifted young people would exploit others, especially if identified openly and grouped together in classes, they tend to be altruistic and have an active social conscience. Their sense of personal responsibility is keen, and they typically feel more disturbed about injustices than do classmates. It's apt to be the bright boy or girl who tries to play competitive games according to the rules, who stands up for the underdog, who is aware of the feelings and emotions of others.

Because gifted children are better than most youngsters at applying what they know to new situations and in seeing relationships, they rate high in traits like common sense. They are also adept at finding good but unusual ways in which to solve problems or to reach goals.

Most gifted youngsters like school—unless it pressures them too much to conform to limited levels of work. They learn quickly, without much repetition, make good grades, and often list difficult subjects as their favorites. They read widely—twice as many books as average students, according to one study.

Gifted young people are more likely than other youngsters to go to college, and they make better grades than classmates when they are in college. They're also more apt to take postgraduate work.

Increasingly, bright children are being viewed as a national asset, as a treasured resource that should be cherished and guarded and helped to flourish. Many schools have started special programs for gifted youngsters, who are identified by a variety of means, such as IQ tests, teacher recommendations, and evidences of unusual talent. Bright children may be assigned to enrichment programs, given opportunities to participate in special art or music classes, allowed to take experimental science courses, or invited to join Saturday programs for the gifted.

Special fast tracks and classes for gifted children are highly controversial in some communities and are often not labeled as such. Efforts may be made to make sure that any child who wishes to be included and do what may seem to be extra work has the opportunity. If your child is bored in school because she already knows the work she is supposed to be learning or has to wait for classmates to catch up, her teacher may be willing to help her find appropriate learning opportunities. At worst, you may have to help her find intellectual challenges at home and be glad that she is probably adept at doing so.

Other new opportunities are opening up. Illinois, for example, has a residential math and science academy for tenth, eleventh, and twelfth graders. Its students are highly successful by measures such as SAT scores, National Merit scholarships, and admission to highly selective colleges. Some large cities have created special elite high schools or magnet schools for bright young people who can win admission.

In some schools, bright children are grouped together in special fast tracks that whiz through an enriched curriculum at a speed more comfortable for them than the pace in a regular classroom. A typical program puts youngsters at least a year ahead of grade level by the time they finish junior high school, then allows them to take advanced college placement courses in high school. It's not unusual for such students to earn a year or more of college credits before high school graduation. They can then finish undergraduate requirements in three years, cutting college costs substantially, and get an earlier start on professional training or a job.

As interest in finding and stimulating the minds of gifted children grows, an increasing number of colleges, universities, and private schools are now offering summer enrichment programs for bright elementary and high school students. Organizations of parents and teachers devoted to the best interests of gifted children are at work in almost every state, making sure that bright youngsters are discovered and helped wherever they can be found. Most state departments of education also push for programs and special resources for the gifted. There are even periodic international conferences held to explore and promote better education for bright and gifted children.

As adults, the gifted typically fulfill the promise of their early youth and become productive, happy, contributing gifted men and women. There is no indication in any scientific research that the old adage of "early ripe, early rot" applies to bright youngsters.

Individuals who were identified as gifted in childhood and who have been followed into middle age have done well in high-level occupations, with earnings and achievements well above not only the general population but also above the average college graduate. Most are highly satisfied with their occupations. They read widely, particularly biography, history, and current drama. They are active in community affairs and organizations; they enjoy sports and have the same superior physical status and health records as they did in childhood. They report their marriages, generally, to be stable and their own lives to be happy to a greater degree than do individuals of average intelligence.

The long-term study begun by Lewis Terman, who followed the lives of a large group of gifted children beginning in 1922, has been continued by associates since his death in 1956. It has confirmed that these bright children generally do grow up to be superior to average individuals in general health, mental health, adult intelligence, income, careers, publications, patents, and other evidences of high achievement and even in contentment with their lives and accomplishments.

Research like this sometimes makes gifted children sound almost too good to be true. Of course, not every bright child has all of these characteristics. Some with superior abilities who aren't challenged enough in school turn into mischievous troublemakers or unhappy introverts. A few are exploited by parents who don't understand that their social and emotional needs are still those of children generally.

But on the whole, bright children are happy, productive, well liked, and have fewer problems than other youngsters. They are a joy to know and to rear. You will be glad if your offspring turns out to be gifted. You will undoubtedly feel that it has been worth the effort to give him a mentally stimulating first six years of life.

References

Chapter 1

1. Carnegie Corporation of New York, *Starting Points: Meeting the Needs of Our Youngest Children,* August 1994.
2. Seymour Papert, *The Connected Family,* Atlanta, Georgia, Longstreet Press, 1996.
3. Burton L. White, *The Origins of Human Competence,* Lexington, Massachusetts, D. C. Heath and Company, 1979.
4. J. McVicker Hunt, *Intelligence and Experience,* New York, Ronald Press, 1961.
5. Dolores Durkin, "Children Who Learned to Read at Home," *Elementary School Journal,* vol. 62, October 1961; and Dolores Durkin, "An Earlier Start in Reading?" *Elementary School Journal,* vol. 63, December 1962; and Dolores Durkin, "Children Who Read Before Grade 1: A Second Study," *Elementary School Journal,* vol. 64, December 1963; and Dolores Durkin, *Children Who Read Early,* New York, Teachers College Press, 1966.
6. Benjamin S. Bloom, Allison Davis, and Robert Hess, *Compensatory Education for Cultural Deprivation,* New York, Holt, Rinehart and Winston, 1965.

7. L. J. Schweinhart, H. V. Barnes, D. P. Weikart, W. S. Barnett, and A. S. Epstein, *Significant Benefits: The High/Scope Perry Preschool Study Through Age 27*, Ypsilanti, Michigan, High/Scope Press, 1993.
8. P. Berrueta-Clement and others, *Changed Lives: The Effects of the Perry Preschool Program on Youths Through Age 19*, Ypsilanti, Michigan, High/Scope Press, 1984.
9. Frances A. Campbell and Craig T. Ramey, "Cognitive and School Outcomes for High-Risk African-American Students at Middle Adolescence: Positive Effects of Early Intervention," *American Educational Research Journal*, vol. 32, no. 4, winter 1995.
10. Craig T. Ramey and Sharon L. Ramey, *Right From Birth*, New York, Goddard Press, 1999.
11. Judy C. Pfannenstiel and Dianne A. Seltzer, *Evaluation Report: New Parents as Teachers Project*, Missouri Department of Elementary and Secondary Education, Jefferson City, Missouri, 1985; "Parents as First Teachers," a series of guides for parents, Ferguson-Florissant School District, Florissant, Missouri, 1985.
12. William Fowler, "Longitudinal Study of Early Stimulation in the Emergence of Cognitive Processes," a paper sponsored by the Social Science Research Council, University of Chicago, February 1966.
13. Richard Lynn, "I.Q. in Japan and the United States Shows a Growing Disparity," *Nature*, vol. 297, 1982.
14. Harold W. Stevenson and James W. Stigler, *The Learning Gap: Why Our Schools Are Failing and What We Can Learn from Japanese and Chinese Education*, New York, Touchstone, 1992.

Chapter 2

1. Ronald Kotulak, "Learning How to Use the Brain," paper presented at the conference "Brain Development in Young

Children: New Frontiers for Research, Policy, and Practice," Chicago, June 1996.

2. P. R. Huttenlocher and Ch. de Courten, "The Development of Synapses in Striate Cortex of Man," *Human Neurology*, vol. 6, spring 1987.

3. Ramey, *op. cit.*

4. Wayne Dennis, "Causes of Retardation among Institutionalized Children: Iran," *Journal of Genetic Psychology*, vol. 96, 1960.

5. Sandra R. Kaler and B. J. Freeman, "Analysis of Environmental Deprivation: Cognitive and Social Development in Romanian Orphans," *Journal of Child Psychology and Psychiatry*, vol. 35, no. 4, 1994.

6. Kim Chisholm, "A Three Year Follow-Up of Attachment and Indiscriminate Friendliness in Children Adopted from Romanian Orphanages," *Child Development*, vol. 69, no. 4, August 1998.

7. Craig T. Ramey and Sharon L. Ramey, "Prevention of Intellectual Disabilities: Early Interventions to Improve Cognitive Development," *Preventative Medicine*, vol. 27, no. 2, March–April 1998.

8. Benjamin S. Bloom, *Stability and Change in Human Characteristics*, New York, John Wiley & Sons, 1964.

9. Marian Diamond and Janet Hopson, *Magic Trees of the Mind*, New York, Plume, 1999.

10. James E. Black, "How a Child Builds Its Brain: Some Lessons from Animal Studies of Neural Plasticity," *Preventative Medicine*, vol. 27, March 1998.

11. T. Elbert, C. Pantev, C. Weinbruch, B. Rockstroh, and E. Taub, "Increased Cortical Representation of the Fingers of the Left Hand in String Players," *Science*, vol. 207, October 13, 1996.

12. Bob Jacobs, Matthew Schall, and Arnold B. Scheibel, "A Quantitative Dendritic Analysis of Wernicke's Area in Humans. II. Gender, Hemispheric, and Environmental Fac-

tors," *Journal of Comparative Neurology,* vol. 327, January 1993; and Arnold B. Scheibel, Tracy Conrad, Sondra Perdue, Uwami Tomiyasu, and Adam Wechsler, "A Quantitative Study of Dendrite Complexity in Selected Areas of the Human Cerebral Cortex," *Brain and Cognition,* vol. 12, January 1990.

13. Harry T. Chugani, "A Critical Period of Brain Development: Studies of Cerebral Glucose Utilization with PET," *Preventative Medicine,* vol. 27, March 1998.

14. Bloom, *op. cit.*

15. Harry T. Chugani, "Metabolic Imaging: A Window on Brain Development and Plasticity," *Neuroscientist,* vol. 5, no. 1, 1999.

16. Frances H. Rauscher, Gordon L. Shaw, and Katherine N. Ky, "Listening to Mozart Enhances Spatial-Temporal Reasoning: Towards a Neurophysiological Basis," *Neuroscience Letters,* vol. 185, 1995; and Frances H. Rauscher, Gordon L. Shaw, Linda J. Levine, Eric L. Wright, Wendy R. Dennis, and Robert L. Newcomb, "Music Training Causes Long-Term Enhancement of Preschool Children's Spatial-Temporal Reasoning," *Neurological Research,* vol. 19, 1997.

17. Maria Montessori, *The Montessori Method,* new edition, Cambridge, Massachusetts, Robert Bentley, 1964.

18. P. K. Kuhl, K. A. Williams, F. Lucevda, K. N. Stevens, and B. Lindbloom, "Linguistic Experience Alters Phonetic Perception in Infants by 6 Months of Age," *Science,* vol. 255, 1992.

19. Janellen Huttenlocher, "Language Input and Language Growth," *Preventative Medicine,* vol. 27, March–April 1998.

20. Wilder Penfield and Lamar Roberts, *Speech and Brain Mechanisms,* Princeton, New Jersey, Princeton University Press, 1959.

21. George Stevens, "Reading for Young Children," in *Building*

the Foundations for Creative Learning, Urban K. Fleege, editor, New York, American Montessori Society, 1964.

22. Charles Leroux and Cindy Schreuder, "Handle With Care: To Thrive, Newborn Babies Require a Vital Touch," *Chicago Tribune*, October 30, 1994.

23. Lewis P. Lipsitt, "Learning and Emotion in Infants," *Pediatrics*, vol. 102, no. 5 supplement, November 1998.

24. Geraldine Dawson, Laura Grofer Klinger, Heracles Panagiotides, Deborah Hill, and Susan Spieker, "Frontal Lobe Activity and Affective Behavior of Infants of Mothers with Depressive Symptoms," *Child Development*, vol. 63, 1992.

25. Mary Carlson and Felton Earls, "Psychological and Neuroendocrinological Sequelae of Early Social Deprivation in Institutionalized Children in Romania," *Annals of the New York Academy of Science*, vol. 807, 1997.

26. Megan R. Gunnar, "Quality of Early Care and Buffering of Neuroendocrine Stress Reactions: Potential Effects on the Developing Human Brain," *Preventative Medicine*, vol. 27, March 1998.

27. Jean Piaget, *The Origin of Intelligence in Children*, New York, International Universities Press, 1952.

28. Robert W. White, "Motivation Reconsidered: The Concept of Competence," *Psychological Review*, vol. 66, 1959.

Chapter 3

1. Kenneth D. Wann, Miriam Selchen Dorn, and Elizabeth Ann Liddle, *Fostering Intellectual Development in Young Children*, New York, Teachers College Press, 1962.

2. Rita Dunn, "Learning Style and Its Relation to Exceptionality at Both Ends of the Spectrum," *Exceptional Children*, April 1983.

3. Robert D. Hess, "Social Class Influences Upon Preschool Early Cognitive Development," an address to the American Montessori Society Seminar, New York, June 1965;

and Robert D. Hess and Virginia Shipman, "Early Blocks to Children's Learning," *Children,* vol. 12, September–October 1965.

4. Ellen Sheiner Moss, "Mothers and Gifted Preschoolers: Teaching and Learning Strategies," a paper presented at the annual meeting of the American Educational Research Association, Montreal, April 1983.

5. Wann, *op. cit.*

6. Victor Goertzel and Mildred G. Goertzel, *Cradles of Eminence,* Boston, Little, Brown, 1962.

7. Merle B. Karnes, Allan M. Shwedel, and Susan A. Linnemeyer, "The Young Gifted/Talented Child: Programs at the University of Illinois," *Elementary School Journal,* vol. 82, January 1982.

8. Benjamin S. Bloom, "The Role of Gifts and Markers in the Development of Talent," *Exceptional Children,* vol. 48, April 1982.

9. Margie Kitano, "Young Gifted Children: Strategies for Preschool Teachers," *Young Children,* vol. 37, May 1982.

Chapter 4

1. Lewis P. Lipsitt, "Critical Conditions in Infancy," *American Psychologist,* vol. 34, October 1979.

2. Leon Eisenberg, "Reading Retardation: Psychiatric and Sociologic Aspects," *Pediatrics,* vol. 37, February 1966.

3. Anneliese F. Korner and Rose Grobstein, "Visual Alertness as Related to Soothing in Neonates: Implications for Maternal Stimulation and Early Deprivation," *Child Development,* vol. 37, December 1966.

4. Hunt, *op. cit.*

5. Newell C. Kephart, "Teaching the Child with Learning Disabilities," an address given to the West Suburban Association for the Other Child, Glen Ellyn, Illinois, January 1968.

Chapter 5

1. Ernst L. Moerk, "The Mother of Eve—As a First Language Teacher," a paper given at a meeting of the Society for Research in Child Development, San Francisco, March 1979.
2. American Academy of Pediatrics, Committee on Accident Prevention, "Responsibility Means Safety for Your Child," 1964.
3. American Academy of Pediatrics, Committee on Psychosocial Aspects of Child and Family Health, "Guidance for Effective Discipline," *Pediatrics,* vol. 101, April 1998.
4. Jack Prelutsky, *A New Kid on the Block,* New York, Greenwillow Books, a division of William Morrow, 1984; reprinted with permission.
5. Robert Lewis Stevenson, *A Child's Garden of Verses,* 1885.

Chapter 6

1. Wann, *op. cit.*

Chapter 7

1. Mabel Morphett and Carleton Washburne, "When Should Children Begin to Read?" *Elementary School Journal,* vol. 31, March 1931.
2. Montessori, *op. cit.*
3. Durkin, *op. cit.,* 1966.
4. LynNell Hancock and Pat Wingert, "If You Can Read This . . ." *Newsweek,* May 13, 1996.
5. Sally Shaywitz, "Dyslexia," *Scientific American,* November 1996.
6. *Chicago Tribune,* "Short Cuts to Reading You Can Teach Your Child," adapted by Joan Beck and Becky, from "Listen and Learn with Phonics," by Dorothy Taft Watson, *Chicago Tribune,* August–November 1964.
7. Joseph E. Brzeinski and John L. Hayman Jr., "The Effectiveness of Parents in Helping Their Preschool Children to

Begin to Read," Denver, Denver Public Schools, September 1962.

8. William H. Teale, "Positive Environments for Learning to Read: What Studies of Early Readers Tell Us," *Language Arts,* vol. 55, November–December 1978.

9. Dolores Durkin, "A Fifth Year Report on the Achievement of Early Readers," *Elementary School Journal,* vol. 65, November 1964.

10. Paul McKee and Joseph E. Brzeinski, "The Effectiveness of Teaching Reading in Kindergarten," Denver, Denver Public Schools, 1966.

Chapter 8

1. E. Paul Torrance, "Education and Creativity," in *Creativity: Progress and Potential,* Calvin W. Taylor, ed., New York, McGraw-Hill, 1964.

2. E. Paul Torrance, *Guiding Creative Talent,* Englewood Cliffs, NJ, Prentice-Hall, 1962.

3. Torrance, *op. cit.,* 1964.

Chapter 9

1. Montessori, *op. cit.*

2. Paula Polk Lillard, *Montessori Today,* New York, Schocken Books, 1996.

Chapter 10

1. Papert, *op. cit.*

2. Ann McCormick Pirstrup, "A Computer in the Nursery School," in *Intelligent Schoolhouse: Readings on Computers and Learning,* Dale Peterson, ed., Reston, Va., Reston Publishing, 1984.

3. Steve Bennett, *The Plugged-In Parent,* New York, Random House, 1998.

4. Papert, *op. cit.*

5. Seymour Papert, "Child Power: Keys to the Learning of

the Digital Century," The Eleventh Colin Cherry Memorial Lecture on Communication, London, Imperial College, June 1998.

Chapter 11

1. Richard L. Masland, "Mental Retardation," in *Birth Defects,* Morris Fishbein, ed., Philadelphia, J. B. Lippincott, 1963.
2. American Academy of Pediatrics, Committee on Infectious Diseases, "Age for Routine Administration of the Second Dose of Measles-Mumps-Rubella Vaccine," *Pediatrics,* vol. 101, January 1998.
3. American Academy of Pediatrics, Committee on Research and Committee on Accident and Poison Prevention, "Reducing the Toll of Injuries in Childhood Requires Support for a Focused Research Effort," *Pediatrics,* vol. 72, November 1983.
4. American Academy of Pediatrics, Committee on Injury and Poison Prevention, "Injuries Associated with Infant Walkers," *Pediatrics,* vol. 95, May 1996.
5. ———, "Selecting and Using the Most Appropriate Car Safety Seats for Children," *Pediatrics,* vol. 97, May 1996.
6. ———, "Air Bag Safety," "Bag Safety Q & A," "Buckle Up America," "Presidential Initiative for Increasing Seat Belt Use Nationwide," *www.aap.org.,* 1999.
7. ———, "Skateboard Injuries," *Pediatrics,* vol. 95, April 1995.
8. American Academy of Pediatrics, Committee on Sports Medicine and Fitness, "Participation in Boxing by Children, Adolescents, and Young Adults," *Pediatrics,* vol. 99, January 1997.
9. American Academy of Pediatrics, Committee on Environmental Health, "Screening for Elevated Blood Lead Levels," *Pediatrics,* vol. 101, June 1998.

Chapter 12

1. Robert J. Havighurst, "Conditions Productive of Superior Children," *Teachers College Record,* vol. 62, April 1961.

Bibliography

Adams, Judith, and Craig R. Ramey, "Structural Aspects of Maternal Speech to Infants Reared in Poverty," *Child Development,* vol. 51, December 1980.

Albert, Robert S., "Exceptionally Gifted Boys and Their Parents," *Gifted Child Quarterly,* vol. 24, fall 1980.

Almay, Millie, Edward Chittenden, and Paula Miller, *Young Children's Thinking,* New York, Teachers College Press, 1966.

American Academy of Pediatrics, Committee on Environmental Health, "Screening for Elevated Blood Lead Levels," *Pediatrics,* vol. 101, June 1998.

————, Joint Committee on Infant Hearing, "1994 Position Statement," *Pediatrics,* vol. 95, January 1994.

————, Committee on Practice and Ambulatory Medicine, Section on Ophthalmology, "Eye Examination and Vision Screening in Infants, Children, and Young Adults," *Pediatrics,* vol. 98, July 1996.

————, Committee on Sports Medicine and Fitness, "Participation in Boxing by Children, Adolescents, and Young Adults," *Pediatrics,* vol. 99, January 1997.

————, Committee on Injury and Poison Prevention, "Skateboard Injuries," *Pediatrics,* vol. 95, April 1995.

————, Committee on Infectious Diseases, "Age for Routine Administration of the Second Dose of Measles-Mumps-Rubella Vaccine," *Pediatrics,* vol. 101, January 1998.

————, Committee on Injury and Poison Prevention, "Injuries Associated with Infant Walkers," *Pediatrics,* vol. 95, May 1996.

————, Committee on Injury and Poison Prevention, "Selecting and Using the Most Appropriate Car Safety Seats for Growing Children: Guidelines for Counseling Parents," *Pediatrics,* vol. 97, May 1996.

————, "Air Bag Safety Card," "Bag Safety Q & A," "Buckle Up America," "Presidential Initiative for Increasing Seat Belt Use Nationwide," *www.aap.com,* 1999.

————, Committee on Injury and Poison Prevention, "Bicycle Helmets," *Pediatrics,* vol. 95, April 1995.

Anger, W. Kent, "Neurobehavioral Testing in the Workplace," a paper presented at the annual meeting of the American Association for the Advancement of Science, Washington, D.C., January 1982.

Annest, Joseph L., and others, "Chronological Trend in Blood Lead Levels Between 1976 and 1980," *New England Journal of Medicine,* vol. 308, June 9, 1983.

Anthony, Sylvia, "Suggestions to 'Turn On' Bright Children at Home," *G/C/T,* November–December 1982.

Apgar, Virginia, and Joan Beck, *Is My Baby All Right?* New York, Simon & Schuster, 1972.

Backman, Joan, "The Role of Psycholinguistic Skills in Reading

Acquisition: A Look at Early Readers," *Reading Research Quarterly*, vol. 18, summer 1983.

Bakeman, Roger, and Josephine V. Brown, "Early Interaction: Consequences for Social and Mental Development at Three Years," *Child Development*, vol. 51, June 1980.

Banks, Martin S., "The Development of Visual Accommodation During Early Infancy," *Child Development*, vol. 51, September 1980.

Barnett, W. Steven, "Long-Term Cognitive and Academic Effects on Early Childhood Education on Children in Poverty," *Preventative Medicine*, vol. 27, March 1998.

Barrera, Maria E., and Daphne Maurer, "Discrimination of Strangers by the Three-Month-Old," *Child Development*, vol. 52, June 1981.

Bates, John E., and others, "Dimensions of Individuality in the Mother–Infant Relationship at Six Months of Age," *Child Development*, vol. 53, April 1982.

Beck, Joan, *Best Beginnings*, New York, G. P. Putnam's Sons, 1983.

———, *Effective Parenting*, New York, Simon & Schuster, 1975.

Begley, Sharon, and Mary Hager, "Your Child's Brain," *Newsweek*, February 19, 1996.

Belsky, Jay, "The Determinants of Parenting: A Process Model," *Child Development*, vol. 55, February 1984.

Belsky, Jay, Mary Kay Goode, and Robert K. Most, "Maternal Stimulation and Infant Exploratory Competence: Cross-Sectional, Correlational, and Experimental Analyses," *Child Development*, vol. 51, December 1980.

Benbow, Camilla P., and Julian C. Stanley, "Intellectually Talented Students: Family Profiles," *Gifted Child Quarterly*, vol. 24, summer 1980.

Benbow, Camilla P., and Julian C. Stanley, editors, *Academic*

Precocity: Aspects of Its Development, Baltimore, The Johns Hopkins University Press, 1983.

Bennett, Steve, *The Plugged-In Parent,* New York, Times Books, a division of Random House, 1998.

Berger, Lawrence R., and others, "Promoting the Use of Car Safety Devices for Infants: An Intensive Health Education Approach," *Pediatrics,* vol. 74, July 1984.

Berlin, Lisa J., Jeanne Brooks-Gunn, Cecelia McCarton, and Marie C. McCormick, "The Effectiveness of Early Intervention: Examining Risk Factors and Pathways to Enhanced Development," *Preventative Medicine,* vol. 27, March 1998.

Berrueta-Clement, P., and others, *Changed Lives,* Ypsilanti, Michigan, High/Scope Press, 1984.

Black, James E., "How a Child Builds Its Brain: Some Lessons from Animal Studies of Neural Plasticity," *Preventative Medicine,* vol. 27, March 1998.

Blanton, William E., "Preschool Reading Instruction: A Literature Search, Evaluation, and Interpretation," National Center for Educational Communication, Department of Health, Education, and Welfare, Washington, D.C., June 1972.

Bloom, Benjamin, editor, *Developing Talent in Young People,* New York, Ballantine, 1985.

―――, "The Role of Gifts and Markers in the Development of Talent," *Exceptional Children,* vol. 48, April 1982.

―――, *Stability and Change in Human Characteristics,* New York, John Wiley & Sons, 1964.

Boegehold, Betty D., and others, *Education Before Five: A Handbook on Preschool Education,* New York, Bank Street College of Education, 1977.

Bowlby, John, *Attachment,* New York, Basic Books, 1969.

―――, *Separation,* New York, Basic Books, 1973.

Bowman, Barbara T., "Do Computers Have a Place in Preschools?" a paper presented at a meeting of the New Mexico Association for the Education of Young Children, Albuquerque, February 1983.

Bradley, Robert H., and Bettye M. Caldwell, "Early Home Environment and Changes in Mental Test Performances in Children from Six to 36 Months," a paper presented at the American Educational Research Association meeting, Washington, D.C., 1975.

———, "The Relation of Home Environment, Cognitive Competence, and I.Q. Among Males and Females," *Child Development*, vol. 51, December 1980.

Brazelton, T. Berry, "The Joint Regulation of Infant-Adult Interaction," a paper presented at the annual meeting of the American Association for the Advancement of Science, Denver, February 1977.

———, *On Becoming a Family: The Growth of Attachment*, New York, Delacorte Press/Seymour Lawrence, 1981.

Brenner, Barbara, and Mari Endreweit, *Bank Street's Family Computer Book*, New York, Ballantine Books, 1984.

Brock, William M., "The Effects of Day Care: A Review of the Literature," Southwest Regional Laboratory for Educational Research and Development, Los Alamitos, California, 1980.

Brunell, Philip A., "Prevention and Treatment of Neonatal Herpes," *Pediatrics*, vol. 66, November 1980.

Brzeinski, Joseph E., and John L. Hayman Jr., "The Effectiveness of Parents in Helping Their Preschool Children to Begin to Read," Denver, Denver Public Schools, September 1962.

Brzeinski, Joseph E., and Will Howard, "Early Reading—How, Not When!" *Reading Teacher*, vol. 25, 1971.

Burton, Barbara K., and Henry L. Nadler, "Antenatal Diagnosis of Metabolic Disorders," *Clinical Obstetrics and Gynecology,* vol. 24, December 1981.

Campbell, Frances A., and Craig T. Ramey, "Cognitive and School Outcomes for High-Risk African-American Students at Middle Adolescence," *American Educational Research Journal,* vol. 32, no. 4, winter 1995.

Carew, Jean V., "Experience and the Development of Intelligence in Young Children at Home and in Day Care," *Monographs of the Society for Research in Child Development,* vol. 45, 1980.

———, "Predicting I.Q. from the Young Child's Everyday Experience," a paper presented at the symposium "Soziale Bedingungen fur die Entwicklung der Lernfahigkeit," Bad Homburg, West Germany, October 1975.

Carew, Jean V., and others, "Observed Intellectual Competence and Tested Intelligence: Their Roots in the Young Child's Transactions with His Environment," a paper presented at the Eastern Psychological Association meeting, New York, April 1975.

Carlson, Mary, and Felton Earls, "Psychological and Neuroendocrinological Consequences of Early Social Deprivation in Institutionalized Children in Romania," *Annals of the New York Academy of Science,* vol. 807, 1997.

Carnegie Corporation of New York, *Starting Points: Meeting the Needs of Our Youngest Children,* August 1994.

Carrelli, Anne O'Brien, "Sex Equity and the Gifted," *G/C/T,* November–December 1982.

Chall, Jeanne, *Learning to Read: The Great Debate,* New York, McGraw-Hill, 1967.

Charney, Evan, and others, "Childhood Lead Poisoning," *New England Journal of Medicine,* vol. 309, November 3, 1983.

Chattin-McNichols, John P., "The Effects of Montessori School Experience," *Young Children,* vol. 36, July 1981.

"Children in Crashes," Insurance Institute for Highway Safety, Washington, D.C., December 1980.

Children's Defense Fund, "Give More Children a Head Start," Washington, D.C., CDF Publications, 1983.

Chisholm, Kim, "A Three Year Follow-Up of Attachment and Indiscriminate Friendliness in Children Adopted from Romanian Orphanages," *Child Development,* vol. 69, no. 4, August 1998.

Chugani, Harry T., "A Critical Period of Brain Development: Studies of Cerebral Glucose Utilization with PET," *Preventative Medicine,* vol. 27, March 1998.

———, "Biological Basis of Emotions: Brain Systems and Brain Development," *Pediatrics,* vol. 102, no. 5 supplement, November 1998.

———, "Metabolic Imaging: A Window on Brain Development and Plasticity," *Neuroscientist,* vol. 5, no. 1, 1999.

Clarke-Stewart, Alison, *Child Care in the Family: A Review of Research and Some Propositions for Policy,* New York, Academic Press, 1977.

Cohen, Leslie B., "Our Developing Knowledge of Infant Perception and Cognition," *American Psychologist,* vol. 34, October 1979.

Cohen, Sarale E., and Leila Beckwith, "Preterm Infant Interaction with the Caregiver in the First Year of Life and Competence at Age Two," *Child Development,* vol. 50, September 1979.

Coleman, Dona, "Parenting the Gifted: Is This a Job for Superparent?" *G/C/T,* March–April 1982.

Colletti, Richard B., "Hospital-Based Rental Programs to Increase Car Seat Usage," *Pediatrics,* vol. 71, May 1983.

Consortium on Developmental Continuity, "The Persistence of Preschool Effects: A Long-Term Follow-Up of 14 Infant and Preschool Experiments," Washington, D.C., Department of Health, Education, and Welfare, September 1977.

Cuffaro, Harriet K., "Microcomputers in Education: Why Is Earlier Better?" *Teachers College Record,* vol. 85, summer 1984.

Cunningham, Anne E., and Keith E. Stanovich, "Early Reading Acquisition and Its Relation to Reading Experience and Ability 10 Years Later," *Developmental Psychology,* vol. 33, no. 6, 1997.

Davidson, Jane, "Wasted Time: The Ignored Dilemma," *Young Children,* vol. 35, May 1980.

Dawson, Geraldine, Laura Grofer Klinger, Heracles Panagiotides, Deborah Hill, and Susan Spieker, "Frontal Lobe Activity and Affective Behavior of Infants of Mothers with Depressive Symptoms," *Child Development,* vol. 63, 1992.

Day, David E., *Early Childhood Education: A Human Ecological Approach,* Glenview, IL, Scott, Foresman, and Company, 1983.

Day, Mary Carol, and Ronald K. Parker, editors, *The Preschool in Action: Exploring Early Childhood Programs,* Boston, Allyn and Bacon, 1977.

Diamond, Marian, and Janet Hopson, *Magic Trees of the Mind,* New York, Penguin Putnam, 1999.

D'Ignazio, Fred, "Can Toddlers Tackle Computers? *Compute!'s PC and PC jr.* vol. 1, August 1984.

Douglas, Jane T., "Dollars and Sense: Employer-Supported Child Care: A Study of Child Care Needs and the Realities of Employer-Support," Washington, D.C., Office of Child Development, Department of Health, Education, and Welfare, 1976.

Drash, Philip W., and Arnold L. Stolberg, "Acceleration of Cognitive, Linguistic and Social Development in the Normal Infant," Tallahassee, Florida, Florida State Department of Health and Rehabilitative Services, 1977.

Dunn, Rita, "Learning Style and Its Relation to Exceptionality at Both Ends of the Spectrum," *Exceptional Children,* April 1983.

Durkin, Dolores, "Children Who Learned to Read at Home," *Elementary School Journal,* vol. 62, October 1961.

———, "Children Who Read Before Grade 1: A Second Study," *Elementary School Journal,* vol. 63, December 1962.

———, *Children Who Read Early,* New York, Teachers College Press, 1966.

———, "An Earlier Start in Reading?" *Elementary School Journal,* vol. 63, December 1962.

———, *Getting Reading Started,* Boston, Allyn and Bacon, 1982.

———, "A Six-Year Study of Children Who Learned to Read in School at the Age of Four," *Reading Research Quarterly,* vol. 10, 1974.

Earls, Felton, "The Fathers (Not the Mothers): Their Importance and Influence with Infants and Young Children," in *Annual Progress in Child Psychiatry and Child Development,* Sella Chess and Alexander Thomas, editors, New York, Brunner Mazel, 1977.

Eisenberg, "Social Context of Child Development," *Pediatrics,* vol. 68, November 1981.

Elardo, Richard, and others, "A Longitudinal Study of the Relation of Infants' Home Environments to Language Development at Age Three," Center for Early Development and Education, Department of Health, Education, and Welfare, Washington, D.C.

Elardo, Richard, Robert Bradley, and Bettye M. Caldwell, "The Relation of Infants' Home Environment to Mental Test Performance from Six to 36 Months: A Longitudinal Analysis," *Child Development,* vol. 46, March 1975.

Elbert, T., C. Pantev, C. Weinbruch, B. Rockstroh, and E. Taub, "Increased Cortical Representation of the Fingers of the Left Hand in String Players," *Science,* vol. 207, October 13, 1997.

Eliason, Claudia Furiman, and Loa Thomson Jenkins, *A Practical Guide to Early Childhood Curriculum,* St. Louis, C. V. Mosby, 1981.

Emery, Donald G., *Teach Your Preschooler to Read,* New York, Simon & Schuster, 1975.

Engelmann, Siegfried, Phyllis Haddox, and Elaine Bruner, *Teach Your Child to Read in 100 Easy Lessons,* New York, Cornerstone Library, Simon & Schuster, 1983.

Epstein, Carol B., "The Gifted and Talented: Programs That Work," National School Public Relations Association, Arlington, VA, 1979.

Eveloff, Herbert H., "Some Cognitive and Affective Aspects of Early Learning Development," *Child Development,* vol. 42, December 1971.

Family Policy Panel of the Economic Policy Council of UNA–USA, "Work and Family in the United States: A Policy Initiative," New York, 1985.

Fantz, Robert L., and Joseph F. Fagan III, "Visual Attention to Size and Number of Pattern Details by Term and Preterm Infants During the First Six Months," *Child Development,* vol. 46, March 1975.

Fehrle, Carl C., and others, "The Most-Asked Questions about Gifted Children: Answers for Parents and Educators," Extension Publications, University of Missouri/Columbia, 1982.

Field, Jeffrey, and others, "Infants' Orientation to Lateral Sounds from Birth to Three Months," *Child Development*, vol. 51, March 1980.

Field, Tiffany, and Reena Greenberg, "Temperament Ratings by Parents and Teachers of Infants, Toddlers, and Preschool Children," *Child Development*, vol. 53, February 1982.

Field, Tiffany, "Maternal Depression Effects on Infants and Early Interventions," *Preventative Medicine*, vol. 27, March 1998.

Fisher, Lianne, Elinor W. Ames, Kim Chisholm, and Lynn Savoie, "Problems Reported by Parents of Romanian Orphans Adopted to British Columbia," *International Journal of Behavioral Development*, vol. 20, 1997.

Flank, Sandra, "Little Hands on the Computer," *G/C/T*, November/December 1982.

Flavell, John H., *Cognitive Development*, Englewood Cliffs, NJ, Prentice-Hall, 1977.

Fowler, William, "Structural Dimensions of the Learning Process in Early Reading," *Child Development*, vol. 35, December 1964.

———, "Teaching a Two-Year-Old to Read: An Experiment in Early Childhood Learning," *Genetic Psychology Monographs*, vol. 66, 1962.

Fox, Lynn H., "Preparing Gifted Girls for Future Leadership Roles," *G/C/T*, March–April 1981.

Gallas, Howard B., and Michael Lewis, "Mother–Infant Interaction and Cognitive Development in the 12-Week-Old Infant," a paper presented at the Society for Research in Child Development, New Orleans, March 1977.

Gelman, Rochel, "Preschool Thought," *American Psychologist*, vol. 34, October 1979.

Geschwind, Norman, "Neurological Foundations of Hemispheric Functional Asymmetry," a paper presented at the annual meeting of the American Association for the Advancement of Science, Houston, January 1979.

Ginsberg-Riggs, Gina, "Being Comfortable with Gifted Children," *G/C/T*, March–April 1981.

Gladieux, Rosemary, "How to Help Your Gifted Child: It's as Easy as ABC," *G/C/T*, September–October 1981.

Goodman, Norman, and Joseph Andrews, "Cognitive Development of Children in Family and Group Day Care," *American Journal of Orthopsychiatry*, vol. 51, April 1981.

Gordon, Ira, "Parent Oriented Home-Based Early Childhood Education Program: Research Report," Gainesville, Florida, Florida University, Institute for Development of Human Resources, May 1975.

Gould, Toni S., *Home Guide to Early Reading*, New York, Walker and Company, 1976.

Green, James A., Gwen E. Gustofson, and Meredith J. West, "Effects of Infant Development on Mother–Infant Interactions," *Child Development*, vol. 51, March 1980.

Greenberg, David J., and William J. O'Donnell, "Infancy and the Optimal Level of Stimulation," *Child Development*, vol. 43, June 1972.

Greenfield, Patricia Marks, *Minds and Media: The Effects of Television, Video Games, and Computers*, Cambridge, MA, Harvard University Press, 1984.

Grotberg, Edith H., and Bernard Brown, "Research on Child Care," a paper presented at the Research Forum on Children and Youth, Washington, D.C., May 1981.

Guilford, Arthur M., Jane Scheuerie, and Susan Shonburn, "Aspects of Language Development in the Gifted," *Gifted Child Quarterly*, vol. 25, fall 1981.

Guillory, Andrea, "The First Four Months: Development of Affect, Cognition, and Synchrony," a paper presented at the

American Psychological Association meeting, Washington, D.C., August 1982.

Gunnar, Megan R., "Quality of Early Care and Buffering of Neuroendocrine Stress Reactions: Potential Effects on the Developing Human Brain," *Preventative Medicine,* vol. 27, March 1998.

Gurren, Louise, and Ann Hughes, "Intensive Phonics vs. Gradual Phonics in Beginning Reading: A Review," *Journal of Educational Research,* vol. 58, April 1965.

Hancock, LynNell, and Pat Wingert, "If You Can Read This . . ." *Newsweek,* May 13, 1996.

Hertz, Thomas H., "The Impact of Federal Early Childhood Programs on Children," Washington, D.C., Department of Health, Education, and Welfare, July 1977.

Hess, Robert D., "The Effects of Parent Training Programs on Child Performance and Parent Behavior," a paper presented at the annual meeting of the American Association for the Advancement of Science, Denver, February 1977.

Hock, Ellen, "Alternative Approaches to Child Rearing and Their Effects on the Mother–Infant Relationship: Final Report," Washington, D.C., Department of Health, Education, and Welfare, 1976.

———, "Working and Nonworking Mothers and Their Infants: A Comparative Study of Maternal Caregiving Characteristics and Infant Social Behavior," *Merrill-Palmer Quarterly,* vol. 26, April 1980.

Holden, George W., "Avoiding Conflict: Mothers as Tacticians in the Supermarket," *Child Development,* vol. 54, 1983.

Holton, Felicia Antonelli, *CompuKids: A Parents' Guide to Computers and Learning,* New York, New American Library, 1985.

317

Holtzman, Mathilda, "The Verbal Environment Provided by Mothers for Their Very Young Children," *Merrill-Palmer Quarterly,* vol. 20, January 1974.

Holtzman, Neil A., and others, "Effect of Informed Parental Consent on Mothers' Knowledge of Newborn Screening," *Pediatrics,* vol. 72, December 1983.

Hunt, J. McV., *Intelligence and Experience,* New York, Ronald Press, 1961.

Huttenlocher, Janellen, "Language Input and Language Growth," *Preventative Medicine,* vol. 27, March–April 1998.

Huttenlocher, P. R., and Ch. de Courten, "The Development of Synapses in Striate Cortex of Man," *Human Neurobiology,* vol. 6, spring 1987.

Jacobs, A., M. Schall, and A. Scheibel, "A Quantitative Dendritic Analysis of Wernicke's Area in Humans. II. Gender, Hemispheric, and Environmental Factors," *Journal of Comparative Neurology,* vol. 327, January 1993.

Jennings, Kay D., and Robin E. Conners, "Children's Cognitive Development and Free Play: Relations to Maternal Behavior," paper presented at the Society for Research in Child Development meeting, Detroit, April 1983.

Jensen, Rita A., and John Wedman, "The Computer's Role in Gifted Education," *G/C/T,* November–December 1983.

Kagan, Jerome, "The Effect of Day Care on the Infant," a paper prepared for the Department of Health, Education, and Welfare, Washington, D.C., June 1976.

———, "The Effects of Infant Day Care on Psychological Development," a paper presented at the annual meeting of the American Association for the Advancement of Science, Boston, February 1976.

Kagan, Jerome, and Margaret Hamburg, "The Enhancement of Memory in the First Year," *Journal of Genetic Psychology,* vol. 138, 1981.

Kagan, Jerome, Richard B. Kearsley, and Philip R. Zelazo, *Infancy: Its Place in Human Development,* Cambridge, MA, Harvard University Press, 1978.

Kaler, Sandra R., and B. J. Freeman, "Analysis of Environmental Deprivation: Cognitive and Social Development in Romanian Orphans," *Journal of Child Psychiatry,* vol. 35, no. 4, 1994.

Kalter, Harold, and Josef Warkany, "Congenital Malformations: Etiologic Factors and Their Role in Prevention," *New England Journal of Medicine,* vol. 308, February 24, 1983.

Karger, Rex H., "Synchrony in Mother–Infant Interaction," *Child Development,* vol. 50, September 1979.

Karnes, Frances A., and M. Ray Karnes, "Parents and Schools: Educating Gifted and Talented Children," *Elementary School Journal,* vol. 82, January 1982.

Karnes, Merle B., Allan M. Shwedel, and Susan A. Linnemeyer, "The Young Gifted/Talented Child: Programs at the University of Illinois," *Elementary School Journal,* vol. 82, January 1982.

Katz, Samuel L., "International Symposium on Measles Immunization: Summary and Recommendations," *Pediatrics,* vol. 71, 1983.

Kierscht, Marcia, "Correlates of Early Infant Competence: A Multivariate Approach, Final Report, Part I," Washington, D.C., Department of Health, Education, and Welfare, August 1975.

Kilmer, Sally, "Infant-Toddler Group Day Care: A Review of Research," a paper sponsored by the National Institute of Education, Washington, D.C., December 1977.

Kitano, Margie, "Young Gifted Children: Strategies for Preschool Teachers," *Young Children,* vol. 37, May 1982.

Klein, Ronald D., "An Inquiry into the Factors Related to

Creativity," *Elementary School Journal,* vol. 82, January 1982.

Kotulak, Ronald, *Inside the Brain,* Kansas City, MO, Andrews McMeel Publishing, 1996.

——, "Inside the Brain: Revolutionary Discoveries of How the Mind Works," *Preventative Medicine,* vol. 27, March 1998.

——, "Learning How to Use the Brain," paper presented at the "Brain Development in Young Children: New Frontiers for Research, Policy and Practice" conference, Chicago, June 1996.

——, "Mental Workouts Pump Up Brain Power," "Research Discovers Secrets of How Brain Learns to Talk," "Epidemic of Violence and Stress is Devastating Kids' Brains," "Reshaping Brain for Better Future," *Chicago Tribune,* April 11–15, 1993.

Kuhl, P. K., K. A. Williams, F. Lacerda, K. N. Stevens, and B. Lindbloom, "Linguistic Experience Alters Phonetic Perception in Infants by 6 Months of Age," *Science,* vol. 205, 1992.

Lamb, Michael E., "Development and Function of Parent–Infant Relationships in the First Two Years of Life," a paper given at the Society for Research in Child Development meeting, New Orleans, March 1977.

Laosa, Luis M., "Maternal Teaching Strategies and Cognitive Styles in Chicano Families," *Journal of Educational Psychology,* vol. 72, 1980.

Ledson, Sidney, *Teach Your Child to Read in 60 Days,* New York, W. W. Norton and Company, 1975.

Levin, Stephen R., Thomas V. Petros, and Florence W. Petrella, "Preschoolers' Awareness of Television Advertising," *Child Development,* vol. 53, August 1982.

Lewkowicz, David J., and Gerald Turkewitz, "Intersensory Interaction in Newborns: Modifications of Visual Preferences Following Exposure to Sounds," *Child Development,* vol. 52, September 1981.

Lillard, Paula Polk, *Montessori Today,* New York, Schocken Books, 1996.

Lipper, Evelyn, and others, "Determinants of Neurobehavioral Outcomes in Low-Birth-Weight Infants," *Pediatrics,* vol. 67, April 1981.

Lipsitt, Lewis P., "Critical Conditions in Infancy," *American Psychologist,* vol. 34, October 1979.

———, "Learning and Emotion in Infants," *Pediatrics,* vol. 102, no. 5 supplement, November 1998.

Lipsitt, Lewis P., and John S. Werner, "The Infancy of Human Learning Processes," *Developmental Plasticity,* E. S. Gollin, editor, New York, Academic Press, 1981.

Longo, Lawrence D., "Maternal Smoking: Effects on the Fetus and Newborn Infant," a paper given at the annual meeting of the American Association for the Advancement of Science, San Francisco, January 1980.

Lowman, Kaye, *Of Cradles and Careers,* Franklin Park, IL, La Leche League International, 1984.

Lynn, Richard, "I.Q. in Japan and the United States Shows a Growing Disparity," *Nature,* vol. 297, May 20, 1982.

Lytton, Hugh, and Denise Watts, "Continuities and Discontinuities in Cognitive and Social Characteristics from Age 2 to Age 9," a paper presented at the Society for Research in Child Development meeting, Boston, April 1981.

Malone, Thomas W., "Guidelines for Designing Educational Computer Programs," *Childhood Education,* March–April 1983.

March of Dimes Science News Information File, *Radiation and Birth Defects,* March of Dimes Birth Defects Foundation, August 1979.

Marland, Sidney P., Jr., "Education of the Gifted and Talented," report to the Congress of the United States by the U.S. Commissioner of Education, Washington, D.C., U.S. Government Printing Office, 1972.

Mass, Leslie Noyes, "Developing Concepts of Literacy in Young Children," *Reading Teacher,* vol. 35, March 1982.

McCall, Robert B., "Environmental Effects on Intelligence: The Forgotten Realm of Discontinuous Nonshared Within-in Family Factors," *Child Development,* vol. 44, April 1983.

McHardy, Roberta, "Planning for Preschool Gifted Education," *G/C/T,* September–October 1983.

McKee, Paul, and Joseph Brzeinski, "The Effectiveness of Teaching Reading in Kindergarten," Denver, Denver Public Schools, 1966.

McQuilkin, Charlette E., "Parents of the Gifted—Look Homeward," *G/C/T,* March–April 1981.

Meltzoff, Andrew N., and M. Keith Moore, "Newborn Infants Imitate Adult Facial Gestures," *Child Development,* vol. 54, June 1983.

Metzl, Marilyn Newman, "Teaching Parents a Strategy for Enhancing Infant Development," *Child Development,* vol. 51, June 1980.

Miller, Bernard S., and Merle Price, editors, *The Gifted Child, the Family, and the Community,* New York, American Association for Gifted Children, 1981.

Miller, Louise B., and Rondeall P. Bizzell, "Long-Term Effects of Four Preschool Programs: Sixth, Seventh, and Eighth Grades," *Child Development,* vol. 54, 1983.

Moerk, Ernst L., "The Mother of Eve—As a First Language Teacher," a paper given at the Society for Research in Child Development meeting, San Francisco, March 1979.

Montessori, Maria, *The Absorbent Mind,* New York, Holt, Rinehart, and Winston, 1967.

————, *The Discovery of the Child,* New York, Ballantine Books, 1972.

————, *A Montessori Handbook,* R. C. Orem, editor, New York, G. P. Putnam's Sons, 1965.

————, *The Montessori Method,* new edition, Cambridge, MA, Robert Bentley, 1964.

————, *The Secret of Childhood,* New York, Ballantine Books, 1972.

Moore, Nancy Delano, "The Joys and Challenges in Raising a Gifted Child," *G/C/T,* November–December 1982.

Moran, James D., III, Roberta M. Milgram, Janet K. Sawyers, and Victoria R. Fu, "Original Thinking in Preschool Children," *Child Development,* vol. 54, August 1983.

Morison, Sara J., Elinor W. Ames, and Kim Chisholm, "The Development of Children Adopted from Romanian Orphanages," *Merrill-Palmer Quarterly,* vol. 41, no. 4., October 1995.

Moss, Ellen Sheiner, "Mothers and Gifted Preschoolers: Teaching and Learning Strategies," a paper presented at the annual meeting of the American Educational Research Association, Montreal, Canada, April 1983.

Motz, Sister Mary, *Montessori Matters: A Language Manual,* Cincinnati, Ohio, Sisters of Notre Dame de Namur, 1980.

Moxley, Roy, *Writing and Reading in Early Childhood,* Englewood Cliffs, NJ, Educational Technology Publications, 1982.

Murray, Ann D., "Maternal Employment Reconsidered: Effects on Infants," *American Journal of Orthopsychiatry,* vol. 45, October 1975.

Nash, Madeleine J., "Fertile Minds," *Time,* February 3, 1997.

Ogbu, John U., "Origins of Human Competence: A Cultural-

Ecological Perspective," *Child Development*, vol. 52, June 1981.

Omenn, Gilbert, "Eco-genetics: Human Variation in Susceptibility to Environmental Agents," a paper presented at the annual meeting of the American Association for the Advancement of Science, Toronto, January 1981.

Oviatt, Sharon, L., "Inferring What Words Mean: Early Development in Infants' Comprehension of Common Object Names," *Child Development*, vol. 53, February 1982.

Palmer, Francis H., "The Effects of Early Childhood Intervention," a paper presented at the annual meeting of the American Association for the Advancement of Science, Denver, February 1977.

Papert, Seymour, *The Connected Family*, Atlanta, GA, Longstreet Press, 1996.

————, "Child Power: Keys to the Learning of the Digital Century," The Eleventh Colin Cherry Memorial Lecture on Communication, London, Imperial College, June 1998.

————, *Mindstorms: Children, Computers, and Powerful Ideas*, New York, Basic Books, 1980.

Pass, Robert F., and others, "Increased Frequency of Cytomegalovirus Infection in Children in Group Day Care," *Pediatrics*, vol. 74, July 1984.

————, "Outcome of Symptomatic Congenital Cytomegalovirus Infection: Results of Long-Term Longitudinal Follow-Up," *Pediatrics*, vol. 66, November 1980.

Passow, A. Harry, "The Nature of Giftedness and Talent," *Gifted Child Quarterly*, vol. 25, winter 1981.

Penfield, Wilder, *The Second Career*, Boston, Little, Brown, 1963.

Penfield, Wilder, and Lamar Roberts, *Speech and Brain Mechanisms*, Princeton, NJ, Princeton University Press, 1959.

Perino, Sheila C., and Joseph Perino, *Parenting the Gifted: Developing the Promise*, New York, R. R. Bowker, 1981.

Peterson, Dale, editor, *Intelligent Schoolhouse: Readings on Computers and Learning*, Reston, VA, Reston Publishing, 1984.

Phillips, John L., *The Origins of Intellect: Piaget's Theory*, San Francisco, W. H. Freeman, 1969.

Piaget, Jean, *The Language and Thought of the Child*, Cleveland, World Book, 1955.

————, *The Origin of Intelligence in Children*, New York, International Universities Press, 1952.

————, *Psychology of Intelligence*, Paterson, NJ, Littlefield, Adams, 1963.

Pincus, Cynthia S., Leslie Elliott, and Trudy Schlachter, *The Roots of Success*, Englewood Cliffs, NJ, Prentice-Hall, 1980.

Pines, Maya, "Baby, You're Incredible," *Psychology Today*, vol. 16, September 1979.

Plomin, Robert, "Developmental Behavioral Genetics," *Child Development*, vol. 54, April 1983.

Portnoy, Fern C., and Carolyn H. Simmons, "Day Care and Attachment," *Child Development*, vol. 49, March 1978.

Price, Eunice H., "How Thirty-seven Gifted Children Learned to Read," *Reading Teacher*, vol. 30, 1976.

Provence, Sally, Audrey Naylor, and June Patterson, *The Challenge of Daycare*, New Haven, CT, Yale University Press, 1977.

Ramey, Craig T., Dale C. Farren, and Frances A. Campbell, "Predicting I.Q. from Mother–Infant Interactions," *Child Development*, vol. 50, June 1979.

Ramey, Craig T., "High-Risk Children and I.Q.: Altering Intergenerational Patterns," *Intelligence*, vol. 16, 1992.

Ramey, Craig T., D. M. Bryant, B. H. Wasik, J. J. Sparling, K. H.

Fendt, and L. M. LaVange, "Infant Health and Development Programs for Low Birth Weight, Premature Infants: Program Elements, Family Participation, and Child Intelligence," *Pediatrics,* vol. 89, March 1992.

Ramey, Craig T., and Sharon L. Ramey, "Prevention of Intellectual Disabilities: Early Interventions to Improve Cognitive Development," *Preventative Medicine,* vol. 27, no. 2, March–April 1998.

Ramey, Craig T., and Sharon L. Ramey, *Right From Birth,* New York, Goddard Press, 1999.

Ricciuti, Henry N., "Effects of Infant Day Care Experience on Behavior and Development: Research and Implications for Social Policy," Washington, D.C., a review prepared for the Department of Health, Education, and Welfare, 1976.

Rinehart, Ward, and Adrienne Kols, with Sidney H. Moore, "Healthier Mothers and Children Through Family Planning," *Population Reports,* May–June 1984.

Rosenzweig, Mark R., and others, "Heredity, Environment, Learning, and the Brain," a paper presented at the annual meeting of the American Association for the Advancement of Science, Berkeley, California, December 1965.

Rothbart, Mary Klevjord, "Measurement of Temperament in Infancy," *Child Development,* vol. 52, June 1981.

Rovee-Colliers, Carolyn K., and Lewis P. Lipsitt, "Learning, Adaptions, and Memory in the Newborn," *Psychobiology of the Human Newborn,* P. Stratton, editor, New York, John Wiley & Sons, 1982.

Royster, Eugene C., and others, "A National Survey of Head Start Graduates and Their Peers," Cambridge, MA, Abt Associates, 1978.

Rubenstein, Judith L., and Carollee Howes, "Caregiving and Infant Behavior in Day Care and in Homes," *Developmental Psychology,* vol. 12, January 1979.

Ruddy, Margaret G., and Marc H. Bornstein, "Cognitive Correlates of Infant Attention and Maternal Stimulation over the First Year of Life," *Child Development,* vol. 53, February 1982.

Rutter, Michael, "Social-Emotional Consequences of Day Care for Preschool Children," *American Journal of Orthopsychiatry,* vol. 51, January 1981.

Sakamoto, Takahiko, "Preschool Reading in Japan," *Reading Teacher,* vol. 29, December 1975.

Sameroff, Arnold J., Ronald Seifer, and Penelope Kelly Elias, "Sociocultural Variability in Infant Temperament Ratings," *Child Development,* vol. 51, February 1982.

Sawyer, Robert N., "By-Mail Options for Brilliant Middle School Youth," a paper presented at the annual meeting of the American Academy of Pediatrics, Chicago, September 1984.

Schachter, Frances Fuchs, "Toddlers with Employed Mothers," *Child Development,* vol. 52, September 1981.

Scheibel, A., T. Conrad, S. Perdue, U. Tomiyasa, and A. Wechsler, "A Quantitative Study of Dendrite Complexity in Selected Areas of the Human Cerebral Cortex," *Brain Cognition,* vol. 12, January 1990.

Schetky, Diane H., "The Emotional and Social Development of the Gifted Child," *G/C/T,* May–June 1981.

Schubert, Jan Bascom, Sharon Bradley-Johnson, and James Nuttal, "Mother–Infant Communication and Maternal Employment," *Child Development,* vol. 51, March 1980.

Schwartz, Lita Linzer, "Are You a Gifted Parent of a Gifted Child?" *Gifted Child Quarterly,* vol. 25, winter 1981.

Schwartz, Pamela, "Length of Day-Care Attendance and Attachment Behavior in Eighteen-Month-Old Infants," *Child Development,* vol. 54, August 1983.

Schwarz, Eitan D., and Bruce D. Perry, "The Post-Traumatic Response in Children and Adolescents," *Psychiatric Clinics of North America,* vol. 17, June 1994.

Schweinhart, L. J., H. V. Barnes, D. P. Weikart, W. S. Barnett, and A. S. Epstein, *Significant Benefits: The High/Scope Perry Preschool Study Through Age 27,* Ypsilanti, MI, High/Scope Press, 1993.

Seitz, Victoria, "Long-Term Effects of Intervention: A Longitudinal Investigation," a paper presented at the annual meeting of the American Association for the Advancement of Science, Denver, February 1977.

Shaywitz, Sally, "Dyslexia," *Scientific American,* November 1996.

Shwedel, Allan, "A New Direction in the Identification of Children for a Preschool Gifted Program," a paper presented at the annual meeting of the American Educational Research Association, Boston, April 1980.

Siegal, Linda A., "Infant Tests as Predictors of Cognitive and Language Development at Two Years," *Child Development,* vol. 52, June 1981.

Siegel, Linda S., "Reproductive, Perinatal, and Environmental Factors as Predictors of the Cognitive and Language Development of Preterm and Full-Term Infants," *Child Development,* vol. 53, August 1982.

Siegelbaum, Laura, and Susan Rotner, "Ideas and Activities for Parents of Preschool Gifted Children," *G/C/T,* January–February 1983.

Silva, P. A., and J. Bradshaw, "Some Factors Contributing to Intelligence at Age of School Entry," *British Journal of Educational Psychology,* vol. 50, 1980.

Smith, Allen N., and Carl M. Spence, "National Day Care Study: Optimizing the Day Care Environment," *American Journal of Orthopsychiatry,* vol. 50, October 1980.

Snyder, Solomon H., "Neurosciences: An Integrative Discipline," *Science,* vol. 225, September 21, 1984.

Spencer, Mina, and Linda Baskin, "Microcomputers in Early Childhood Education," a report for the National Institute of Education, Washington, D.C., 1983.

Spitzer, Dean R., *Concept Formation and Learning in Early Childhood,* Columbus, OH, Charles E. Merrill Publishing, 1977.

Stein, Zena A., "Adverse Reproductive Outcomes and the Environment," a paper presented at the annual meeting of the American Association for the Advancement of Science, New York, May 1984.

Stevenson, Harold W., "Making the Grade: School Achievement in Japan, Taiwan, and the United States," from the Annual Report of the Center for Advanced Study in the Behavioral Sciences, Ann Arbor, MI, 1984.

Stevenson, Harold W., and James W. Stigler, *The Learning Gap,* New York, Touchstone, a division of Simon & Schuster, 1992.

Stewig, John Warren, *Teaching Language Arts in Early Childhood,* New York, CBS College Publishing, Holt, Rinehart, and Winston, 1982.

Strobino, Barbara Reiber, Jennie Kline, and Zena Stein, "Chemical and Physical Exposures of Parents: Effects on Human Reproduction and Offspring," *Journal of Early Human Development,* vol. 1, February 1978.

Sutton, Marjorie Hunt, "Children Who Learned to Read in Kindergarten: A Longitudinal Study," *Reading Teacher,* vol. 22, April 1969.

Sylva, Kathy, "Critical Periods in Childhood Learning," *British Medical Bulletin,* vol. 53, January 1997.

Teale, William H., *Early Reading: An Annotated Bibliography,* Newark, DE, International Reading Association, 1980.

————, "Positive Environments for Learning to Read: What Studies of Early Readers Tell Us," *Language Arts,* vol. 55, November–December 1978.

————, "Toward a Theory of How Children Learn to Read and Write Naturally," *Language Arts,* vol. 59, September 1982.

Thompson, Ross A., Michael E. Lamb, and David Estes, "Stability of Infant–Mother Attachment and Its Relationship to Changing Life Circumstances, in an Unselected Middle-Class Sample," *Child Development,* vol. 53, February 1982.

Tittle, Bess M., "Why Montessori for the Gifted?" *G/C/T,* May–June 1984.

Torrance, E. Paul, *Guiding Creative Talent,* Englewood Cliffs, NJ, Prentice-Hall, 1962.

————, *Rewarding Creative Behavior,* Englewood Cliffs, NJ, Prentice-Hall, 1965.

Truss, Carroll V., and others, "Parent Training in Preprimary Competence," a paper presented at the American Psychological Association meeting, San Francisco, August 1977.

Tulkin, Steven R., and Jerome Kagan, "Mother–Child Interaction in the First Year of Life," *Child Development,* vol. 43, March 1972.

Turkle, Sherry, *The Second Self: Computers and the Human Spirit,* New York, Simon & Schuster, 1984.

Uzgiris, Ina C., "Patterns of Cognitive Development in Infancy," *Merrill-Palmer Quarterly,* vol. 19, October 1973.

Walbert, Herbert J., and others, "Childhood Traits and Environmental Conditions of Highly Eminent Adults," *Gifted Child Quarterly,* vol. 25, summer 1981.

Wann, Kenneth D., Miriam Selchen Dorn, and Elizabeth Ann Liddie, *Fostering Intellectual Development in Young Children,* New York, Teachers College Press, 1962.

Watrin, Rita, and Paul Hanly Furfey, *Learning Activities for the Young Preschool Child,* New York, D. Van Nostrand, 1978.

Watt, Dan, "Teaching Turtles," *Popular Computing,* July 1982.

Weikart, David P., "Changing Early Childhood Development through Educational Intervention," *Preventative Medicine,* vol. 27, March–April 1998.

Weissbourd, Bernice, and Judith Musick, editors, *Infants: Their Social Environments,* Washington, D.C., National Association for the Education of Young Children, 1981.

Werner, John S., and Lewis P. Lipsitt, "The Infancy of Human Sensory Systems," from *Developmental Plasticity,* E. S. Gollin, editor, New York, Academic Press, Inc., 1981.

Weyer, Stephen A., "Computers for Communication," *Childhood Education,* March–April 1983.

Whelan, Elizabeth M., *A Smoking Gun,* Philadelphia, George F. Stickley, 1984.

White, Burton L., "Critical Influences in the Origins of Competence," *Merrill-Palmer Quarterly,* vol. 21, October 1975.

———, "Early Stimulation and Behavioral Development," in *Genetics, Environment and Intelligence,* A. Oliverior, editor, Elsevier/North Holland, Biomedical Press, 1977.

———, "Guidelines for Parent Education, 1977," a paper presented at the Planning Education Conference, Flint, MI, September 1977.

———, *Human Infants: Experience and Psychological Development,* Englewood Cliffs, NJ, Prentice-Hall, 1971.

———, *The New First Three Years of Life,* New York, a Fireside Book, Simon & Schuster, 1997.

———, *The Origins of Human Competence,* Lexington, MA, D. C. Heath and Company, 1979.

————, "Should You Stay Home with Your Baby?" *Educational Horizons,* fall 1980.

White, Burton L., and Peter Castle, "Visual Exploratory Behavior Following Postnatal Handling of Human Infants," *Perceptual and Motor Skills,* vol. 18, 1964.

White, Burton L., and Jean Carew Watts, *Experience and Environment,* Englewood Cliffs, NJ, Prentice-Hall, 1973.

White, Burton L., and others, "Child Rearing Practices and the Development of Competence, Final Report," Cambridge, MA, Harvard University Graduate School of Education, 1974.

White House Conference on Early Childhood Development and Learning Policy Announcements, April 17, 1997.

Willerman, Lee, "Effects of Families on Intellectual Development," *American Psychologist,* vol. 34, October 1979.

Williams, Frank E., "Developing Children's Creativity at Home and in School," *G/C/T,* September–October 1982.

Wilson, Christopher B., and others, "Development of Adverse Sequelae in Children Born with Subclinical Congenital Toxoplasma Infection," *Pediatrics,* vol. 66, November 1980.

Wilson, James G., and Margery W. Shaw, editors, *Handbook of Teratology,* New York, Plenum Press, 1977.

Wynder, Ernst L., "Introduction to the Report on the Conference on the 'Critical' Period of Brain Development," *Preventative Medicine,* vol. 27, March 1998.

Young, Karl W., and Teri Young, "Putting Montessori and the Computer Together," *Constructive Triangle,* vol. 11, summer 1984.

Yurchak, Mary-Jane H., and others, *Infant-Toddler Curriculum of the Brookline Early Education Project,* Brookline, MA, Brookline Early Education Project, November 1975.

Yussen, Steven R., "Performance of Montessori and Traditionally Schooled Nursery Children on Social Cognitive Tasks
and Memory Problems," *Contemporary Educational Psychology,* vol. 5, April 1980.

Ziajka, Alan, "Microcomputers in Early Childhood Education?" *Young Children,* July 1983.

Zigler, Edward F., and Edmund W. Gordon, editors, *Day Care:
Scientific and Social Policy Issues,* Boston, Auburn House
Publishing, 1982.

Zigler, Edward F., and Jeanette Valentine, editors, *Project
Head Start: A Legacy of the War on Poverty,* New York,
Free Press, 1979.

About the Author

The late Joan Beck wrote the award-winning "You and Your Child" column for the *Chicago Tribune* for many years, in which she pioneered coverage of new research on brain development, the battle against birth defects, and the struggles of parents to balance family and careers—all the while raising two children herself. Later, she became the first woman member of the *Tribune*'s editorial board and her twice-weekly op-ed columns were syndicated in hundreds of newspapers nationwide. A member of the Chicago Journalism Hall of Fame, Ms. Beck was also the author of four books: *Best Beginnings, Effective Parenting, Is My Baby All Right?* with Dr. Virginia Apgar, and *How to Raise a Brighter Child,* which has been translated into eight languages and published widely around the world.